Welcome to our neighborhood...

As a residential builder or developer, you will find in this catalogue the solutions to many of the most difficult problems you may face in the day-to-day business of new home development.

This **Special Edition** will serve as an introduction to Nelson Design Group, LLC, Residential Planners - Designers, a national full-service design firm that specializes in an uncompromising commitment to total customer service, regardless of the size of the client.

At NDG, it's not just a home…It's a neighborhood. We don't just sell home plans - we sell beautifully functional neighborhoods, a lifestyle, a theme for living spaces. We offer marketing expertise and materials to make your planned community from concept to a 'brick and mortar' reality.

We are a nationally known design firm with plans published by *Garlinghouse, Home Design Alternatives, Builder Magazine, Home Planners, Architectural Designs, Better Homes & Gardens*, and many more. During our move into the national marketplace in the 1990's, it quickly became apparent that residential builders and developers were not receiving the type of prompt service routinely offered by NDG, nor were they being offered the marketing materials necessary to successfully sell their homes during the raw construction stages - a sales period absolutely crucial to the builder's success.

Filling the void in customer service is top priority for NDG. Serving our customers and providing prompt answers to your questions - is just routine business for us. This commitment is not just empty words; we have numerous customers who will testify to our continued response to critical issues and our old-style Southern hospitality.

Our more than 15 years of experience in both the residential design and real estate markets have allowed us to see the need for professional marketing materials and services to be readily available and affordable for builders and developers. We offer a complete marketing package of materials for presentation in model homes including full color feature sheets, matted color renderings and other items for display.

The lack of diversity in planned community designs has allowed us to bring fresh and exciting ideas into developments around the country. NDG's community designs incorporate a neighborhood continuity and ease of lifestyle that is in such great demand among today's homebuyer.

In the pages of this catalogue you will find home collections that are warm and inviting, yet remarkably functional. All of our plans can be easily and inexpensively modified to meet your customers' individual needs. The satisfaction of living in a Nelson Design Group home - a home that was built under your company name - will translate into a goodwill message from your homebuyer to others that no amount of money could ever produce.

We believe that, in Nelson Design Group, you have found not only a source for all of your home plan needs, but also a partner upon whom you can fully rely.

With Nelson Design Group, it's not just a home…It's a neighborhood.

Best Regards,

Michael E. Nelson
President

MICHAEL E. NELSON

Home Plan Marketing Ideas

Nelson Design Group offers marketing materials for each of our home plans and can easily customize them to fit your specific needs. A developer whether large or small can have cost effective marketing tools on the property while under construction and in the office framed, or available for handouts.

About Our Plans

Our goal is to provide our clients with a design that perpetuates a constant feeling of pride. Each home owner should step into their dream home each day knowing they made the best possible decision, not only with their home design, but with their surroundings. Our experienced staff offers creativity and efficiency, and can modify any of our plans to suit your needs, saving time and guaranteeing customer satisfaction.

Table of Contents

Nelson Design Group Collections

CHARTED Neighborhoods™

"Solutions for Master Planned Communities"
Planning - Home Design - Marketing

A "Charted Neighborhood" is Nelson Design Group's approach for design *"plus"* marketing services making your job easier when developing "Master Planned Communities." As the name implies, a *Charted Neighborhood*™ *represents a distinctive new direction and concept in residential design and marketing – an approach that is unique to Nelson Design Group.*

*T*oday, a public awakening now highly values its heritage of great neighborhoods. Updated interiors of the homes many of us grew up in are now incorporated into Neo-Traditional, or Traditional Neighborhood Design. Hence, the pursuit of the American Dream has taken an indirect path, away from suburban sprawl and back to a renewed appreciation of development patterns of our predecessors. Some of these planning and design principals date back to the late 1800's.

*I*n more recent years, New Urbanism has caused a revival among historic towns, cities and villages, where the home-buying public wants more than just a place to sleep after work. A new appreciation for a richer social and civic life is integral to today's Master Planned Communities, in which families can get to know their neighbors by relaxing on spacious front porches and walking along tree covered streets and sidewalks.

*I*n response to the demand of Traditional Neighborhood Designs, today's building professional is looking for a design firm that can be much more than just a vendor of stock plans. Until now, builders and developers have indicated that a true "total resource" for planning, design, cost-analysis and value-added marketing services, is almost unheard of. Most builders need a home plan source that essentially functions as their very own "in-house, complete source" for new home design and associated services. Nelson Design Group is a firm that concentrates on true personal service, and one that will modify plans as necessary, always delivering much more.

No longer will you need several firms to provide plans or modifications, and still be on your own to market the project afterwards. Regardless of your Company's size and volume, whether builder or developer, we want to be your "personal design and promotional partner." We are happy to consult with you on individual plans or small in-fill projects, and yet we are large enough to work with you on the design of new large-scale Charted Neighborhood communities. Quite simply, we do it all - always with a personal touch and at a reasonable fee.

Because builders and developers across the country already rely on us to provide their plans and marketing resources, we cater daily to a diverse marketplace with a broad mix of consumers, real estate professionals and home builders. We know what buyers want, how builders 'build,' and how to design and

market homes that sell quickly. Each Nelson Design Group plan offers stunning elevations and fresh interior floor plans with unique features such as kids nooks, hearth rooms, and grilling porches to attract homeowner interests and promote a carefree lifestyle. Our designs are supported with our wide array of economical customized marketing materials to promote your project during construction, and then facilitate a quick sale-often at premium appraisal values.

*I*n the following pages, you will find individual designs and also several different groups of plans such as our new *Wellington, Renaissance and Florida Collections.* Our designs have complementary themes that work together to build a single home, a neighborhood, or a full-scale development. There is certainly something you can immediately incorporate into your building program.

*W*hen online, point your browser to our comprehensive website, nelsondesigngroup.com. Our site features a handy "search" option where you can select from hundreds of plans to simplify locating designs that accommodate your lot dimensions and preferred architectural style. Give us a call or send us an E-mail. Above all, please let us know if you have any questions or special requirements. We are always interested in hearing about your projects and how we might serve you now, and in the future.

*A*s we say, "Welcome to our Neighborhood." On behalf of Michael E. Nelson and our entire staff of friendly designers, marketing specialists, cost-analysts and customer service team, we are pleased to introduce Nelson Design Group, LLC, America's fastest growing home design, planning, and marketing firm.

Village at
WINDSTONE

When you choose a Nelson Design Group collection, you not only create beautiful homes, you achieve ideal master planned communities. The Village at Windstone Collection features living spaces of 1,800 to 2,800 square feet replicating historical Southern style designs. Each of these plans complement the other, resulting in an effective Traditional Neighborhood Design theme — making development easy for you. All plans are designed to fit lots of 50 feet to 80 feet. Nelson Design Group also offers complementary collections with the same traditional appeal and quality as our Village at Windstone Collection.

Nelson Design Group LLC

RESIDENTIAL PLANNERS - DESIGNERS

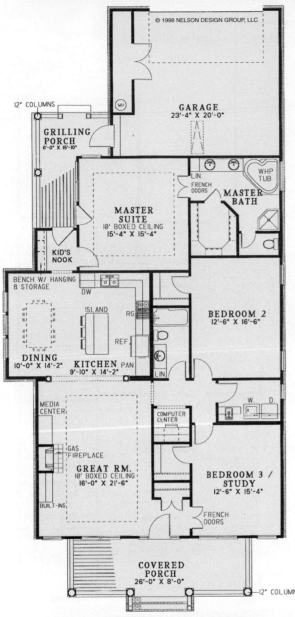

© 1998 NELSON DESIGN GROUP, LLC

12" COLUMNS

GARAGE
23'-4" X 20'-0"

GRILLING
PORCH
6'-0" X 15'-10"

WHP
TUB

LIN.
FRENCH
DOORS

MASTER
BATH

MASTER
SUITE
10' BOXED CEILING
15'-4" X 15'-4"

KID'S
NOOK

BENCH W/ HANGING
& STORAGE

DW

ISLAND

RG

REF.

DINING
10'-0" X 14'-2"

KITCHEN
9'-10" X 14'-2"

PAN

LIN

BEDROOM 2
12'-6" X 16'-6"

MEDIA
CENTER

COMPUTER
CENTER

W. D.

GAS
FIREPLACE

GREAT RM.
10' BOXED CEILING
16'-0" X 21'-6"

BUILT-INS

BEDROOM 3 /
STUDY
12'-6" X 15'-4"

FRENCH
DOORS

COVERED
PORCH
26'-0" X 8'-0"

12" COLUMNS

312 Windstone Place

Windstone Collection I

A beautifully-designed eight foot covered porch with 12 inch columns is just one of the elements that makes this Nelson Design Group home such a treasure. Southern charm surrounds the formal foyer leading to an impressive great room with gas fireplace and built-in shelves and media center. Beyond the great room is the kitchen and dining area. Enjoy hours of privacy in your secluded master suite with access to a rear covered grilling porch. The porch also leads to the dining and kitchen areas, providing hours of hassle-free entertainment.

Width: 39' 0"	Main Ceiling: 9 ft.
Depth: 81' 0"	Bedrooms: 3
Total Living: 1,832 sq. ft.	Baths: 2
Price Tier: B	Foundation: Crawl, Slab

BEST SELLER
Designers
Choice
NELSON DESIGN GROUP

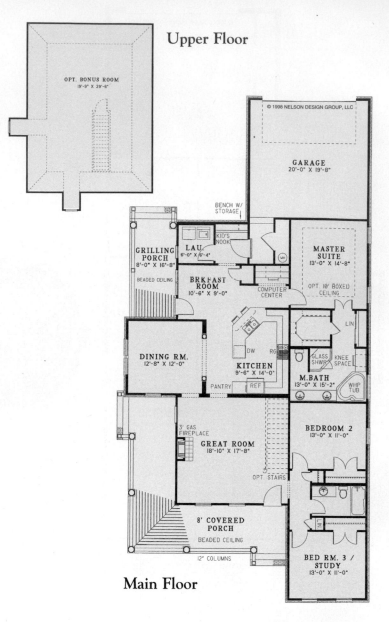

Upper Floor

OPT. BONUS ROOM
19'-9" X 29'-6"

© 1998 NELSON DESIGN GROUP, LLC

GARAGE
20'-0" X 19'-8"

BENCH W/ STORAGE

GRILLING PORCH
8'-0" X 16'-8"
BEADED CEILING

LAU.
6'-0" X 6'-4"

KID'S NOOK

MASTER SUITE
13'-0" X 14'-8"

BRKFAST ROOM
10'-6" X 9'-0"

COMPUTER CENTER

OPT. 10' BOXED CEILING

DINING RM.
12'-8" X 12'-0"

KITCHEN
9'-6" X 14'-0"

LIN

PANTRY   REF

M.BATH
13'-0" X 15'-2"

GLASS SHWR

KNEE SPACE

WHP TUB

3' GAS FIREPLACE

GREAT ROOM
18'-10" X 17'-8"

BEDROOM 2
13'-0" X 11'-0"

OPT. STAIRS

8' COVERED PORCH
BEADED CEILING

12" COLUMNS

BED RM. 3 / STUDY
13'-0" X 11'-0"

Main Floor

321 Windstone Place

Windstone Collection I

An eight foot wrap-around entry porch with classic southern columns allows you to enjoy an exquisite view from every direction of this Nelson Design Group home. Take advantage of hours of quality family time in a marvelous great room with an open stairway leading to the upper level. A double bedroom area with connecting full bath is ideal for kids of all ages. A bright breakfast area with access to a spacious kitchen and rear grilling porch conveniently provides entertaining and relaxing family dinners. Traveling to the upper level, find a huge bonus area for use as a game room or even another private suite.

Width: 41' 4"

Depth: 83' 8"

Total Living: 1,845 sq. ft.*

*Optional Bonus: 1,191 sq. ft.

Price Tier: B

Main Ceiling: 9 ft.

Upper Ceiling: 8 ft.

Bedrooms: 3

Baths: 2

Foundation: Crawl, Slab, Optional Basement
Optional Daylight Basement

To order call 1.800.590.2423 or to view the rest of this collection visit www.nelsondesigngroup.com

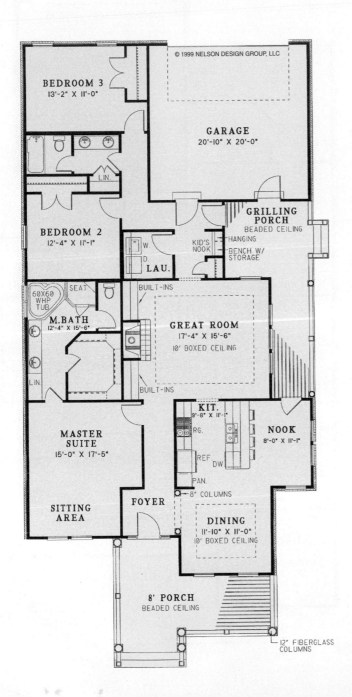

BEDROOM 3
13'-2" X 11'-0"

© 1999 NELSON DESIGN GROUP, LLC

GARAGE
20'-10" X 20'-0"

LIN.

BEDROOM 2
12'-4" X 11'-1"

GRILLING PORCH
BEADED CEILING

HANGING

KID'S NOOK

BENCH W/ STORAGE

W D

LAU.

60X60 WHP TUB

SEAT

BUILT-INS

M.BATH
12'-4" X 15'-6"

GREAT ROOM
17'-4" X 15'-6"
10' BOXED CEILING

LIN.

BUILT-INS

KIT.
9'-8" X 11'-1"

RG.

NOOK
8'-0" X 11'-1"

REF DW

MASTER SUITE
15'-0" X 17'-5"

PAN.

8" COLUMNS

SITTING AREA

FOYER

DINING
11'-10" X 11'-0"
10' BOXED CEILING

8' PORCH
BEADED CEILING

12" FIBERGLASS COLUMNS

338 Windstone Place

Windstone Collection II

Step inside this traditional Nelson Design Group home and leave the world behind. Enjoy comfortable evenings relaxing in your spacious great room, complete with gas fireplace and built-in shelving. Dinner parties are a breeze in the comfort of your formal dining area enhanced by eight inch wood columns. For more casual gatherings, invite friends over for a delicious cookout on your grilling porch, accessible from the breakfast nook and garage. Finally, relish in the privacy of your large master suite and relax in the corner whirlpool tub of the master bath.

Width: 38' 0"

Depth: 79' 6"

Total Living: 1,848 sq. ft.

Price Tier: B

Main Ceiling: 9 ft.

Bedrooms: 3

Baths: 2

Foundation: Crawl, Slab

317 Windstone Place

Windstone Collection I

This master-planned Nelson Design Group home is designed to capture the classic style and splendor of historical Southern architecture. Let summer days slip away on a traditional eight foot covered front porch. An elegant foyer leads directly to a marvelous great room complete with a built-in media center, computer nook and efficient gas fireplace. Pass through remarkable wooden columns into a formal dining area — perfect for elegant dinner parties and conveniently located with fluid access to the kitchen. Invite friends over for a cookout using the side covered grilling porch. Intricate french doors lead to a grand master suite and adjoining full master bath with all the amenities you've come to expect.

Width: 39' 0"

Depth: 72' 0"

Total Living: 1,915 sq. ft.

Price Tier: B

Main Ceiling: 10 ft.

Bedrooms: 3

Baths: 2

Foundation: Crawl, Slab

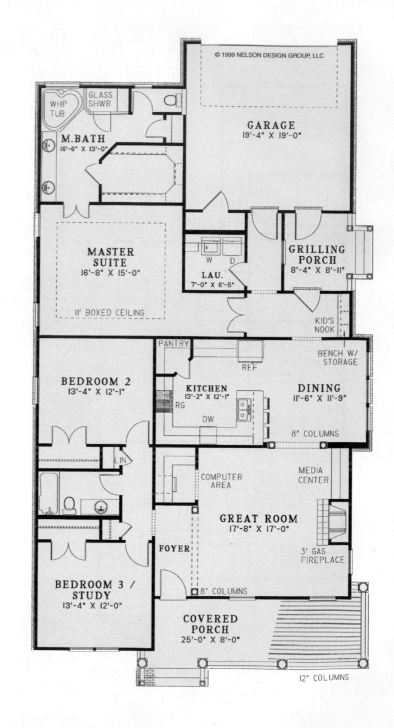

© 1999 NELSON DESIGN GROUP, LLC

GARAGE
19'-4" X 19'-0"

WHP TUB

GLASS SHWR

M. BATH
16'-6" X 13'-0"

MASTER SUITE
16'-8" X 15'-0"

11' BOXED CEILING

LAU.
7'-0" X 6'-5"

GRILLING PORCH
8'-4" X 8'-11"

KID'S NOOK

PANTRY

REF

BENCH W/ STORAGE

BEDROOM 2
13'-4" X 12'-1"

KITCHEN
13'-2" X 12'-1"

RG

DW

DINING
11'-6" X 11'-9"

8" COLUMNS

LIN

COMPUTER AREA

MEDIA CENTER

GREAT ROOM
17'-8" X 17'-0"

FOYER

3' GAS FIREPLACE

BEDROOM 3 / STUDY
13'-4" X 12'-0"

8" COLUMNS

COVERED PORCH
25'-0" X 8'-0"

12" COLUMNS

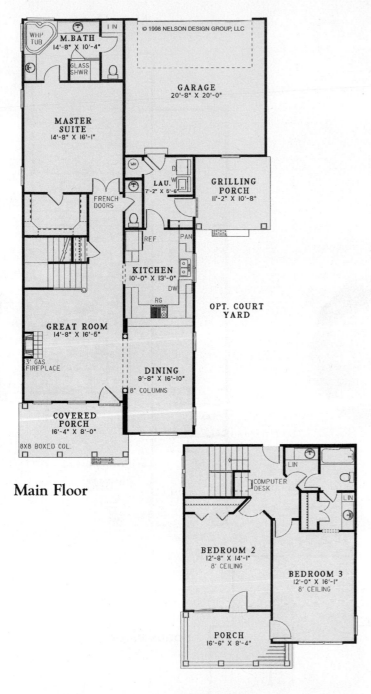

Main Floor

WHP TUB

M. BATH
14'-8" X 10'-4"

© 1998 NELSON DESIGN GROUP, LLC

I IN

GLASS SHWR

GARAGE
20'-8" X 20'-0"

MASTER SUITE
14'-8" X 16'-1"

FRENCH DOORS

LAU.
7'-2" X 5'-6"

GRILLING PORCH
11'-2" X 10'-8"

REF   PAN

KITCHEN
10'-0" X 13'-0"

DW

RG

OPT. COURT YARD

GREAT ROOM
14'-8" X 16'-5"

3' GAS FIREPLACE

DINING
9'-8" X 16'-10"

8" COLUMNS

COVERED PORCH
16'-4" X 8'-0"

8X8 BOXED COL.

Upper Floor

LIN

COMPUTER DESK

LIN

BEDROOM 2
12'-8" X 14'-1"
8' CEILING

BEDROOM 3
12'-0" X 16'-1"
8' CEILING

PORCH
16'-6" X 8'-4"

316 Windstone Place

Windstone Collection I

Forget the fast-paced hustle and bustle and embrace quiet times of yesterday when you enjoy the view from a spacious covered front porch on a warm spring day in this Nelson Design Group home. An extraordinary great room with gas fireplace, accented with open stairs leading to the upper floor, will certainly provide countless hours of entertainment for the entire family. Attached to the great room is a formal dining area – perfect for elegant dinner parties and enhanced by beautifully-crafted wood columns. Past the stairway, and accessible only through privacy french doors, is the master suite and bath. The upper floor is a perfect haven for children of all ages, complete with a built-in computer desk and balcony porch.

Width: 36' 4"	Main Ceiling: 9 ft.
Depth: 64' 10"	Upper Ceiling: 8 ft.
Main Floor: 1,298 sq. ft.	Bedrooms: 3
Upper Floor: 624 sq. ft.	Baths: 2 1/2
Total Living: 1,922 sq. ft.	Foundation: Crawl, Slab, Optional Basement
Price Tier: B	Optional Daylight Basement

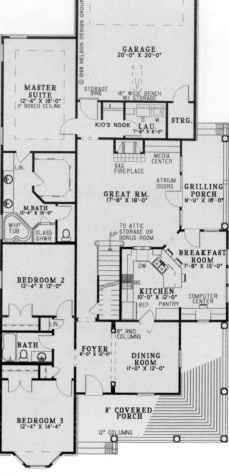

355 Windstone Place

Windstone Collection II

Imagine yourself in this Nelson Design Group home. Each day is a dream come true as you enjoy quiet summer evenings over iced tea and conversation on your covered front porch. Become the perfect host or hostess of charming dinners in your dining room easily and conveniently accessible to the kitchen and breakfast room. A side grilling porch just off the breakfast room provides ample space for entertaining as well. After dining, adjourn to the great room for coffee in front of a gas fireplace. Then retreat to a wonderful master suite complete with master bath including a whirlpool tub and double vanity. But don't worry about the kids, they'll have plenty of space to play in the proposed upper level bonus area with nine foot ceilings.

Width: 39' 0"

Depth: 82' 4"

Total Living: 1,927 sq. ft.*

*Optional Bonus: 909 sq. ft.

Price Tier: B

Main Ceiling: 10 ft.

Bonus Ceiling: 9 ft.

Bedrooms: 3

Baths: 2

Foundation: Crawl, Slab, Basement, Daylight Basement

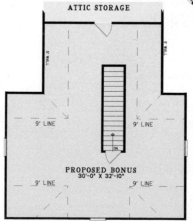

Bonus Floor

To order call 1.800.590.2423 or to view the rest of this collection visit www.nelsondesigngroup.com

Upper Floor

ATTIC STRG.

BED RM. 2
13'-0" X 11'-10"

LOFT

OPEN TO BELOW

WINDOW SEAT

LIN.

BED RM. 3
13'-0" X 10'-10"

© 1998 NELSON DESIGN GROUP, LLC

GARAGE
19'-4" X 20'-0"

GRILLING PORCH
10'-10" X 8'-0"

BRKFAST RM.
10'-6" X 8'-0"

KID'S NOOK
BENCH W/ STORAGE

STORAGE BINS

LAU.

D

STORAGE
6'-4" X 5'-6"

W H

PANTRY

HANGING

DW

KITCHEN
13'-0" X 10'-8"

RG.

REF.

LIN

UP

MASTER SUITE
13'-0" X 14'-6"
10' BOXED CEILING

DINING RM.
13'-0" X 10'-8"

8" COLUMNS

8" COLUMNS

WHP TUB

COMPUTER CENTER

M. BATH
13'-0" X 12'-10"

GAS FIREPLACE

8" COLUMNS

BATH

GREAT RM.
17'-0" X 15'-0"

MEDIA CENTER

FOYER

COVERED PORCH
21'-0" X 8'-0"

GUEST RM. / STUDY
13'-0" X 11'-10"

12" COLUMNS

Main Floor

309 Windstone Place
Windstone Collection I

This traditional Nelson Design Group home is enhanced by historical southern style. After enjoying hours of relaxation on your covered front porch, retreat to the great room with its romantic gas fireplace and built-in media center. Attached is the formal dining area with elegant eight inch wood columns, perfect for lovely dinner parties or quiet romantic evenings. A spacious kitchen and breakfast area opens to a rear covered grilling porch and kid's nook complete with built-in storage bench, storage bins and hanging space. Traveling upstairs you'll find two spacious bedrooms accented by an open loft with a view of the foyer below.

Width: 36' 4"	Main Ceiling: 9 ft.
Depth: 73' 6"	Upper Ceiling: 8 ft.
Main Floor: 1,558 sq. ft.	Bedrooms: 4
Upper Floor: 429 sq. ft.	Baths: 3
Total Living: 1,987 sq. ft.	Foundation: Crawl, Slab, Optional Basement, Optional Daylight Basement
Price Tier: B	

529 Windstone Place

Windstone Collection III

This Nelson Design Group design offers the utmost living environment. Enter the front door and begin a journey of truly inspired family areas. The breakfast nook, a room of its own, adjoins the kitchen complete with extra bar seating and an open view of the great room. For a central location, the computer desk is conveniently placed in a hall nook outside of the great room. The master suite located on the main floor, has a ten foot boxed ceiling, a bathroom filled with amenities and a large walk-in closet. This split bedroom plan has two bedrooms upstairs, each with a private access vanity. An optional media/TV room is available as well as a huge bonus room located above the garage.

Width: 35' 6"

Depth: 74' 8"

Main Floor: 1,485 sq. ft.

Upper Floor: 531 sq. ft.

Total Living: 2,016 sq. ft.*

*Optional Bonus: 426 sq. ft.

Price Tier: C

Main Ceiling: 9 ft.

Upper Ceiling: 8 ft.

Bedrooms: 3

Baths: 2 1/2

Foundation: Crawl, Slab, Optional Basement, Optional Daylight Basement

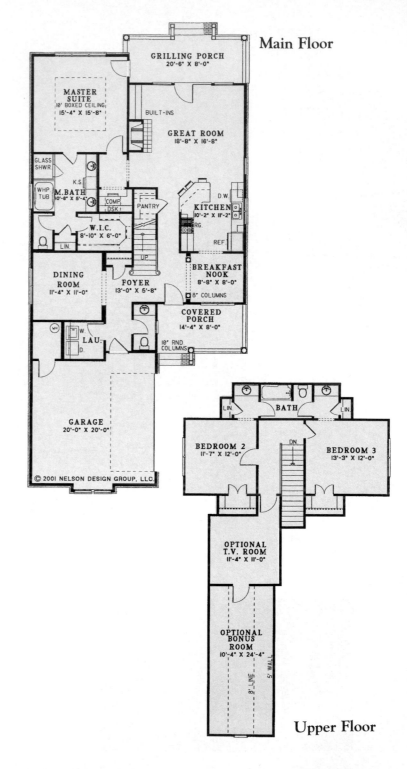

Main Floor

© 2001 NELSON DESIGN GROUP, LLC.

Upper Floor

Main Floor

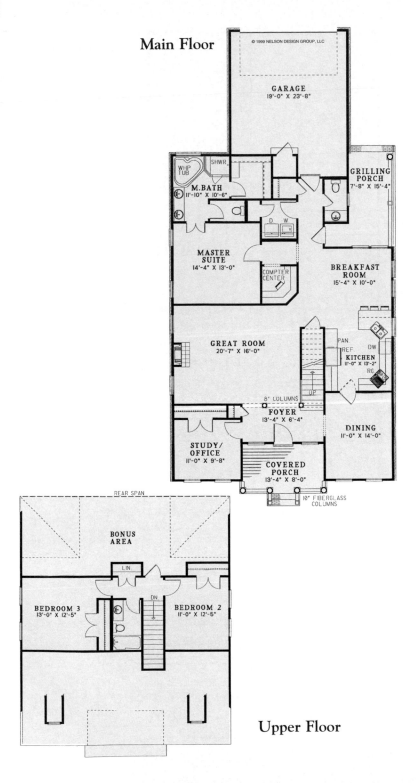

© 1999 NELSON DESIGN GROUP, LLC

GARAGE
19'-0" X 23'-8"

WHP TUB

SHWR

M. BATH
11'-10" X 10'-6"

GRILLING PORCH
7'-8" X 15'-4"

D W

MASTER SUITE
14'-4" X 13'-0"

COMPTER CENTER

BREAKFAST ROOM
15'-4" X 10'-0"

GREAT ROOM
20'-7" X 16'-0"

PAN.
REF.
DW

KITCHEN
11'-0" X 13'-2"

RG.

UP

8" COLUMNS

FOYER
13'-4" X 6'-4"

DINING
11'-0" X 14'-0"

STUDY/ OFFICE
11'-0" X 9'-8"

COVERED PORCH
13'-4" X 8'-0"

10" FIBERGLASS COLUMNS

REAR SPAN

BONUS AREA

LIN.

DN.

BEDROOM 3
13'-0" X 12'-5"

BEDROOM 2
11'-0" X 12'-5"

Upper Floor

337 Windstone Place
Windstone Collection II

Stepping onto the covered entry porch and through the main floor of this Nelson Design Group home, you'll instantly feel the grandeur of traditional southern style. Enjoy hours of family entertainment in your huge great room adjacent to a formal dining room — perfect for elegant parties or casual gatherings. A convenient swinging door allows access from the dining room to a wonderful kitchen area, providing ultimate ease in the preparation and presentation of your favorite meals. After a long day, retreat to a secluded master suite, while the kids enjoy two spacious bedrooms on the upper floor. An upstairs bonus area can be easily converted to an extraordinary game room or quiet study space.

Width: 36' 8"	Main Ceiling: 9 ft.
Depth: 75' 6"	Upper Ceiling: 8 ft.
Main Floor: 1,690 sq. ft.	Bedrooms: 3
Upper Floor: 450 sq. ft.	Baths: 2 1/2
Total Living: 2,140 sq. ft.	Foundation: Crawl, Slab, Optional Basement,
Price Tier: C	Optional Daylight Basement

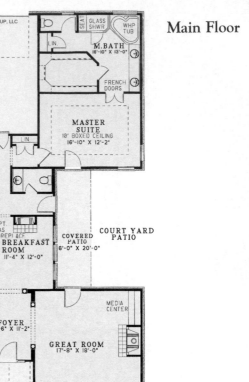

Main Floor

© 1999 NELSON DESIGN GROUP, LLC

GARAGE
21'-0" X 20'-0"

M.BATH
18'-10" X 13'-0"

SEAT GLASS SHWR

WHP TUB

LIN.

FRENCH DOORS

MASTER SUITE
10' BOXED CEILING
16'-10" X 12'-2"

LAU.
7'-0" X 5'-6"

UP

OPT. GAS FIREPLACE

BREAKFAST ROOM
11'-4" X 12'-0"

KITCHEN
12'-3" X 12'-0"

REF.

PANTRY

COVERED PATIO
6'-0" X 20'-0"

COURT YARD PATIO

8" COLUMNS

FOYER
7'-6" X 11'-2"

MEDIA CENTER

DINING
11'-8" X 14'-0"

GREAT ROOM
17'-8" X 18'-0"

PORCH
21'-6" X 8'-0"

VAULTED CEILING

391 Windstone Place

Windstone Collection III

Welcome your friends and family to this traditional Nelson Design Group home. Leading your guests into the foyer, they'll notice all the beautiful columns surrounding all entrances from the foyer to the adjoining rooms. Your spacious great room has a warm fireplace for those cold mornings. The gorgeous courtyard can be viewed by accessing the side covered patio from either the great room or master suite. The optional fireplace in the breakfast room will create a cozy environment for family breakfasts. Upstairs, you'll find two more bedrooms with walk-thru access to the bath.

Width: 38' 10"
Depth: 70' 4"
Main Floor: 1,654 sq. ft.
Upper Floor: 492 sq. ft.
Total Living: 2,146 sq. ft.
Price Tier: C

Main Ceiling: 9 ft.
Upper Ceiling: 8 ft.
Bedrooms: 3
Baths: 2 1/2
Foundation: Crawl, Slab, Optional Basement, Optional Daylight Basement

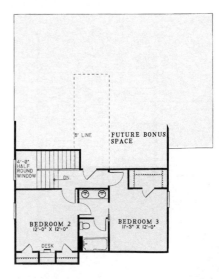

8' LINE

FUTURE BONUS SPACE

4'-0" HALF ROUND WINDOW

DN.

BEDROOM 2
12'-0" X 12'-0"

BEDROOM 3
11'-3" X 12'-0"

DESK

Upper Floor

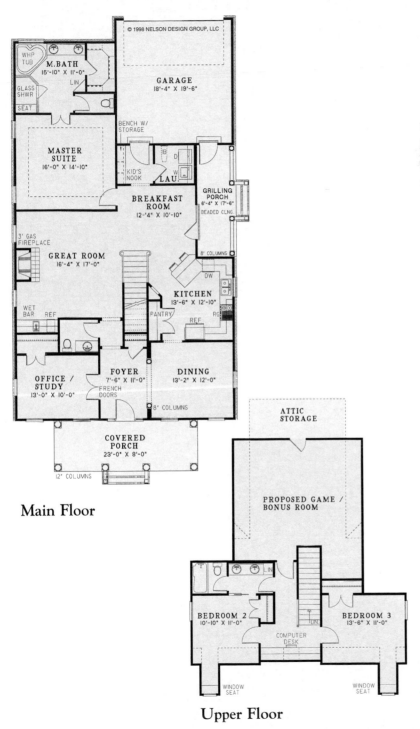

Main Floor

Upper Floor

318 Windstone Place
Windstone Collection I

Pamper yourself with Southern charm when you select this Nelson Design Group home. Become instantly immersed in tradition as you step into an elegant foyer designed with an open entrance to the formal dining room. Brilliant french doors open to a private study for late night work or quiet time with your favorite book. Enjoy romantic nights in front of a roaring fire while you sip drinks from the built-in wet bar in the great room. Plan a fun cookout and show off your famous barbeque skills while utilizing the side grilling porch. A spacious upper level with a bonus room – perfect for a game or study area – allows plenty of space for the kids.

Width: 35' 4"
Depth: 71' 6"
Main Floor: 1,698 sq. ft.
Upper Floor: 533 sq. ft.
Total Living: 2,231 sq. ft.*
*Optional Bonus: 394 sq. ft.
Price Tier: C

Main Ceiling: 9 ft.
Upper Ceiling: 8 ft.
Bedrooms: 3
Baths: 2 1/2
Foundation: Crawl, Slab, Basement, Daylight Basement

343 Windstone Place
Windstone Collection II

Upon entering this Nelson Design Group home notice the elegant dining room, adjoined to a butler pantry, creating fluid entry to a marvelously spacious kitchen. The great room, complete with a romantic gas fireplace and built-in media center, is at the heart of the design with an open entry to a breakfast room. Enjoy countless possibilities entertaining on your convenient grilling porch. Stairs with left and right hand volutes take you to the spacious upper level. Two bedrooms with window seats, a full bath and bonus area with attic storage provide plenty of room for the kids.

Width: 32' 0"

Depth: 83' 4"

Main Floor: 1,831 sq. ft.

Upper Floor: 455 sq. ft.

Total Living: 2,286 sq. ft.

Price Tier: C

Main Ceiling: 9 ft.

Upper Ceiling: 8 ft.

Bedrooms: 4

Baths: 3

Foundation: Crawl, Slab, Basement, Daylight Basement

Main Floor

Upper Floor

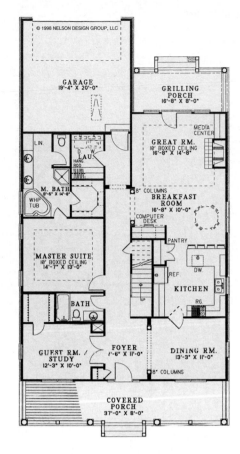

Main Floor

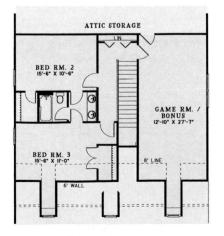

Upper Floor

307 Windstone Place
Windstone Collection I

This Nelson Design Group home is full of all the amenities of true southern style. Lazy summer afternoons slip by as you sit and visit with friends and family on the traditional eight foot covered entry porch. A formal foyer with eight inch wood columns leads you through to an elegant dining area. A master suite and bath will pamper you as you enjoy the luxury of a corner whirlpool tub with privacy glass block windows, large walk-in closet, corner glass shower and double 'his and hers' vanities with linen cabinet. The rear grilling porch with atrium doors leads to the great room – perfect for entertaining any time of year. The upper floor creates a wonderful area for kids of all ages with two spacious bedrooms with walk-through bath and a large game room.

Width: 37' 0"	Main Ceiling: 9 ft.
Depth: 73' 0"	Upper Ceiling: 8 ft.
Main Floor: 1,713 sq. ft.	Bedrooms: 3
Upper Floor: 610 sq. ft.	Baths: 3
Total Living: 2,323 sq. ft.*	Foundation: Crawl, Slab, Optional Basement, Optional Daylight Basement
*Optional Bonus: 384 sq. ft.	
Price Tier: C	

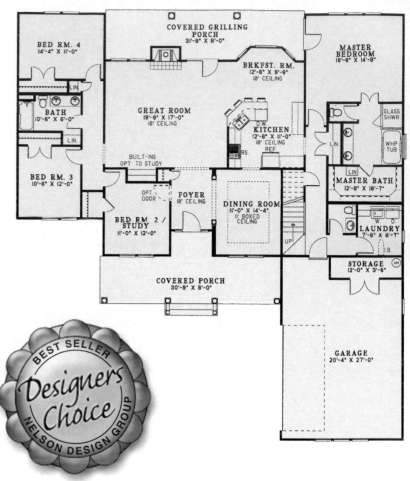

Main Floor

COVERED GRILLING PORCH
31'-8" X 8'-0"

BED RM. 4
14'-4" X 11'-0"

MASTER BEDROOM
16'-6" X 14'-8"

BRKFST. RM.
12'-6" X 9'-6"
10' CEILING

LIN

BATH
10'-6" X 6'-0"

GREAT ROOM
19'-6" X 17'-0"
10' CEILING

GLASS SHWR

D.W.
KITCHEN
12'-6" X 11'-0"
10' CEILING

LIN

WHP TUB

REF.

LIN

BED RM. 3
10'-6" X 12'-0"

BUILT-INS OPT TO STUDY

MASTER BATH
12'-8" X 16'-7"

OPT. DOOR

FOYER
10' CEILING

DINING ROOM
11'-0" X 14'-4"
11' BOXED CEILING

LIN

W. D.

LAUNDRY
7'-6" X 8'-7"

BED RM. 2 / STUDY
11'-0" X 12'-0"

UP

STORAGE
12'-0" X 3'-6"

WH

COVERED PORCH
30'-9" X 8'-0"

GARAGE
20'-4" X 27'-0"

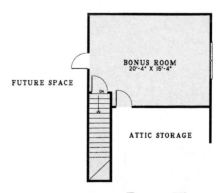

528 Windstone Place

Windstone Collection III

Cedar shake and a cozy porch with round columns introduce this split bedroom plan. Our Nelson Design Group home is elegant enough for the elite and conservative at the same time. Once inside the foyer, a ten foot ceiling continues through to the great room for a grand effect. The dining room has a column entry with access to the kitchen enhanced with an eleven foot boxed ceiling and with open bar seating. The kitchen and breakfast room both with ten foot ceilings, enjoy an outside view looking through a large covered grilling porch. An elegant master suite includes a large walk-in closet, whirlpool tub, shower and separate toilet room. A large laundry room and half bathroom lead to a courtyard entry garage. An upstairs bonus room is available if desired.

BONUS ROOM
20'-4" X 15'-4"

FUTURE SPACE

ON

ATTIC STORAGE

Bonus Floor

Width: 66' 0"	Main Ceiling: 9 ft.
Depth: 72' 7"	Bonus Ceiling: 8 ft.
Total Living: 2,354 sq. ft.*	Bedrooms: 4
*Optional Bonus: 326 sq. ft.	Baths: 2 1/2
Price Tier: C	Foundation: Crawl, Slab, Optional Basement, Optional Daylight Basement

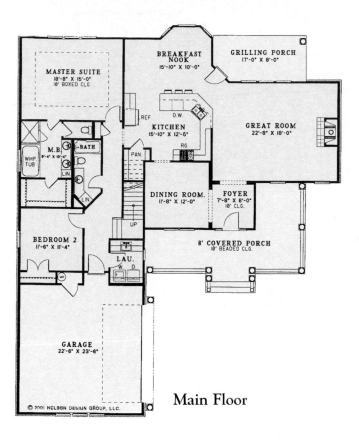

MASTER SUITE
18'-8" X 15'-0"
10' BOXED CLG.

BREAKFAST NOOK
15'-10" X 10'-0"

GRILLING PORCH
17'-0" X 8'-0"

REF.   D.W.

KITCHEN
15'-10" X 12'-6"

GREAT ROOM
22'-8" X 18'-0"

M.B.-BATH

WHP. TUB   M.B.
9'-4" X 10'-4"

LIN

RG.

PAN.

LIN

DINING ROOM.
11'-8" X 12'-0"

FOYER
7'-8" X 8'-0"
10' CLG.

UP

BEDROOM 2
11'-6" X 11'-4"

8' COVERED PORCH
10' BEADED CLG.

LAU.
W   D

GARAGE
22'-6" X 23'-6"

© 2001 NELSON DESIGN GROUP, LLC.

Main Floor

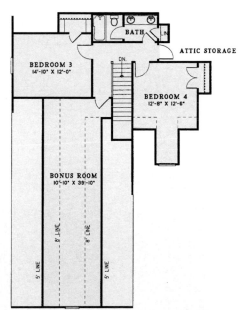

BATH

ATTIC STORAGE

BEDROOM 3
14'-10" X 12'-0"

DN.

BEDROOM 4
12'-8" X 12'-6"

BONUS ROOM
10'-10" X 39'-10"

8' LINE   8' LINE

5' LINE   5' LINE

Upper Floor

538 Windstone Place
Windstone Collection III

A wrap-around porch with a ten foot beaded ceiling, round columns and gentle arches welcomes you into this Nelson Design Group home. The foyer also carries a ten foot ceiling and leads into a great room with fireplace and a view overlooking the grilling porch. A wide walkway leads you into the breakfast nook adjoining the kitchen and through to the formal dining room. Entertaining will be enjoyable for both you and guests with this easy flowing floor plan. The master suite adorned with a boxed ceiling, as well as one bedroom and full bath are on the main floor. Upstairs has two additional bedrooms, a full bath and large bonus room located over the garage.

Width: 58' 6"
Depth: 71' 10"
Main Floor: 1,992 sq. ft.
Upper Floor: 643 sq. ft.
Total Living: 2,635 sq. ft.*
*Optional Bonus: 468 sq. ft.
Price Tier: D

Main Ceiling: 9 ft.
Upper Ceiling: 9 ft.
Bedrooms: 4
Baths: 3
Foundation: Crawl, Slab, Optional Basement, Optional Daylight Basement

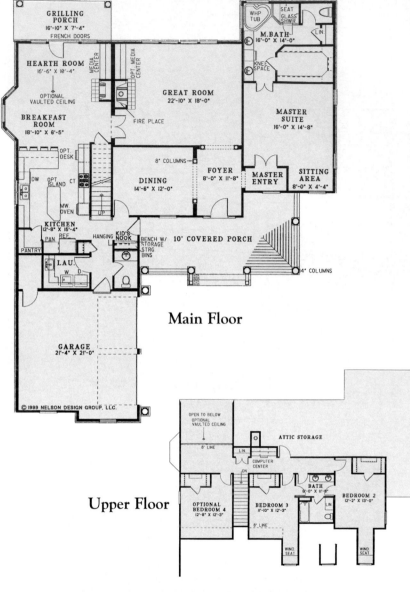

Main Floor

Upper Floor

354 Windstone Place
Windstone Collection II

This grand one and a half story Nelson Design Group home combines historic southern charm with modern technology and design. A spacious two-car garage and engaging covered front porch with 14 inch columns allow optimum convenience. A marvelous foyer leads directly to an elegant dining room and comfortable great room — perfect for family fun. A separate entrance opens to a sitting area joined to the master suite, providing ample privacy and comfort. The family will love cookouts on your grilling porch — accessible to both a hearth room and breakfast nook by way of French doors. Traveling to the upper level you'll find ample bedrooms for the kids — complete with a computer area.

Width: 59' 4"
Depth: 74' 2"
Main Floor: 2,082 sq. ft.
Upper Floor: 695 sq. ft.
Total Living: 2,777 sq. ft.*
*Optional Bonus: 310 sq. ft.
Price Tier: D

Main Ceiling: 9 ft.
Upper Ceiling: 8 ft.
Bedrooms: 4
Baths: 2
Foundation: Crawl, Slab, Optional Basement, Optional Daylight Basement

To order call 1.800.590.2423 or to view the rest of this collection visit www.nelsondesigngroup.com

Arts&Crafts™ collection

"A step back in time"

This collection of timeless home designs celebrates the most functional use of space and building materials. With emphasis on simplicity, these designs feature lovely front porches, columns and built-ins and are suitable for narrow lots. These beautiful designs focus on family areas while allowing adequate storage to help create an uncluttered environment. Although these designs have been updated to suit today's busy lifestyle, the integrity of the Arts and Crafts era is maintained by using craftsman quality interior and exterior finishes.

Nelson Design Group LLC

RESIDENTIAL PLANNERS - DESIGNERS

626 Fir

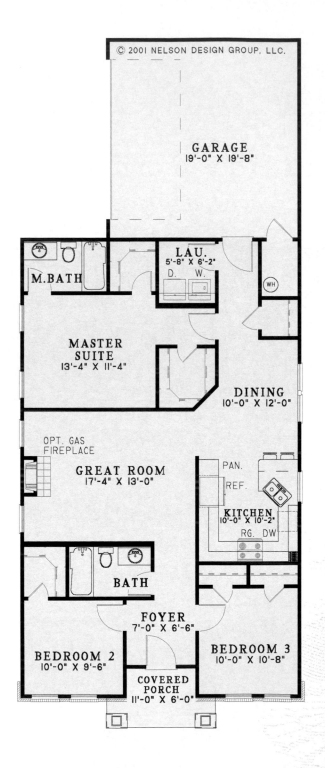

© 2001 NELSON DESIGN GROUP, LLC.

GARAGE
19'-0" X 19'-8"

LAU.
5'-8" X 6'-2"
D. W.

M.BATH

WH

MASTER
SUITE
13'-4" X 11'-4"

DINING
10'-0" X 12'-0"

OPT. GAS
FIREPLACE

GREAT ROOM
17'-4" X 13'-0"

PAN.
REF.

KITCHEN
10'-0" X 10'-2"

RG. DW

BATH

FOYER
7'-0" X 6'-6"

BEDROOM 2
10'-0" X 9'-6"

BEDROOM 3
10'-0" X 10'-8"

COVERED
PORCH
11'-0" X 6'-0"

Greet your family and friends on the lovely covered porch of this Nelson Design Group Arts and Crafts style home. The warmth of this split bedroom design will capture the attention your guests as they enter the foyer. Two bedrooms are gently placed at the front of the home for privacy and possibly used as a study if desired. An attractive great room offers you the perfect place to relax and has an abundance of wall space for treasured antiques. The convenience of the kitchen to dining room will keep dinnertime less hectic and more enjoyable. As evening falls find seclusion in the master suite complete with spacious walk-in closet and private bathroom.

Width: 28' 4" • Depth: 69' 0" • Total Living: 1,259 sq. ft.
Main Ceiling: 9 ft. • Bedrooms: 3 • Baths: 2
Foundation: Crawl, Slab, Opt. Basement and Opt. Daylight Basement
Price Tier: A

To order call 1.800.590.2423 or to view similar plans visit www.nelsondesigngroup.com

© 2001 NELSON DESIGN GROUP, LLC.

GARAGE
19'-0" X 20'-0"

MASTER SUITE
12'-8" X 12'-0"

DINING
14'-6" X 10'-0"

PANTRY

BATH

LAUNDRY
5'-6" X 7'-6"

W. D.

DW

KIT.
14'-6" X 10'-8"

RG.

REF.

STORAGE

BEDROOM 2
11'-4" X 10'-6"

LIN.

GREAT ROOM
14'-8" X 16'-10"

OPT. GAS
FIREPLACE

BATH

FOYER

BEDROOM 3
11'-6" X 10'-0"

COVERED PORCH
23'-2" X 6'-0"

628 Mulberry

Indulge yourself in this timeless Arts and Crafts style home by Nelson Design Group. Columns and a beaded ceiling gracefully adorn the front covered porch. Relax with family in the spacious great room with optional fireplace. A lovely step saver kitchen with angled bar counter and a large pantry adjoins the dining room for the ultimate dinner gathering. The laundry room is located just steps away from the kitchen for convenience and if two bedrooms are sufficient, use the third as an optional study or den. The master suite is quietly placed at the rear of the home and has plenty of wall space, a spacious walk-in closet, and a private bathroom.

Width: 32' 8" • Depth: 65' 2" • Total Living: 1,348 sq. ft.
Main Ceiling: 9 ft. • Bedrooms: 3 • Baths: 2
Foundation: Crawl, Slab, Opt. Basement and Opt. Daylight Basement
Price Tier: A

To order call 1.800.590.2423 or to view similar plans visit www.nelsondesigngroup.com

625 Sycamore

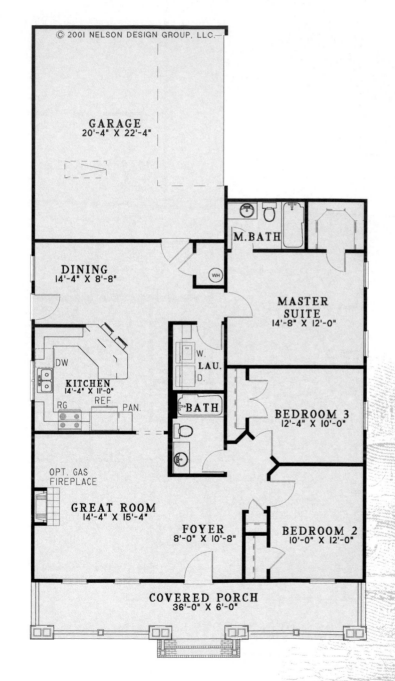

© 2001 NELSON DESIGN GROUP, LLC.

GARAGE
20'-4" X 22'-4"

M.BATH

DINING
14'-4" X 8'-8"

WH

MASTER SUITE
14'-8" X 12'-0"

DW

KITCHEN
14'-4" X 11'-0"

W. LAU. D.

RG   REF   PAN.

BATH

BEDROOM 3
12'-4" X 10'-0"

OPT. GAS FIREPLACE

GREAT ROOM
14'-4" X 15'-4"

FOYER
8'-0" X 10'-8"

BEDROOM 2
10'-0" X 12'-0"

COVERED PORCH
36'-0" X 6'-0"

A covered porch with brick columns and railing add great street appeal to this Nelson Design Group Arts and Crafts style home. Enjoy conversation with friends and loved ones in the great room with cozy fireplace. Easy access from the kitchen to the dining room across an angled bar counter makes serving your meals a delight. This design offers a double bedroom area with full bath that is ideal for the kids or overnight guests while separate from the master suite entry. For privacy and convenience the master suite is located at the rear of the house and has a private bathroom and large walk-in closet.

Width: 36' 0" • Depth: 65' 0" • Total Living: 1,374 sq. ft.
Main Ceiling: 9 ft. • Bedrooms: 3 • Baths: 2
Foundation: Crawl, Slab, Opt. Basement and Opt. Daylight Basement
Price Tier: A

629 Redwood

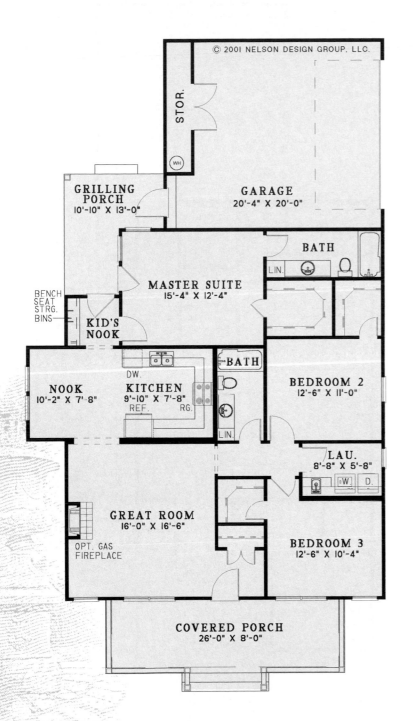

STOR.

GRILLING PORCH
10'-10" X 13'-0"

GARAGE
20'-4" X 20'-0"

WH

BATH

MASTER SUITE
15'-4" X 12'-4"

LIN.

BENCH SEAT STRG. BINS

KID'S NOOK

BATH

DW.

NOOK
10'-2" X 7'-8"

KITCHEN
9'-10" X 7'-8"

REF.   RG.

BEDROOM 2
12'-6" X 11'-0"

LIN.

LAU.
8'-8" X 5'-8"

W   D.

GREAT ROOM
16'-0" X 16'-6"

OPT. GAS FIREPLACE

BEDROOM 3
12'-6" X 10'-4"

COVERED PORCH
26'-0" X 8'-0"

This Nelson Design Group home has detail and style reminiscent of the Arts and Crafts era. Enjoy a cup of coffee with neighbors on the expansive front porch detailed with double columns and railing. Upon entry notice a large closet perfect for seasonal storage and on to the large great room complete with a cozy fireplace for cherished family time. A breakfast nook is attached to the kitchen and just steps from the grilling porch entry. A nearby kid's nook keeps clutter at a minimum. The master suite has a private bath, a large walk-in closet and is located at the rear of the home. For convenience, the laundry room is centrally located next to the two additional bedrooms and bathroom.

Width: 39' 0" • Depth: 68' 6" • Total Living: 1,399 sq. ft.
Main Ceiling: 9 ft. • Bedrooms: 3 • Baths: 2
Foundation: Crawl, Slab, Opt. Basement and Opt. Daylight Basement
Price Tier: A

To order call 1.800.590.2423 or to view similar plans visit www.nelsondesigngroup.com

630 Maple

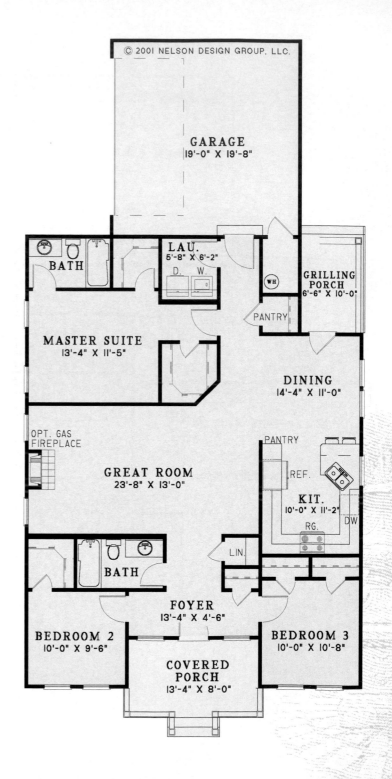

This Nelson Design Group home is styled in the Arts and Crafts era with an updated floor plan. Once inside the foyer, bedrooms on either side are away from the private master suite at the rear of the home. An expansive great room with fireplace is centrally located and opens to a large dining room. The U-shaped kitchen is a step saver and includes a bar counter for serving buffet style. Dining will be fun for the whole family with easy access to the grilling porch. After the kids are in bed, find solitude in your master suite with private bath and 'his and her' walk-in closets.

Width: 34' 8" • Depth: 69' 0" • Total Living: 1,442 sq. ft.
Main Ceiling: 9 ft. • Bedrooms: 3 • Baths: 2
Foundation: Crawl, Slab, Opt. Basement and Opt. Daylight Basement
Price Tier: A

589 Magnolia

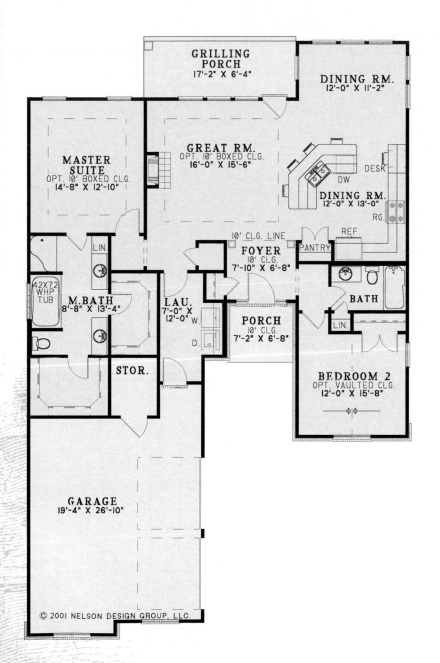

GRILLING PORCH
17'-2" X 6'-4"

DINING RM.
12'-0" X 11'-2"

MASTER SUITE
OPT. 10' BOXED CLG.
14'-8" X 12'-10"

GREAT RM.
OPT. 10' BOXED CLG.
16'-0" X 15'-6"

DESK

DW

DINING RM.
12'-0" X 13'-0"

RG.

10' CLG. LINE

REF.

LIN.

FOYER
10' CLG.
7'-10" X 6'-8"

PANTRY

42X72 WHP TUB

M. BATH
8'-8" X 13'-4"

LAU.
7'-0" X 12'-0"

W.

BATH

PORCH
10' CLG.
7'-2" X 6'-8"

LIN.

D.

STOR.

BEDROOM 2
OPT. VAULTED CLG.
12'-0" X 15'-8"

GARAGE
19'-4" X 26'-10"

© 2001 NELSON DESIGN GROUP, LLC.

Nelson Design Group has created an elegant design reflective of the Arts and Crafts era. Copper roofing and carriage style garage doors warmly welcome guests into this split bedroom plan. Ten foot ceilings and an abundance of windows allow natural light to flow throughout. An elegant master suite is fully suited as a private hideaway while the opposite side of the home includes a large kitchen and dining room with large bar island for additional seating. A courtyard entry garage allows for the utmost in security and convenience.

Width: 43' 0" • Depth: 66' 6" • Total Living: 1,474 sq. ft.
Main Ceiling: 9 ft. • Bedrooms: 2 • Baths: 2
Foundation: Crawl and Slab • Price Tier: A

627 PineOak

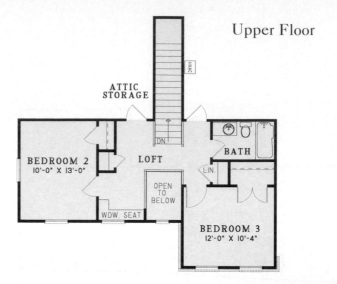

Main Floor

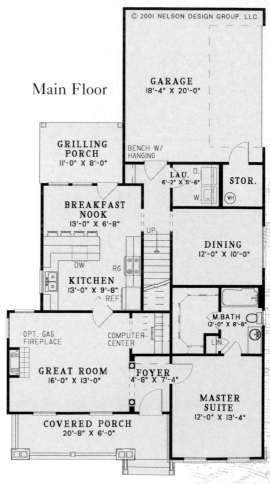

This Arts and Crafts style home by Nelson Design Group is simple yet elegant. A beaded ceiling and double columns set atop brick pillars enhancing the covered front porch. As you enter the foyer, admire eight-inch columns inviting you into a spacious great room with fireplace and swinging door to the kitchen. Family can enjoy a sunny breakfast nook adjoining the kitchen and accessing a rear-grilling porch. Just across the hall is a formal dining room for large family gatherings. For privacy and convenience, this split bedroom plan places the spacious master suite on the main level. Two additional two bedrooms, a full bath and a loft area with window are located upstairs.

Width: 34' 4" • Depth: 59' 6"
Main Floor: 1,063 sq. ft. • Upper Floor: 496 sq. ft.
Total Living: 1,559 sq. ft. • Main Ceiling: 9 ft. • Upper Ceiling: 8 ft.
Bedrooms: 3 • Baths: 2
Foundation: Crawl, Slab, Opt. Basement, Opt. Daylight Basement
Price Tier: B

To order call 1.800.590.2423 or to view similar plans visit www.nelsondesigngroup.com

588 Cypress

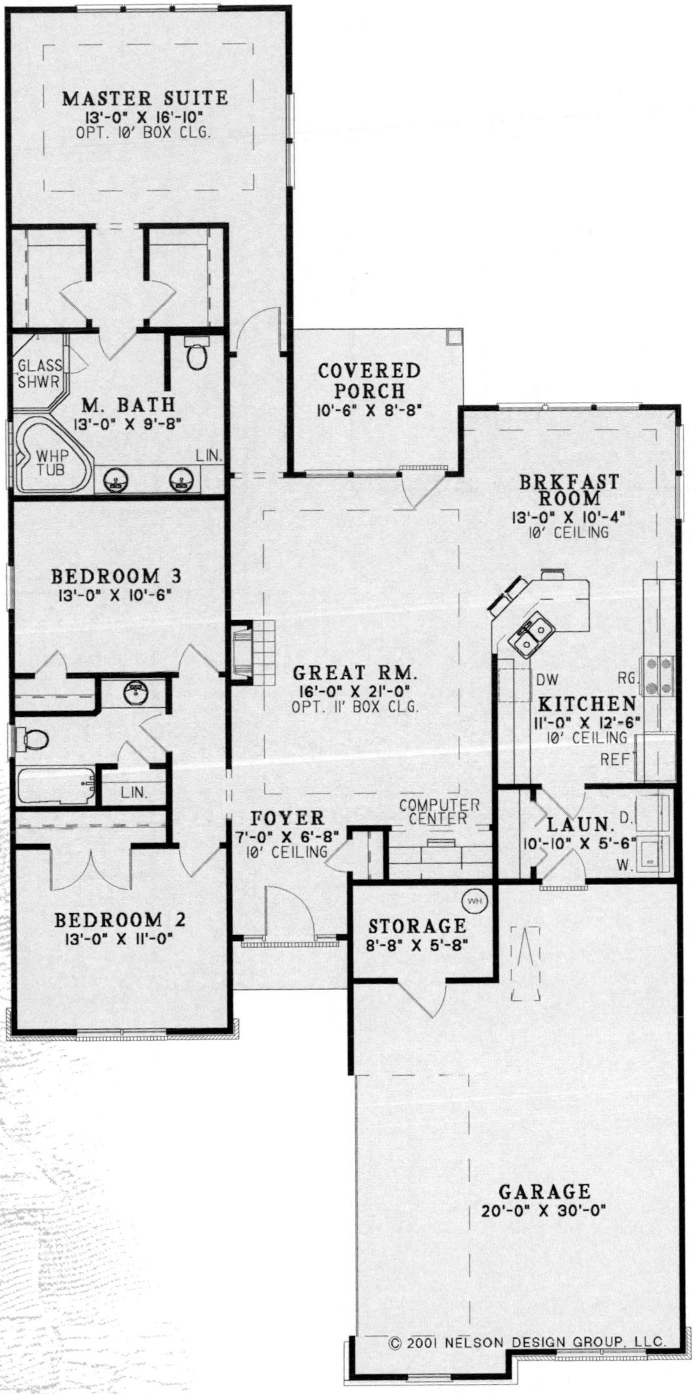

Floor plan labels:

MASTER SUITE
13'-0" X 16'-10"
OPT. 10' BOX CLG.

GLASS SHWR

M. BATH
13'-0" X 9'-8"

WHP TUB

LIN.

COVERED PORCH
10'-6" X 8'-8"

BRKFAST ROOM
13'-0" X 10'-4"
10' CEILING

BEDROOM 3
13'-0" X 10'-6"

GREAT RM.
16'-0" X 21'-0"
OPT. 11' BOX CLG.

DW   RG.

KITCHEN
11'-0" X 12'-6"
10' CEILING

REF

COMPUTER CENTER

LIN.

FOYER
7'-0" X 6'-8"
10' CEILING

LAUN. D.

W.

BEDROOM 2
13'-0" X 11'-0"

STORAGE
8'-8" X 5'-8"

WH

GARAGE
20'-0" X 30'-0"

© 2001 NELSON DESIGN GROUP, LLC.

This crafty design by Nelson Design Group combines a rustic exterior with an elegant interior. Ten-foot ceilings and an abundance of windows enhance the family areas for plenty of natural lighting. The breakfast room and kitchen are combined and enjoy a bar counter for additional seating. A large laundry room with pantry is located between the kitchen and garage access for convenience. On the opposite side of the home are two bedrooms, a full bath and a luxurious master suite with 10' boxed ceiling, his and her walk in closets and large bathroom with glass shower, whirlpool tub and double vanity.

Width: 41' 4" • Depth: 84' 2" • Total Living: 1,747 sq. ft.
Main Ceiling: 9 ft. • Bedrooms: 3 • Baths: 2
Foundation: Crawl and Slab • Price Tier: B

595 Jasmine

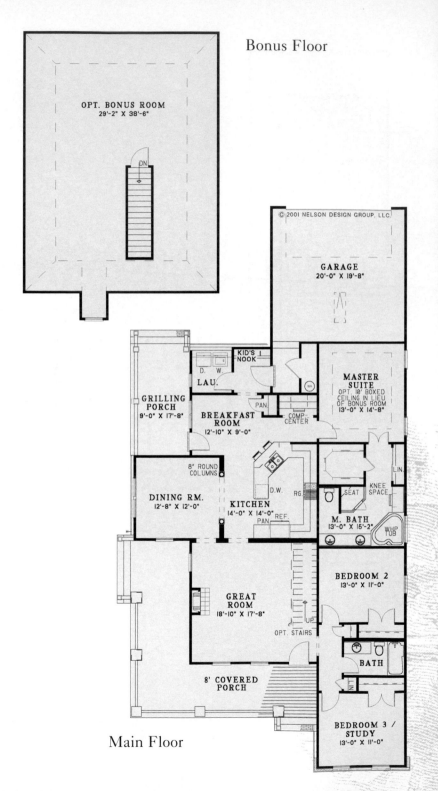

Bonus Floor

OPT. BONUS ROOM
29'-2" X 38'-6"

DN

© 2001 NELSON DESIGN GROUP, LLC.

GARAGE
20'-0" X 19'-8"

KID'S NOOK

D.W.

LAU.

GRILLING PORCH
9'-0" X 17'-8"

BREAKFAST ROOM
12'-10" X 9'-0"

PAN.

WH

COMP. CENTER

MASTER SUITE
OPT. 10' BOXED CEILING IN LIEU OF BONUS ROOM
13'-0" X 14'-8"

8" ROUND COLUMNS

DINING RM.
12'-8" X 12'-0"

KITCHEN
14'-0" X 14'-0"

D.W.

PAN.

REF.

RG.

LIN.

SEAT

KNEE SPACE

M. BATH
13'-0" X 15'-2"

WHP TUB

GREAT ROOM
18'-10" X 17'-8"

UP

OPT. STAIRS

BEDROOM 2
13'-0" X 11'-0"

BATH

8' COVERED PORCH

BEDROOM 3 / STUDY
13'-0" X 11'-0"

Main Floor

Nelson Design Group has created a cozy historical home with a corner wrapped wooden porch and large brick columns with railing. This split floor plan has a great room immediately upon entry with access to the two bedrooms and full bath. An efficient kitchen with an angled bar counter allows for additional seating and adjoins a large breakfast room and access to a side grilling porch. Also nearby is a convenient kid's nook located near the rear load garage entry. The luxurious master suite is enhanced with an optional ten-foot boxed ceiling and has French door access to the master bathroom packed with amenities. An optional bonus room is available upstairs for future needs.

Width: 41' 10" • Depth: 83' 8"
Main Floor: 1,836 sq. ft. • Opt. Bonus Floor: 1,116 sq. ft.
Total Living: 1,836 sq. ft. • Main Ceiling: 9 ft. • Bonus Ceiling: 8 ft.
Bedrooms: 3 • Baths: 2
Foundation: Crawl and Slab • Price Tier: B

586 Ivy

Upper Floor

BEDROOM 2
11'-0" X 13'-4"

8' LINE

4' WALL

BATH

BEDROOM 3
12'-8" X 13'-10"

8' LINE

5' WALL

DN.

WH

ATTIC STORAGE

Main Floor

WHP. TUB

M.BATH
14'-0" X 15'-0"

LIN.

W.I.C.   **W.I.C.**

GRILLING PORCH
12'-4" X 6'-0"

MASTER SUITE
14'-0" X 13'-6"

BREAKFAST ROOM
12'-0" X 9'-6"

STORAGE

COMPUTER CENTER

LAU.
6'-10" X 6'-10"

W. D.

GARAGE
17'-8" X 19'-4"

D.W.

RG.

ISLAND

UP

KITCHEN
REF. 12'-0" X 14'-0"

BUILT-INS

© 2001 NELSON DESIGN GROUP, LLC.

DINING
11'-8" X 12'-0"

GREAT RM.
14'-0" X 13'-8"

COVERED PORCH
20'-4" X 7'-0"

This Nelson Design Group home is reminiscent of days gone by. A lovely front covered porch is enhanced with railing and square tapered columns atop brick pillars. Upon entering a quaint foyer, the great room welcomes you with a large fireplace and built-ins while leading you into a large formal dining room opening into the kitchen and breakfast room. The master suite is located on the main floor for convenience and privacy. Upstairs you'll find two additional bedrooms with angled ceilings, a full bathroom and a large attic storage area.

Width: 45' 0" • Depth: 67' 2"
Main Floor: 1,412 sq. ft. • Upper Floor: 494 sq. ft.
Total Living: 1,906 sq. ft. • Main Ceiling: 9 ft. • Upper Ceiling: 8 ft.
Bedrooms: 3 • Baths: 2 1/2
Foundation: Crawl, Slab, Opt. Basement, Opt. Daylight Basement
Price Tier: B

596 Elm

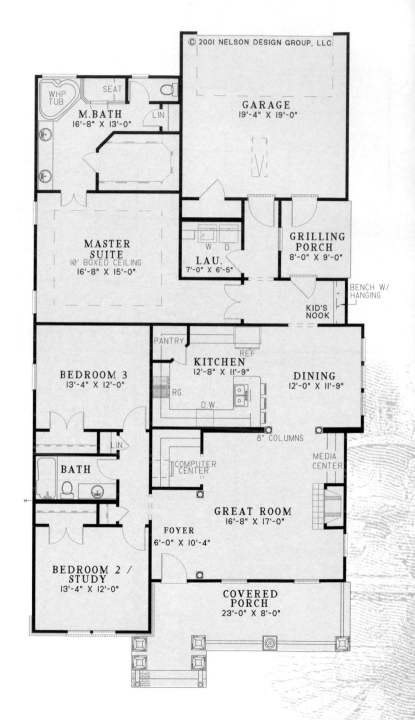

The detailing of this Nelson Design Group home warmly invites friends and family into a home reflective of the Craftsman Era. A covered porch leads to a foyer separating the guest bedrooms from the rest of the home. The great room entry has eight-inch columns, media center, a cozy fireplace and a hidden computer center. A spacious kitchen with bar seating adjoins the dining room and has a wall of windows for plenty of natural lighting. Conveniently located near the garage entry is a kid's nook with bench to help keep areas clutter free. A ten-foot boxed ceiling, a large walk-in closet, whirlpool tub and a separate shower with seat enhance the master suite for the ultimate privacy and relaxation.

Width: 37' 0" • Depth: 74' 4" • Total Living: 1,933 sq. ft.
Main Ceiling: 9 ft. • Bedrooms: 3 • Baths: 2
Foundation: Crawl and Slab • Price Tier: B

To order call 1.800.590.2423 or to view similar plans visit www.nelsondesigngroup.com

590 Willow

Main Floor

© 2001 NELSON DESIGN GROUP, LLC.

- GARAGE 21'-0" X 20'-0"
- SEAT
- WHP TUB
- M.BATH 16'-10" X 13'-0"
- LIN.
- W.I.C.
- FRENCH DOORS
- MASTER SUITE 10' BOXED CEILING 16'-10" X 12'-2"
- W. D LAU.
- WH
- UP
- COURT YARD PATIO
- BREAKFAST ROOM 11'-3" X 12'-0"
- GRILLING PORCH 6'-0" X 20'-0"
- RG DW KITCHEN 12'-4" X 12'-0"
- REF
- PANTRY
- BUILT-INS
- DINING 11'-8" X 14'-0"
- FOYER 7'-6" X 11'-3"
- GREAT ROOM 17'-8" X 18'-0"
- COVERED PORCH 22'-0" X 8'-0"

Upper Floor

- FUTURE BONUS SPACE
- 8' WALL
- DN.
- BEDROOM 2 12'-0" X 14'-4"
- DESK
- BEDROOM 3 11'-3" X 12'-0"
- 8' WALL

Gables, columns and architectural detailing give this Nelson Design Group home a warm feeling reminiscent of your grandmother's home. A cozy porch gently welcomes you into a foyer lined with columns and separating the formal dining room from a large great room with fireplace. The kitchen and breakfast room is centrally located and views a lovely courtyard patio perfect for entertaining. Your perfect hideaway awaits you in a spacious master suite with large walk-in closet and bathroom packed with amenities. The upstairs as two bedrooms each with private access to a full bathroom as well as future bonus space when desired.

Width: 38' 10" • Depth: 70' 4"
Main Floor: 1,654 sq. ft. • Upper Floor: 492 sq. ft.
Total Living: 2,146 sq. ft. • Main Ceiling: 9 ft. • Upper Ceiling: 8 ft.
Bedrooms: 3 • Baths: 2 1/2
Foundation: Crawl and Slab • Price Tier: C

594 Holly

Upper Floor

Main Floor

This Nelson Design Group home has dormers with copper roofing and a covered porch for lovely street appeal. The large great room with built-in wet bar and a large fireplace are centrally located for a family oriented atmosphere. A large breakfast room accesses the covered grilling porch perfect for entertaining. After a long day retire to your master bedroom with French door entry to your elegant master bathroom complete with whirlpool tub, separate shower and large walk-in closet. The upstairs has a built-in computer desk for study time, two bedrooms, a full bath, and a large optional game/bonus room.

Width: 37' 8" • Depth: 71' 6"
Main Floor: 1,708 sq. ft. • Upper Floor: 529 sq. ft.
Total Living: 2,237 sq. ft. • Optional Bonus: 436 sq. ft.
Main Ceiling: 9 ft. • Upper Ceiling: 8 ft.
Bedrooms: 3 • Baths: 2 1/2
Foundation: Crawl, Slab, Opt. Basement, Opt. Daylight Basement
Price Tier: C

Main Floor

BEDROOM 2
12'-8" X 13'-4"

GRILLING PORCH
18'-8" X 12'-6"

M.BATH
9'-0" X 17'-10"

LIN

WHP TUB

MASTER SUITE
12'-10" X 17'-10"

BUILT-INS

PORCH
6'-6" X 11'-0"

HEARTH RM. / BRKFAST RM.
17'-0" X 10'-0"

DINING RM.
17'-10" X 11'-6"

UP

12" BOX COLUMNS

BUFFET

DW

KITCHEN
19'-0" X 11'-0"

MEDIA CENTER

BUILT-INS

RG   REF.   PAN.

D.   W.

WH

GREAT RM.
15'-0" X 18'-0"

FOYER
6'-9" X 9'-8"

GARAGE
19'-4" X 20'-8"

COVERED PORCH
22'-6" X 8'-0"

ATTIC STORAGE

© 2001 NELSON DESIGN GROUP, LLC.

OPTIONAL BONUS/ BEDROOM

LIN.

W.I.C.

DN.

BEDROOM 3
17'-10" X 20'-0"

8' LINE

WALL LINE BELOW

WINDOW SEAT

Upper Floor

587 Wisteria

Nelson Design Group has created a beautiful design that resembles a home that your grandfather might have built. Double columns atop brick pillars enhance the front covered porch. An open foyer leads through a great room with corner fireplace and built in media center. A formal dining room accesses the cozy hearth room and kitchen divided by a bar counter for additional seating. Also on the main floor are the master suite, an additional bedroom and a full bathroom. Foyer stairs lead up to a large room with private bath as well as an optional bonus area.

Width: 42' 0" • Depth: 70' 10"
Main Floor: 1,903 sq. ft. • Upper Floor: 385 sq. ft.
Total Living: 2,288 sq. ft. • Main Ceiling: 9 ft. • Upper Ceiling: 8 ft.
Bedrooms: 3 • Baths: 3
Foundation: Crawl, Slab, Opt. Basement, Opt. Daylight Basement
Price Tier: C

THE Burlington COLLECTION

634 Burlington Cove

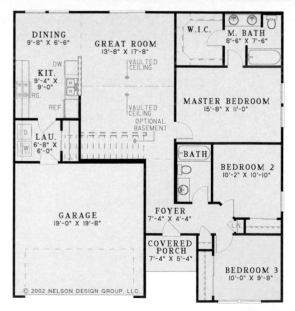

Width: 40' 0" • Depth: 43' 2" • Total living: 1,270 sq. ft.
Main Ceiling: 8 ft. • Bedrooms: 3 • Baths: 2

635 Burlington Cove

Upper Floor

Main Floor

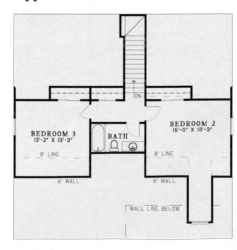

Width: 39' 0" • Depth: 39' 10"
Main Floor: 1,048 sq. ft. • Upper Floor: 620 sq. ft. • Total living: 1,668 sq. ft.
Main Ceiling: 8 ft. • Upper Ceiling: 8 ft. • Bedrooms: 3 • Baths: 2

641 PROVIDIAN PLACE   645 PROVIDIAN PLACE

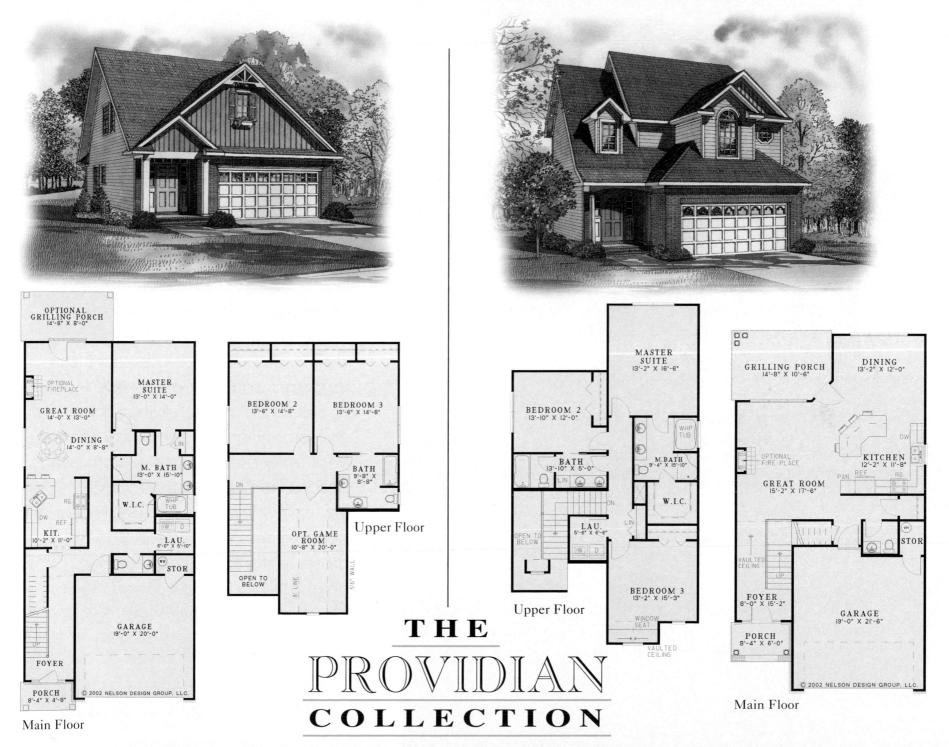

641 PROVIDIAN PLACE

OPTIONAL GRILLING PORCH 14'-8" X 8'-0"

OPTIONAL FIREPLACE

MASTER SUITE 13'-0" X 14'-0"

GREAT ROOM 14'-0" X 13'-0"

DINING 14'-0" X 8'-8"

M. BATH 13'-0" X 15'-10"

LIN

W.I.C.

WHP TUB

KIT. 10'-2" X 11'-0"

RG

DW   REF

W   D

LAU. 6'-0" X 5'-10"

WH   STOR

UP

FOYER

GARAGE 19'-0" X 20'-0"

PORCH 8'-4" X 4'-8"

© 2002 NELSON DESIGN GROUP, LLC.

Main Floor

BEDROOM 2 13'-6" X 14'-8"

BEDROOM 3 13'-6" X 14'-8"

BATH 9'-8" X 8'-8"

DN

OPT. GAME ROOM 10'-8" X 20'-0"

OPEN TO BELOW

8' LINE   5'6" WALL

Upper Floor

645 PROVIDIAN PLACE

MASTER SUITE 13'-2" X 16'-6"

BEDROOM 2 13'-10" X 12'-0"

WHP TUB

BATH 13'-10" X 5'-0"

M.BATH 9'-4" X 15'-10"

LIN

W.I.C.

OPEN TO BELOW

DN

LAU. 5'-6" X 6'-6"

W   D

LIN

BEDROOM 3 13'-2" X 15'-3"

WINDOW SEAT

VAULTED CEILING

Upper Floor

GRILLING PORCH 14'-8" X 10'-6"

DINING 13'-2" X 12'-0"

DW

OPTIONAL FIRE PLACE

KITCHEN 12'-2" X 11'-8"

PAN   REF   RG

GREAT ROOM 15'-2" X 17'-6"

WH   STOR

VAULTED CEILING

UP

FOYER 8'-0" X 15'-2"

PORCH 8'-4" X 6'-0"

GARAGE 19'-0" X 21'-6"

© 2002 NELSON DESIGN GROUP, LLC.

Main Floor

THE
PROVIDIAN
COLLECTION

THE URBAN
COLLECTION

These Traditional Neighborhood Designs represent a growing trend in the New Urbanism movement. Cities are becoming stronger by building historically inspired homes in existing neighborhoods thus preserving communities of 50 to 100 years old. Our Urban Collection offers six plans ranging in square footage from 1,200 to 1,500 with modern living spaces and amenities that families demand. Rear entry garages and private grilling porches are among the many features while offering the safety of a close environment. These plans preserve the integrity of our city neighborhoods and offer an innovative living environment.

Nelson Design Group LLC

RESIDENTIAL PLANNERS - DESIGNERS

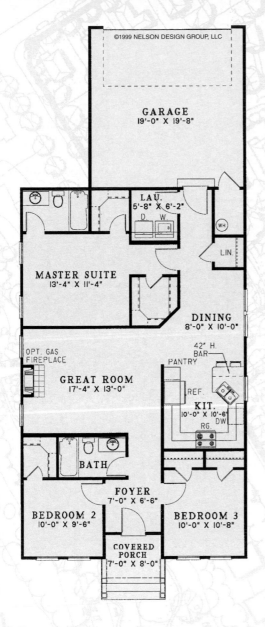

GARAGE
19'-0" X 19'-8"

LAU.
5'-8" X 6'-2"

D W

WH

LIN.

MASTER SUITE
13'-4" X 11'-4"

DINING
8'-0" X 10'-0"

OPT. GAS FIREPLACE

42" H. BAR

PANTRY

GREAT ROOM
17'-4" X 13'-0"

REF.

KIT.
10'-0" X 10'-6"

RG. DW

BATH

FOYER
7'-0" X 6'-6"

BEDROOM 2
10'-0" X 9'-6"

BEDROOM 3
10'-0" X 10'-8"

COVERED PORCH
7'-0" X 8'-0"

Width: 28' 4"

Depth: 66' 0"

Total Living: 1,260 sq. ft.

Main Ceiling: 9 ft.

Price Tier: A

Bedrooms: 3

Baths: 2

Foundation: Crawl, Slab

❁ 398 Urban Lane

Picture yourself greeting your family and friends on the covered entry porch of this Nelson Design Group home. The warmth of this split bedroom design will enchant you and your guests as they enter the foyer. The attractive great room offers you the perfect place to relax and enjoy the company of loved ones in front of the fireplace. Dinner will be delicious and convenient with easy access to the kitchen from the dining room. As evening falls and the guests leave you will find seclusion in the master suite complete with spacious 'his and her' walk-in closets and private bath. This southern traditional style design has all the amenities you've come to expect.

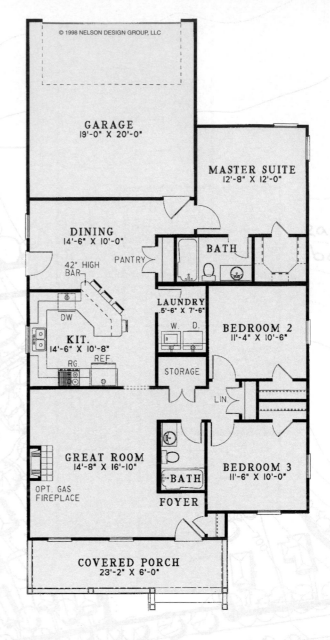

© 1998 NELSON DESIGN GROUP, LLC

GARAGE
19'-0" X 20'-0"

MASTER SUITE
12'-8" X 12'-0"

DINING
14'-6" X 10'-0"

BATH

PANTRY

42" HIGH
BAR

DW

LAUNDRY
5'-6" X 7'-6"

W. D.

KIT.
14'-6" X 10'-8"

BEDROOM 2
11'-4" X 10'-6"

RG. REF.

STORAGE

LIN

GREAT ROOM
14'-8" X 16'-10"

BATH

BEDROOM 3
11'-6" X 10'-0"

OPT. GAS
FIREPLACE

FOYER

COVERED PORCH
23'-2" X 6'-0"

400 Urban Lane

Imagine yourself coming home to this southern traditional Nelson Design Group home. Upon entering the foyer, you can relax away the day in your charming great room with optional fireplace. You will have ample room in the kitchen and dining room to spend some quality time with your family. Helping the kids with their homework or finishing that report for work can be easy with one bedroom converted to a study. As the evening sets in, you will be able to relax in the privacy of the master suite with private bath and spacious walk in closet. This delightful neighborhood design has all the pleasantries you're looking for in your future home.

Width: 32' 8"

Depth: 64' 10"

Total Living: 1,342 sq. ft.

Main Ceiling: 9 ft.

Price Tier: A

Bedrooms: 3

Baths: 2

Foundation: Crawl, Slab, Optional Basement, Optional Daylight Basement

To order call 1.800.590.2423 or to view similar plans visit www.nelsondesigngroup.com

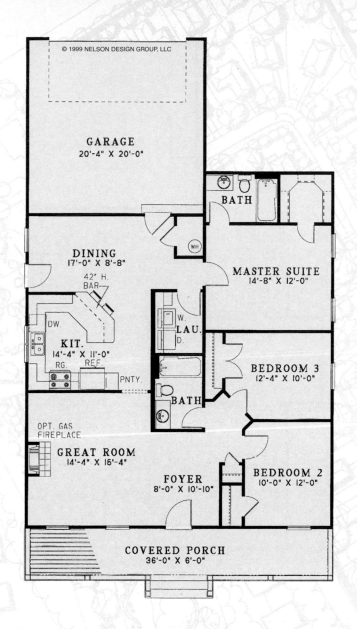

© 1999 NELSON DESIGN GROUP, LLC

GARAGE
20'-4" X 20'-0"

BATH

DINING
17'-0" X 8'-8"

42" H.
BAR

MASTER SUITE
14'-8" X 12'-0"

DW.

KIT.
14'-4" X 11'-0"

RG.   REF.

W.
LAU.
D.

PNTY.

BEDROOM 3
12'-4" X 10'-0"

BATH

OPT. GAS
FIREPLACE

GREAT ROOM
14'-4" X 15'-4"

FOYER
8'-0" X 10'-10"

BEDROOM 2
10'-0" X 12'-0"

COVERED PORCH
36'-0" X 6'-0"

WH

Width: 36' 0"   Bedrooms: 3

Depth: 62' 4"   Baths: 2

Total Living: 1,381 sq. ft.   Foundation: Crawl, Slab,
                                              Optional Basement,
Main Ceiling: 9 ft.   Optional Daylight Basement

Price Tier: A

❀ 397 Urban Lane

Sit back and breathe deeply on the covered porch of this traditional southern style Nelson Design Group home. The great room, with fireplace is the perfect place to converse with your loved ones and friends. Easy access from the dining room to the kitchen makes serving your family a delight on those warm Sunday afternoons. This traditional neighborhood design offers a double bedroom area with full bath that is ideal for the kids or overnight guests. After a full day of activity you can seclude yourself in the master suite with private bath and huge walk-in closet.

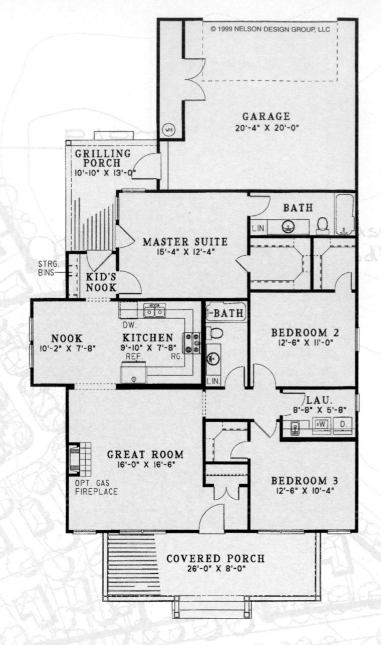

© 1999 NELSON DESIGN GROUP, LLC

GARAGE
20'-4" X 20'-0"

GRILLING PORCH
10'-10" X 13'-0"

BATH

MASTER SUITE
15'-4" X 12'-4"

STRG. BINS

KID'S NOOK

NOOK
10'-2" X 7'-8"

KITCHEN
9'-10" X 7'-8"

DW.

REF. RG.

BATH

LIN.

BEDROOM 2
12'-6" X 11'-0"

LAU.
8'-8" X 5'-8"

W. D.

GREAT ROOM
16'-0" X 16'-6"

OPT. GAS FIREPLACE

BEDROOM 3
12'-6" X 10'-4"

COVERED PORCH
26'-0" X 8'-0"

401 Urban Lane

This Nelson Design Group home has classic southern traditional charm. Picture yourself gazing in the distance on the front covered porch of your new home as the sun sets. Traveling inside you'll feel right at home in the spacious great room with optional fireplace. You'll start family traditions in the cozy breakfast nook with access to the kid's nook which includes built in storage bins. The rear side grilling porch, with access to the master suite will make entertaining a breeze on those warm summer weekends. As night falls you'll find peace in your master suite with private bath and large walk-in closet. Two bedrooms with large walk-in closets complete the design.

Width:	39' 0"	**Bedrooms:**	3
Depth:	70' 6"	**Baths:**	2
Total Living:	1,401 sq. ft.	**Foundation:**	Crawl, Slab
Main Ceiling:	9 ft.	**Price Tier:**	A

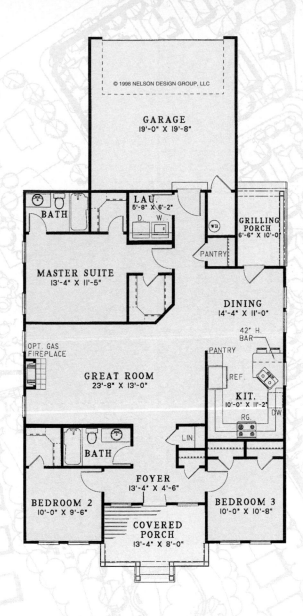

GARAGE
19'-0" X 19'-8"

© 1998 NELSON DESIGN GROUP, LLC

LAU.
5'-8" X 6'-2"

BATH

D. W.

W.H.

GRILLING
PORCH
6'-6" X 10'-0"

PANTRY

MASTER SUITE
13'-4" X 11'-5"

DINING
14'-4" X 11'-0"

42" H.
BAR

OPT. GAS
FIREPLACE

PANTRY

GREAT ROOM
23'-8" X 13'-0"

REF.

KIT.
10'-0" X 11'-2"

RG.

DW

LIN.

BATH

FOYER
13'-4" X 4'-6"

BEDROOM 2
10'-0" X 9'-6"

BEDROOM 3
10'-0" X 10'-8"

COVERED
PORCH
13'-4" X 8'-0"

Width: 34' 8"

Depth: 71' 0"

Total Living: 1,442 sq. ft.

Main Ceiling: 9 ft.

Price Tier: A

Bedrooms: 3

Baths: 2

Foundation: Crawl, Slab

❀ 402 Urban Lane

This adorable Nelson Design Group home is the perfect starter home for you and your new family. Imagine coming home after a long day and basking in the afternoon sun on the cozy covered porch, while watching the kids play. After entering the charming foyer, you'll travel into the spacious great room, which will serve as the heart of your home. Spending time in front of the fireplace will warm the hearts of family and friends. Dining will be fun for the whole family with easy access to the grilling porch. After the kids are in bed, you'll be able to find solitude in your master suite with private bath and 'his and her' closets. This split bedroom traditional style design has all the amenities you'll need to call it home.

To order call 1.800.590.2423 or to view similar plans visit www.nelsondesigngroup.com

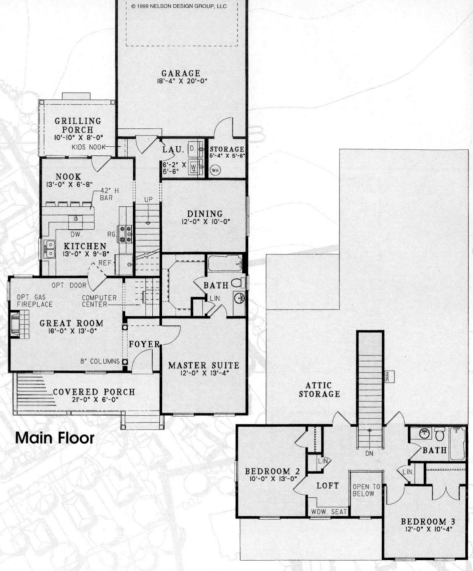

Main Floor

GARAGE
18'-4" X 20'-0"

© 1999 NELSON DESIGN GROUP, LLC

GRILLING PORCH
10'-10" X 8'-0"
KIDS NOOK

LAU.
6'-2" X 5'-6"

STORAGE
5'-4" X 5'-6"

NOOK
13'-0" X 6'-8"

42" H. BAR

UP

DINING
12'-0" X 10'-0"

DW.

R.G.

KITCHEN
13'-0" X 9'-8"

REF

BATH

LIN.

OPT. DOOR

OPT. GAS FIREPLACE

COMPUTER CENTER

GREAT ROOM
16'-0" X 13'-0"

FOYER

8" COLUMNS

MASTER SUITE
12'-0" X 13'-4"

COVERED PORCH
21'-0" X 6'-0"

Upper Floor

ATTIC STORAGE

DN

BEDROOM 2
10'-0" X 13'-0"

LIN

LOFT

OPEN TO BELOW

BATH

LIN

WDW. SEAT

BEDROOM 3
12'-0" X 10'-4"

399 Urban Lane

The simple elegance of this Nelson Design Group home will capture your imagination. As you enter the foyer, you'll admire the graceful appeal of the eight inch columns that invite you into the spacious great room. The warmth of this room will provide the perfect place to create lasting memories with family and friends. Starting the day will be fun for everyone in the charming breakfast nook with access to the rear grilling porch. After everyone is off to work or play, you'll be able to relax upstairs, maybe read your favorite book on the window seat, or retreat to the master suite with private bath complete with a huge walk in closet. This home also features two large bedrooms, loft area, and has ample storage space to suit your needs.

Width: 34' 4"	**Main Ceiling:** 9 ft.
Depth: 61' 6"	**Upper Ceiling:** 8 ft.
Main Floor: 1,063 sq. ft.	**Bedrooms:** 3
Upper Floor: 496 sq. ft.	**Baths:** 2
Total Living: 1,559 sq. ft.	**Foundation:** Crawl, Slab,
Price Tier: B	Optional Basement,
	Optional Daylight Basement

To order call 1.800.590.2423 or to view similar plans visit www.nelsondesigngroup.com

THE Cross Creek COLLECTION

When you choose a Nelson Design Group collection, you not only create beautiful homes, you achieve ideal master planned communities. The Cross Creek Collection features living spaces of 1,300 to 1,700 square feet and front loading garages gently tiered for street appeal. Each of the six plans complement each other, resulting in an effective Traditional European design theme and a complete neighborhood — making development easy for you. All plans are designed to fit a narrow lot of 50 feet to 60 feet. Nelson Design Group also offers complementary collections with the same traditional appeal and quality as our Cross Creek Collection.

Nelson Design Group LLC

RESIDENTIAL PLANNERS · DESIGNERS

Elevation A

Elevation B

299 Cross Creek

If you can picture yourself hosting an elegant dinner party surrounded by friends and family, then step into this Nelson Design Group home. After greeting guests on the covered porch, guide them into the spacious great room. Here, mingling can begin and maybe drinks around the romantic gas fireplace. Conveniently accessible to the kitchen, you can slip away to check on the excellent cuisine you are preparing. A connecting breakfast room can serve as more space for guests or a quiet place just for you. A door opening to a grilling porch allows you to even prepare grilled meats with ease. When all the excitement is over, enjoy the privacy of the master suite or relax in a whirlpool bath.

Width:	48' 0"	**Bedrooms:**	3
Depth:	63' 4"	**Baths:**	2
Total Living:	1,452 sq. ft.	**Foundation:**	Crawl, Slab
Main Ceiling:	9 ft.	**Price Tier:**	A

STRG.
8'-2" X 5'-6"

LAU.
7'-0" X 5'-6"

NOOK
9'-0" X 7'-0"

MASTER SUITE
10'-0" BOXED CEILING
12'-0" X 13'-8"

GARAGE
20'-0" X 20'-0"

KITCHEN
14'-8" X 12'-4"

PANTRY

© 1998 NELSON DESIGN GROUP, LLC

DINING ROOM
10'-8" X 10'-0"

M.BATH
12'-0" X 11'-6"

GLASS BLOCKS

WHP TUB

SHWR

8" COLUMNS

BEDROOM 3
12'-0" X 10'-8"

GREAT ROOM
10'-0" BOXED CEILING
14'-8" X 20'-0"

LIN

BATH

SITTING AREA
9'-0" X 4'-0"

FOYER

BEDROOM 2
12'-0" X 10'-4"

PRCH

Width: 48' 0"

Depth: 60' 4"

Total Living: 1,598 sq. ft.

Main Ceiling: 9 ft.

Bedrooms: 3

Baths: 2

Foundation: Crawl, Slab

Price Tier: B

Elevation A

Elevation B

298 Cross Creek

Elegance radiates through this Nelson Design Group home. Through a traditional foyer, enter a tasteful sitting area — perfect for greeting guests before continuing into the great room with intricate ten foot boxed ceiling. Set off by magnificently crafted wooden columns, the dining room area provides an excellent atmosphere for graceful dinner parties — business or pleasure. A wonderfully open kitchen with island and bright bay window nook will ensure you have all you need.

Elevation A

Elevation B

302 Cross Creek

Entering through majestic columns into the traditional foyer, you instantly feel the grandeur of this Nelson Design Group home. Imagine an evening of exquisite cuisine as you entertain your close friends and colleagues in the elegant dining room enhanced by ten foot ceilings and beautifully crafted columns. A grilling porch, located off the spacious kitchen and breakfast room, provides the ease needed to serve your favorite recipes. Following the festivities, retreat to a private master suite and relax in your whirlpool tub.

Width: 52' 8"	**Bedrooms:**	3
Depth: 60' 6"	**Baths:**	2
Total Living: 1,627 sq. ft.	**Foundation:**	Crawl, Slab
Main Ceiling: 9 ft.	**Price Tier:**	B

BEDROOM 3
12'-8" X 10'-10"

COVERED PORCH
15'-4" X 7'-0"

GLASS BLOCKS

WHP TUB

M.BATH

LIN

SHLVS.

DINING RM. / HEARTH RM.
15'-4" X 12'-0"

MASTER SUITE
10' BOXED CLNG
14'-0" X 13'-0"

LIN

BEDROOM 2
12'-8" X 12'-4"

KITCHEN
13'-0" X 13'-0"

DW

RG.

REF.

PAN.

D

W.H.

L.B.

W

STRG.
7'-8" X 5'-6"

8" COL.

FOYER

GARAGE
19'-8" X 20'-0"

SLOPED CEILING

GREAT RM.
11' FLAT CEILING
15'-4" X 18'-0"

PRCH

MEDIA CENTER

© 1998 NELSON DESIGN GROUP, LLC.

Width: 49' 0"

Depth: 58' 6"

Total Living: 1,654 sq. ft.

Main Ceiling: 9 ft.

Price Tier: B

Bedrooms: 3

Baths: 2

Foundation: Crawl, Slab, Basement, Daylight Basement

Elevation A

Elevation B

301 Cross Creek

A covered entry porch sets the stage for elegance in this Nelson Design Group home. Travel through the foyer and enter a spacious great room with unique sloped ceilings, complete with built-in media center, for hours of family entertainment. Take advantage of the distinguished dining and hearth room with a lovely fireplace. Continue entertaining on your covered rear porch over conversation and a breath-taking view.

Elevation A

Elevation B

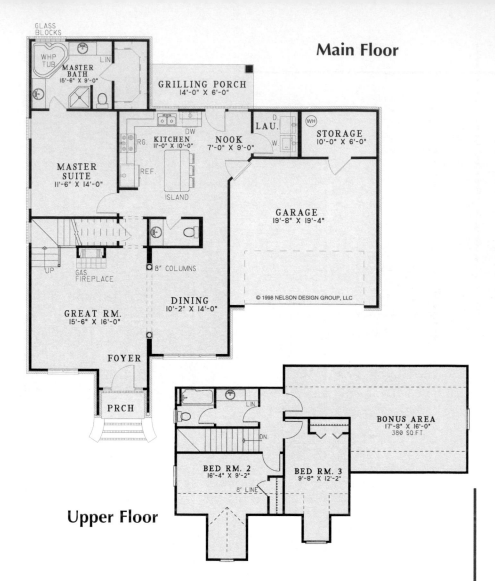

Main Floor

Upper Floor

300 Cross Creek

Become enchanted by European beauty as you enter this Nelson Design Group home. Nine foot ceilings create a marvelous openness throughout the entire plan especially in the great room. Spend hours entertaining friends and family, before journeying to the elegant dining room for a spectacular meal followed by conversation over coffee. A clever grilling porch just off the kitchen area provides ample room and convenience to prepare the cuisine. After the party ends, retreat to your private master suite or relax in the whirlpool tub of your master bath. A large bonus room and two bedrooms, with adjoining bath on the upper level, make an excellent children's suite.

Width: 47' 0"
Depth: 50' 0"
Main Floor: 1,155 sq. ft.
Upper Floor: 529 sq. ft.
Total Living: 1,684 sq. ft.*
***Bonus:** 380 additional sq. ft.
Price Tier: B

Main Ceiling: 9 ft.
Upper Ceiling: 8 ft.
Bedrooms: 3
Baths: 2 1/2
Foundation: Crawl, Slab, Optional Basement, Optional Daylight Basement

Main Floor

BED RM. 2
11'-0" X 10'-8"

BED RM. 3
9'-3" X 11'-0"

ATTIC STORAGE

4' WALL

5' WALL

HVAC

Upper Floor

Designers Choice — BEST SELLER · NELSON DESIGN GROUP

Elevation A

Elevation B

303 Cross Creek

The lovely covered entry porch of this Nelson Design Group home leads you into a traditional foyer — perfect for greeting guests before an elegant dinner party. Through graceful wooden columns, enter the dining area with ten foot ceiling, creating the perfect dining ambiance. Following dinner, retreat with guests to a spacious great room for conversation over coffee and dessert. After a full night of entertaining, retreat to the comfort and privacy of a secluded master suite. The children will be fast asleep on the upper level in the two bedrooms with walk-through bath.

Width: 48' 0"

Depth: 43' 0"

Main Floor: 1,356 sq. ft.

Upper Floor: 441 sq. ft.

Total Living: 1,797 sq. ft.

Price Tier: B

Main Ceiling: 9 ft.

Upper Ceiling: 8 ft.

Bedrooms: 3

Baths: 2 1/2

Foundation: Crawl, Slab, Basement, Daylight Basement

The Village at Wellington

This collection has been put together to ease the selection of a home plan with minimal yet efficient space. Enjoy charming traditional front porches and gently recessed garages for better street appeal. All fourteen plans range between 1,000 to 1,500 square feet and are perfect for narrow lots and Traditional Neighborhood Design. Take a moment and stroll through our Village at Wellington for a beautifully designed plan to suit your needs.

Nelson Design Group LLC

RESIDENTIAL PLANNERS - DESIGNERS

STORAGE
15'-8" X 3'-0"

GARAGE
21'-0" X 19'-0"

© 2000 NELSON DESIGN GROUP, LLC.

PAN

BREAKFAST
14'-8" X 7'-10"

KITCHEN
10'-10" X 8'-0"

REF   RG

D.W.

GREAT
ROOM
14'-8" X 16'-10"
OPT. 9' CEILING

LAU.
6'-2" X
5'-8"

BATH

W.I.C.

MASTER
SUITE
OPT. 9' BOXED
CEILING
11'-8" X 11'-0"

BATH

COVERED
PORCH
15'-5" X 8'-0"

BEDROOM 2
11'-8" X 11'-6"

524 Wellington Lane

This stately Nelson Design Group home has all the amenities you're looking for in a home. The covered front porch is accented by ten inch round columns and a beaded ceiling. As you enter the expansive great room with optional nine foot ceiling, you'll enjoy the openness created by the eat at snack bar open to the kitchen. Starting your day will be fun and easy in the convenient kitchen with breakfast room. After a full day of activity you'll breathe easy in the privacy of the master suite, with full bath and huge walk-in closet. The second bedroom would make a lovely nursery for the family just starting out, or the perfect spare bedroom for overnight guests.

Width: 48' 8"

Depth: 45' 10"

Total Living: 1,067 sq. ft.

Main Ceiling: 8 ft.

Bedrooms: 2

Baths: 2

Foundation: Crawl, Slab

Price Tier: A

59

531 Wellington Lane

Enjoy warm summer evenings under the stars on the front porch of this Nelson Design Group home. Traveling inside you'll feel the ambiance created by the intricate ten foot boxed ceiling in the living room and the elegance of the boxed columns leading to the dining room. The convenient kitchen with eat at snack bar is adjacent to the second bedroom or study. The master suite offers you a world of its own with spacious nine foot boxed ceiling, a large master bath complete with 'his and her' vanities and ample closet space. This Traditional Country design will make your dreams come true.

© 2000 NELSON DESIGN GROUP, LLC

Width: 48' 4"

Depth: 53' 0"

Total Living: 1,169 sq. ft.

Main Ceiling: 8 ft.

Price Tier: A

Bedrooms: 2

Baths: 2

Foundation: Crawl, Slab

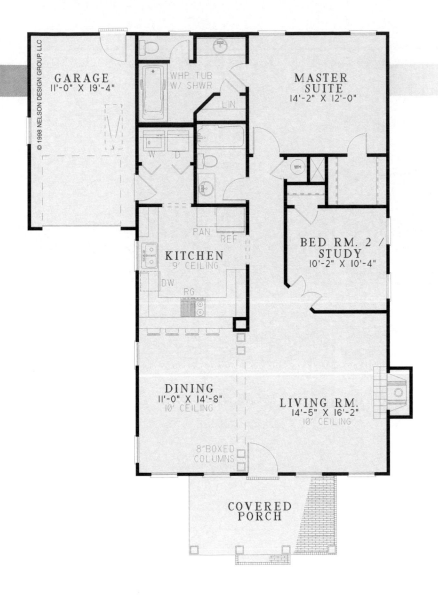

GARAGE
11'-0" X 19'-4"

© 1998 NELSON DESIGN GROUP, LLC

WHP. TUB
W/ SHWR

LIN

W   D

MASTER
SUITE
14'-2" X 12'-0"

PAN   REF

KITCHEN
9' CEILING

DW
RG

BED RM. 2 /
STUDY
10'-2" X 10'-4"

WH

DINING
11'-0" X 14'-8"
10' CEILING

LIVING RM.
14'-5" X 16'-2"
10' CEILING

8" BOXED
COLUMNS

COVERED
PORCH

Width: 37' 0"
Depth: 53' 0"
Total Living: 1,172 sq. ft.
Main Ceiling: 9 ft.
Price Tier: A

Bedrooms: 2
Baths: 2
Foundation: Crawl, Slab

270 Wellington Lane

Charming columns welcome you onto the front porch of this Nelson Design Group home. Inside you'll feel the warmth of the fireplace and an openness created by ten foot ceilings in both the living room and formal dining room, also enhanced with eight inch boxed columns. You'll have extra dinner seating or a buffet line by utilizing the bar area that ties the kitchen to the dining room making entertaining a breeze. A roomy kitchen with a pantry and nine foot ceiling make cooking a joy. The second bedroom can serve as a spare room for overnight guests or be easily converted into a study if you have the luxury of working at home. The master suite with a large walk-in closet and whirlpool tub with shower complete the design.

525 Wellington Lane

Imagine coming home to this enchanting Nelson Design Group home. Friends and family will feel welcomed onto the charming front porch of this traditional neighborhood design. On those cold wintery evenings, you and your family will create lasting memories in front of the fireplace in the great room. Start family traditions in the morning by eating breakfast with your loved ones in the breakfast nook open to the kitchen and eat at bar. After the kids are in their own beds separated by a full bath, you can retreat to the privacy of the master suite complete with nine foot boxed ceiling, walk-in closet, and master bath with 'his and her' vanities.

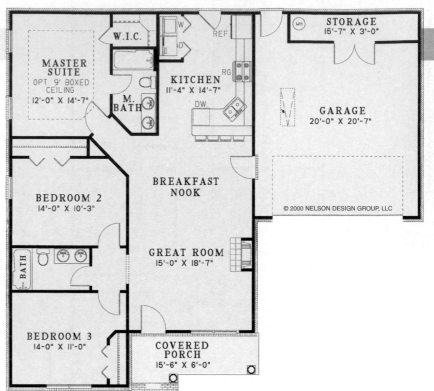

© 2000 NELSON DESIGN GROUP, LLC

Width: 50' 4"	Bedrooms: 3
Depth: 45' 0"	Baths: 2
Total Living: 1,250 sq. ft.	Foundation: Crawl, Slab, Optional Basement, Optional Daylight Basement
Main Ceiling: 8 ft.	
Price Tier: A	

To order call 1.800.590.2423 or to view similar plans visit www.nelsondesigngroup.com

MASTER SUITE
11'-0" X 14'-8"
10' BOXED CEILING

BEDROOM 2
10'-6" X 11'-3"

GARAGE
17'-8" X 20'-0"

© 1998 NELSON DESIGN GROUP, LLC

BEDROOM 3 / OFFICE
10'-6" X 9'-3"

D.

W.

WH

LIN

8" BOXED COLUMNS

DINING RM.
10'-2" X 11'-10"

GREAT RM.
14'-6" X 17'-0"
GAS FIREPLACE

10' BOXED CEILING

PAN

FOYER

DW.

REF

KIT.
10'-6" X 15'-10"

RG.

NOOK

COVERED PORCH
15'-0" X 8'-0"

289 Wellington Lane

Impressive boxed columns surround the covered porch of this Nelson Design Group home. As you enter the foyer, you notice a spacious great room with fireplace that will be a wonderful gathering place for family and friends to begin an evening of entertainment. Serve your elegant cuisine in the dining room detailed with eight inch boxed columns with a view to the kitchen with a quaint breakfast nook. After your guests leave, you can retire to your master suite with ample room in the large walk-in closet.

Width: 44' 0"

Depth: 54' 8"

Total Living: 1,281 sq. ft.

Main Ceiling: 9 ft.

Price Tier: A

Bedrooms: 3

Baths: 2

Foundation: Crawl, Slab

292 Wellington Lane

This traditional neighborhood Nelson Design Group home has a quaint covered porch to welcome friends and family for an afternoon of visiting. Entering through the foyer, your guests will enjoy gathering in the great room with a fireplace to warm themselves from the frigid temperatures that winter brings. During the summer, entertain on your rear grilling porch. After entertaining, you will enjoy quiet time in your master suite, with a large walk-in closet and private bath. Two additional bedrooms complete this design.

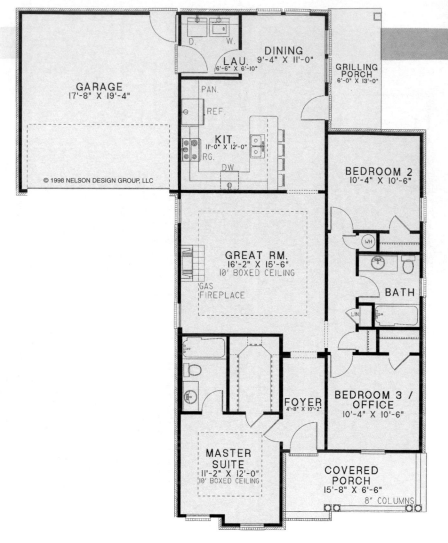

GARAGE
17'-8" X 19'-4"

LAU.
6'-6" X 6'-10"

DINING
9'-4" X 11'-0"

GRILLING PORCH
6'-0" X 13'-0"

PAN.

REF.

KIT.
11'-0" X 12'-0"

RG.

DW

© 1998 NELSON DESIGN GROUP, LLC

BEDROOM 2
10'-4" X 10'-6"

GREAT RM.
16'-2" X 15'-6"
10' BOXED CEILING

GAS FIREPLACE

BATH

LIN

WH

FOYER
4'-8" X 10'-2"

BEDROOM 3 / OFFICE
10'-4" X 10'-6"

MASTER SUITE
11'-2" X 12'-0"
10' BOXED CEILING

COVERED PORCH
15'-8" X 6'-6"
8" COLUMNS

Width: 45' 6"	Bedrooms: 3
Depth: 56' 10"	Baths: 2
Total Living: 1,289 sq. ft.	Foundation: Crawl, Slab
Main Ceiling: 9 ft.	
Price Tier: A	

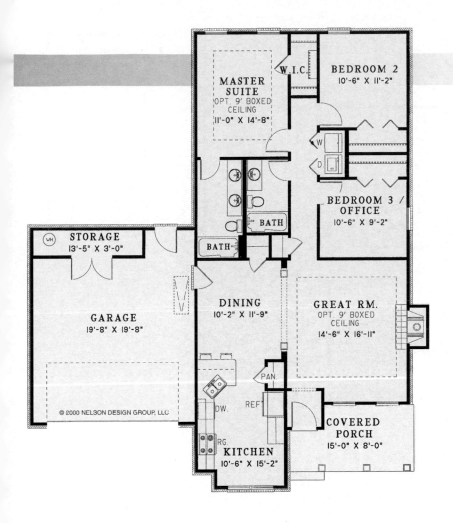

530 Wellington Lane

Beautiful ferns and boxed columns embellish the front porch of this Nelson Design Group home. Upon entering the foyer, you'll be welcomed into the great room with a cozy fireplace and nine foot boxed ceiling. Across and through a column cased opening is the formal dining directly accessing the kitchen for ease in entertaining. Down the hall is the master suite also enhanced by a nine foot ceiling, large walk-in closet with built-ins and a full bathroom with double vanity. The second and third bedrooms or office share a full bathroom located in the hall. This Traditional Country design offers you and your family an array of amenities you've come to look for in your future home.

Width: 46' 0"

Depth: 54' 8"

Total Living: 1,294 sq. ft.

Main Ceiling: 8 ft.

Price Tier: A

Bedrooms: 3

Baths: 2

Foundation: Crawl, Slab

To order call 1.800.590.2423 or to view similar plans visit www.nelsondesigngroup.com

291 Wellington Lane

This split bedroom Nelson Design Group home will turn your dreams into reality. Imagine greeting your family and friends on the front porch adorned with ten inch columns. Upon entering the home you'll notice the expansive great room with fireplace, open to the dining room and kitchen. This will make entertaining guests a cinch. The master suite will be your haven with it's spacious ten foot boxed ceiling and full bath. The second and third bedrooms offer the kids their own part of the home with a full bath complete with 'his and her' vanities, as well as ample closet space.

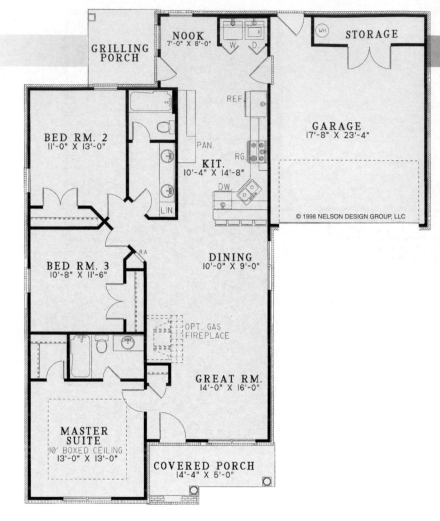

Width: 46' 0"	Bedrooms: 3
Depth: 54' 10"	Baths: 2
Total Living: 1,317 sq. ft.	Foundation: Crawl, Slab, Basement, Daylight Basement
Main Ceiling: 9 ft.	
Price Tier: A	

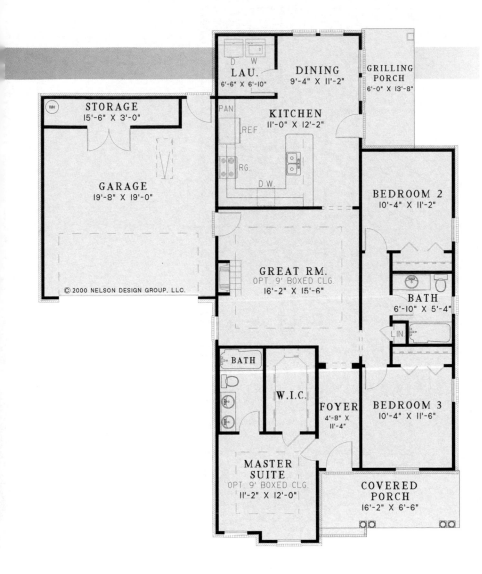

STORAGE
15'-6" X 3'-0"

GARAGE
19'-8" X 19'-0"

© 2000 NELSON DESIGN GROUP, LLC.

LAU.
6'-6" X 6'-10"

DINING
9'-4" X 11'-2"

GRILLING PORCH
6'-0" X 13'-8"

PAN

KITCHEN
11'-0" X 12'-2"

REF

R.G.

D.W.

GREAT RM.
OPT. 9' BOXED CLG.
16'-2" X 15'-6"

BEDROOM 2
10'-4" X 11'-2"

BATH
6'-10" X 5'-4"

LIN

BATH

W.I.C.

FOYER
4'-8" X 11'-4"

BEDROOM 3
10'-4" X 11'-6"

MASTER SUITE
OPT. 9' BOXED CLG.
11'-2" X 12'-0"

COVERED PORCH
16'-2" X 6'-6"

Width: 47' 6"

Depth: 58' 6"

Total Living: 1,321 sq. ft.

Main Ceiling: 8 ft.

Price Tier: A

Bedrooms: 3

Baths: 2

Foundation: Crawl, Slab

532 Wellington Lane

Enjoy the elegant porch with double columns and railing that give life to this traditional Nelson Design Group home. Guests will enjoy hot chocolate and a cozy fireplace in your great room enhanced with a nine foot boxed ceiling. The kitchen adjoins a large dining area and accesses a rear porch giving you the option of grilling or simply relaxing. After entertaining, seclude yourself in the master suite adorned by a nine foot boxed ceiling, full bath and a huge walk-in closet. This split bedroom design offers the children their own privacy on the other side of the house with their own room and full bathroom in between.

271 Wellington Lane

A charming southern traditional home reminiscent of grandmother's house exemplifies this Nelson Design Group home. Impressive boxed columns embrace the entry to the spacious dining room, while beautiful french doors open to the study. Breakfast tradition can begin in your home in the cozy kitchen with view to the dining room. To the rear of the home, you'll find a spacious master suite with ample closet space. Conclude a busy day with a long soak in your whirlpool bath.

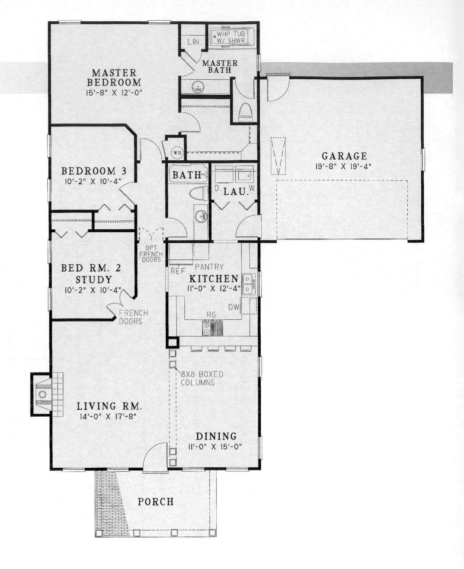

Width: 48' 4"

Depth: 62' 0"

Total Living: 1,404 sq. ft.

Main Ceiling: 9 ft.

Price Tier: A

Bedrooms: 3

Baths: 2

Foundation: Crawl, Slab, Optional Basement, Optional Daylight Basement

To order call 1.800.590.2423 or to view similar plans visit www.nelsondesigngroup.com

GRILLING PORCH
11'-8" X 6'-0"

HEARTH RM.
11'-4" X 12'-0"

OPT. GAS FIREPLACE

MASTER SUITE
14'-8" X 13'-8"
10' BOXED CEILING

WHP TUB

SHWR LIN.

GARAGE
17'-8" X 20'-0"

© 1999 NELSON DESIGN GROUP, LLC

KIT.
11'-4" X 11'-2"
RG. DW REF.

BEDROOM 2
11'-4" X 11'-0"

GREAT RM.
14'-8" X 16'-6"
10' BOXED CEILING

GAS FIREPLACE

LIN.

BATH

LIN.

COVERED PORCH
15'-0" X 8'-0"

10" COLUMNS

BEDROOM 3 / STUDY
11'-4" X 12'-0"

290 Wellington Lane

Enjoy peaceful fall evenings watching the sun set in this Nelson Design Group home. When it gets too cold, you can warm yourself in the comfortable great room, complete with fireplace. Begin each day with coffee and the morning paper in the hearth room with fluid access to the kitchen. The family chef will love displaying his or her skills during an afternoon cookout on the rear grilling porch. After the day has come to a close, you will find it most relaxing to soothe those aches away in the privacy of your master bath.

Width: 45' 0"

Depth: 64' 10"

Total Living: 1,425 sq. ft.

Main Ceiling: 9 ft.

Price Tier: A

Bedrooms: 3

Baths: 2

Foundation: Crawl, Slab

297 Wellington Lane

This split bedroom Nelson Design Group home offers all the amenities you're looking for in a home. Once inside you'll feel an openness created by the spacious great room with fireplace and elaborate ten foot boxed ceiling. The third bedroom or study, with elegant eight inch columns, is open to the great room creating a spacious feel throughout the design. Spending quality time with the family will be a delight in the breakfast room with access to the grilling porch. You'll find solitude in the master suite complete with a heavenly whirlpool tub and huge walk-in closet. A full bath separates bedroom two from the office, completing the design.

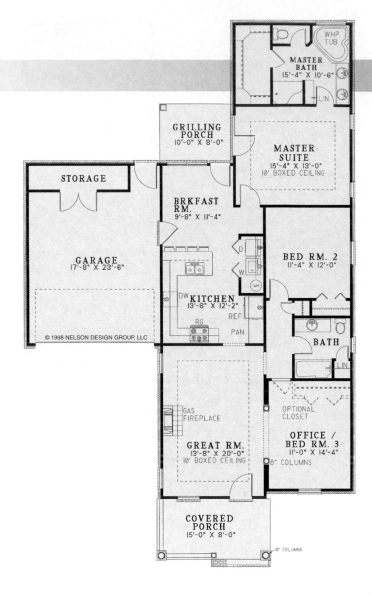

Width: 44' 0"

Depth: 71' 2"

Total Living: 1,449 sq. ft.

Main Ceiling: 9 ft.

Price Tier: A

Bedrooms: 3

Baths: 2

Foundation: Crawl, Slab

To order call 1.800.590.2423 or to view similar plans visit www.nelsondesigngroup.com

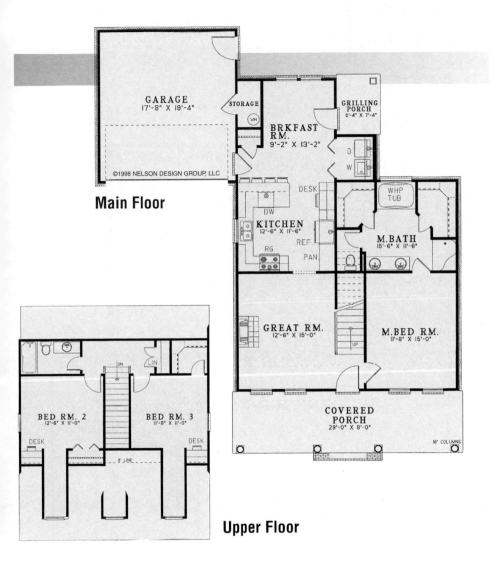

Main Floor

GARAGE
17'-8" X 19'-4"

©1998 NELSON DESIGN GROUP, LLC

STORAGE

WH

BRKFAST RM.
9'-2" X 13'-2"

GRILLING PORCH
6'-4" X 7'-4"

D

W

DESK

DW

KITCHEN
12'-6" X 11'-6"

REF

RG.

PAN.

WHP TUB

M.BATH
15'-6" X 11'-6"

GREAT RM.
12'-6" X 15'-0"

M.BED RM.
11'-8" X 15'-0"

UP

COVERED PORCH
29'-0" X 8'-0"

10' COLUMNS

Upper Floor

DN.

LIN.

BED RM. 2
12'-6" X 11'-0"

BED RM. 3
11'-8" X 11'-0"

DESK

DESK

8' LINE

Width: 47' 0"

Depth: 55' 2"

Main Floor: 980 sq. ft.

Upper Floor: 561 sq. ft.

Total Living: 1,541 sq. ft.

Price Tier: B

Main Ceiling: 9 ft.

Upper Ceiling: 8 ft.

Bedrooms: 3

Baths: 2

Foundation: Crawl, Slab, Basement, Daylight Basement

293 Wellington Lane

A charming front porch attracts everyone in this traditional Nelson Design Group home. Entertaining will be easy on your convenient grilling porch which allows you to prepare dinner with ease. After dinner, your guests can gather in the spacious great room for games and laughter. After the guests leave, you can retire to your private master suite and bath which features an enticing whirlpool bath as well as 'his and her' walk-in closets. Upstairs, the children will be tucked away in their own bedrooms.

296 Wellington Lane

This quaint Nelson Design Group home provides the traditional family all the privacy they need. Beautiful columns welcome you into the great room with a built-in media center and gas fireplace. The grill master of the family can try their luck on the rear grilling porch for those friends who tend to drop by. A spacious kitchen allows you to prepare quick meals with ease. When night falls, travel to your master suite where you'll relax with a corner whirlpool bath, double vanities and separate corner glass shower. Upstairs you'll find two more bedrooms, just right for the kids.

Main Floor

LIN
M.BATH
12'-6" X 8'-8"
WHP TUB

MASTER SUITE
12'-6" X 13'-4"
10' BOXED CEILING

GRILLING PORCH
7'-10" X 5'-0"

STORAGE

PAN.
REF.
DW.
RG

DINING
10'-8" X 11'-6"

KITCHEN
14'-4" X 11'-8"

GARAGE
17'-8" X 23'-0"

W   D.

MEDIA CENTER

© 1999 NELSON DESIGN GROUP, LLC

GREAT RM.
15'-4" X 16'-0"

GAS FIREPLACE

UP

FOYER

8" COLUMNS

COVERED PORCH
22'-0" X 8'-0"

10" COLUMNS

Upper Floor

ATTIC STORAGE
SLOPED CEILING

LIN

BED RM. 2
10'-10" X 10'-8"

BED RM. 3
10'-4" X 12'-9"

Width: 44' 0"	Main Ceiling: 9 ft.
Depth: 59' 4"	Upper Ceiling: 8 ft.
Main Floor: 1,112 sq. ft.	Bedrooms: 3
Upper Floor: 483 sq. ft.	Baths: 2 1/2
Total Living: 1,595 sq. ft.	Foundation: Crawl, Slab, Basement, Daylight Basement
Price Tier: B	

Sage Meadows
COLLECTION

When you choose a Nelson Design Group collection, you not only create beautiful homes, you achieve ideal master planned communities. The Sage Meadows Collection of French Country designs feature living spaces of 1,100 to 1,600 square feet — advantageous for rear access and open views for lake or golf course settings. Each of the twelve plans complement each other, resulting in an effective overall design theme and a complete neighborhood — making development easy for you. All plans are designed to fit a narrow lot of 50 feet to 60 feet. Nelson Design Group also offers complementary collections with the same traditional appeal and quality as our Sage Meadows Collection.

Nelson Design Group LLC

RESIDENTIAL PLANNERS - DESIGNERS

288 Sage Meadows

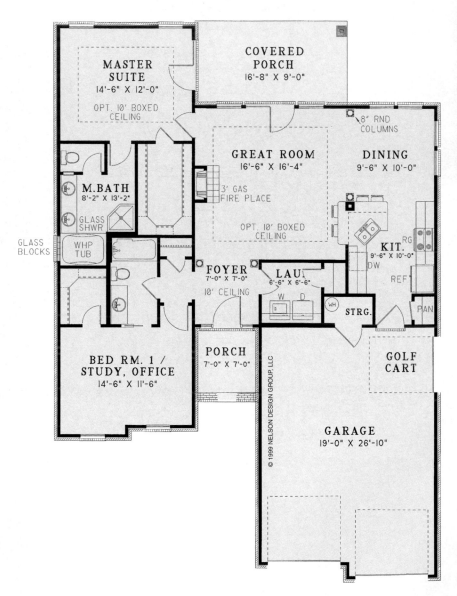

Imagine the luxury of waking to a warm spring morning, walking out an atrium door from your master suite onto a rear covered porch overlooking a beautiful lake or golf course. With this Nelson Design Group home, the dream is a reality. The covered porch makes entertaining friends easy with convenient access to the great room — complete with gas fireplace and ten-foot boxed ceilings.

Width: 41' 10"

Depth: 59' 8"

Total Living: 1,287 sq. ft.

Main Ceiling: 9 ft.

Price Tier: A

Bedrooms: 2

Baths: 2

Foundation: Crawl, Slab, Basement, Daylight Basement

279 Sage Meadows

GRILLING PORCH
14'-6" X 8'-0"

FRENCH DOORS

MASTER SUITE
11'-4" X 15'-0"

FRENCH DOORS

10' BOXED CEILING

LIN.

GREAT ROOM
13'-8" X 17'-6"

10' BOXED CEILING

M.BATH
11'-4" X 12'-4"

GLASS BLOCKS

GLASS SHWR

WHP TUB

D

W LAU.
8'-10" X 6'-6"

8X8 BOXED COLUMNS

GOLF CART
8'-0" X 6'-10"

DINING
13'-8" X 10'-0"

OPT. FRENCH DOORS

BEDROOM 3 / DEN / STUDY
11'-4" X 11'-0"

KIT.
8'-10" X 13'-0"

PAN

GARAGE
19'-8" X 20'-0"

FOYER
4'-6" X 8'-3"

RG

© 1998 NELSON DESIGN GROUP, LLC

DW

REF

PAN

PORCH

BEDROOM 2
11'-4" X 11'-0"

Throughout this Nelson Design Group home, you'll feel the openness achieved by the grandeur of nine foot ceilings. A covered rear porch makes entertaining friends and family a breeze, and perfect for a delicious summer barbecue. Elegant french doors lead you back inside where you'll enjoy conversation in your spacious great room, conveniently accessible to the dining area and kitchen. An additional third bedroom can be converted to a den or study to accommodate everyone.

Width: 46' 0"	Bedrooms: 3
Depth: 60' 4"	Baths: 2
Total Living: 1,359 sq. ft.	Foundation: Crawl, Slab
Main Ceiling: 9 ft.	
Price Tier: A	

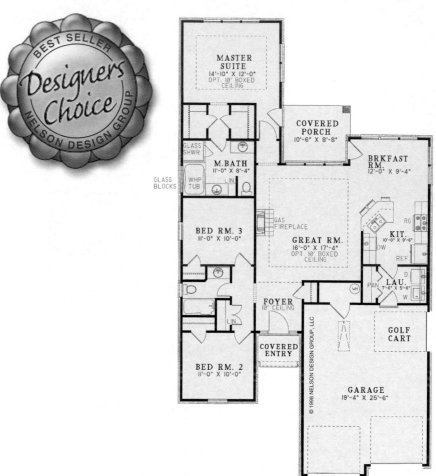

MASTER SUITE 14'-10" X 12'-0" OPT. 10' BOXED CEILING

COVERED PORCH 10'-6" X 8'-8"

GLASS SHWR

M.BATH 11'-0" X 8'-4"

WHP TUB

LIN

BRKFAST RM. 12'-0" X 9'-4"

GLASS BLOCKS

GAS FIREPLACE

BED RM. 3 11'-0" X 10'-0"

GREAT RM. 16'-0" X 17'-4" OPT. 10' BOXED CEILING

KIT. 10'-0" X 9'-6"

RG

DW

REF

PAN

LAU. 7'-6" X 5'-6"

D

W

FOYER 10' CEILING

GOLF CART

COVERED ENTRY

BED RM. 2 11'-0" X 10'-0"

© 1998 NELSON DESIGN GROUP, LLC

GARAGE 19'-4" X 25'-6"

Enter this French Country Nelson Design Group home and find a traditional covered entry porch with marvelous ten foot ceilings. Following through the foyer, you're led into a spacious great room where you can spend cold winter nights in front of a warm fire. In addition, convenient access from the master suite to the covered rear porch provides the atmosphere for private romantic summer evenings.

Width: 38' 4"	**Bedrooms:** 3
Depth: 68' 6"	**Baths:** 2
Total Living: 1,379 sq. ft.	**Foundation:** Crawl, Slab
Main Ceiling: 9 ft.	
Price Tier: A	

281 Sage Meadows

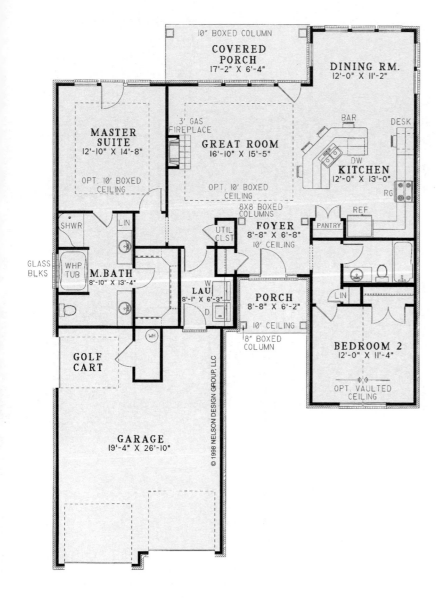

Floor plan labels:

- 10" BOXED COLUMN
- COVERED PORCH 17'-2" X 6'-4"
- DINING RM. 12'-0" X 11'-2"
- BAR
- DESK
- MASTER SUITE 12'-10" X 14'-8"
- 3' GAS FIREPLACE
- GREAT ROOM 16'-10" X 15'-5"
- OPT. 10' BOXED CEILING
- DW
- KITCHEN 12'-0" X 13'-0"
- OPT. 10' BOXED CEILING
- RG
- 8X8 BOXED COLUMNS
- REF
- SHWR
- LIN
- UTIL CLST
- FOYER 8'-8" X 6'-8" 10' CEILING
- PANTRY
- GLASS BLKS
- WHP TUB
- M.BATH 8'-10" X 13'-4"
- W
- LAU 8'-1" X 6'-3"
- D
- PORCH 8'-8" X 6'-2" 10' CEILING
- LIN
- © 1998 NELSON DESIGN GROUP, LLC
- GOLF CART
- WH
- 8" BOXED COLUMN
- BEDROOM 2 12'-0" X 11'-4"
- GARAGE 19'-4" X 26'-10"
- OPT. VAULTED CEILING

After a great game, drive your golf cart right off the course and up to your spacious two-car garage with side golf cart entry in this French Country Nelson Design Group home. Or come up the front walk and enter a beautiful porch with ten foot ceiling and boxed columns leading to an open foyer and great room where you'll enjoy hours of relaxation and entertainment. Share conversation or sit in silent awe as you watch the calming lake from your rear covered porch.

Width: 43'		**Bedrooms:** 2	
Depth: 63' 6"		**Baths:** 2	
Total Living: 1,387 sq. ft.		**Foundation:** Crawl, Slab, Optional Basement, Optional Daylight Basement	
Main Ceiling: 9 ft.			
Price Tier: A			

MASTER SUITE
15'-10" X 12'-0"
OPT. 10' BOXED CEILING

COVERED PORCH
29'-0" X 7'-8"

FRENCH DOORS

LIN.

WHP TUB

GLASS BLOCKS

M. BATH
11'-10" X 16'-4"

GLASS SHWR

GREAT ROOM
14'-0" X 16'-10"

10' BLOCK CEILING

9' CEILING

LIN.

DW

RG

REF.

BRKFST ROOM
7'-6" X 13'-0"

KIT.
10'-2" X 13'-0"

W

LAU.
6'-4" X 5'-6"

PANTRY

STORAGE

WH

D

GOLF CART

© 1998 NELSON DESIGN GROUP, LLC

PORCH
6'-6" X 5'-0"
10' CEILING

BEDROOM 2
8'-8" X 10'-0"

BEDROOM 3
9'-2" X 11'-6"
OPT. VAULTED CEILING

GARAGE
19'-0" X 27'-2"

Begin each day in comfort in this Nelson Design Group home. A spacious breakfast area allows early morning sunshine to peek through wonderful windows. French doors lead onto a spacious rear covered porch, perfect for entertaining or relaxing, which features a private entry to the master suite. French doors from the porch bring you back into the center of the home – the great room. Here, spend hours of quality time with your family playing games or reading a good book before retreating to your private master suite.

Width: 45'

Depth: 64' 2"

Total Living: 1,395 sq. ft.

Main Ceiling: 9 ft.

Price Tier: A

Bedrooms: 3

Baths: 2

Foundation: Crawl, Slab

286 Sage Meadows

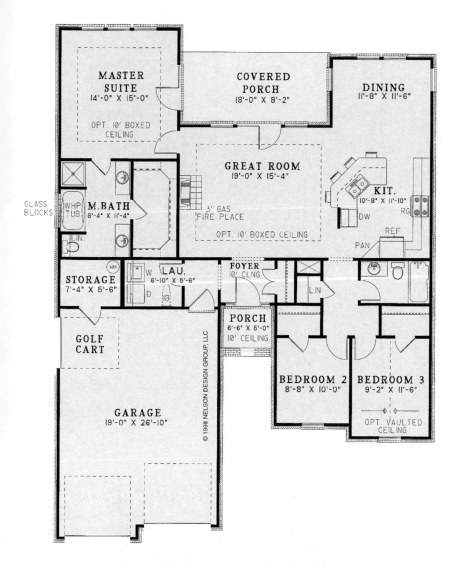

MASTER SUITE
14'-0" X 15'-0"
OPT. 10' BOXED CEILING

COVERED PORCH
18'-0" X 8'-2"

DINING
11'-8" X 11'-6"

GLASS BLOCKS

WHP TUB

M.BATH
8'-4" X 11'-4"

GREAT ROOM
19'-0" X 15'-4"
3' GAS FIRE PLACE
OPT. 10' BOXED CEILING

KIT.
10'-8" X 11'-10"

DW

REF

PAN

STORAGE
7'-4" X 5'-6"

W

LAU.
6'-10" X 5'-6"

D

FOYER
10' CLNG

LIN

GOLF CART

PORCH
6'-6" X 5'-0"
10' CEILING

GARAGE
19'-0" X 26'-10"

BEDROOM 2
8'-8" X 10'-0"

BEDROOM 3
9'-2" X 11'-6"

OPT. VAULTED CEILING

© 1998 NELSON DESIGN GROUP, LLC

Whether entering through the traditional covered porch with ten foot ceiling or the wonderful two-car garage with offset doors and side golf cart storage, this French Country Nelson Design Group home has plenty to offer. Passing through the foyer, you'll find an expansive great room complete with a gas fireplace and atrium doors leading to a rear covered porch, the ideal setting for grilling and entertaining. Enjoy the convenience of preparing meals in a spacious kitchen with angular island and eat-at bar. After a long day of work or play, relax in your private master suite with a beautiful view and access to the rear porch.

Width: 45'	Bedrooms: 3
Depth: 60' 4"	Baths: 2
Total Living: 1,472 sq. ft.	Foundation: Crawl, Slab
Main Ceiling: 9 ft.	
Price Tier: A	

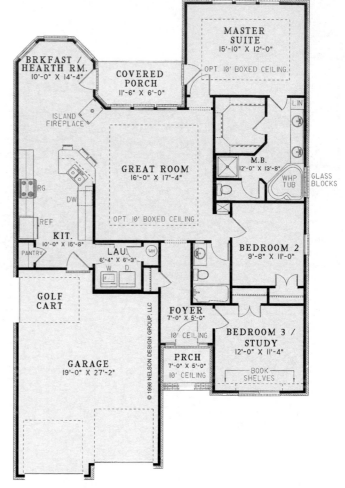

MASTER SUITE
15'-10" X 12'-0"

OPT. 10' BOXED CEILING

BRKFAST / HEARTH RM.
10'-0" X 14'-4"

COVERED PORCH
11'-6" X 6'-0"

ISLAND FIREPLACE

GREAT ROOM
16'-0" X 17'-4"

LIN

M.B.
12'-0" X 13'-8"

WHP TUB

GLASS BLOCKS

OPT. 10' BOXED CEILING

KIT.
10'-0" X 15'-8"

LAU.
6'-4" X 6'-3"

BEDROOM 2
9'-8" X 11'-0"

PANTRY

W D

WH

GOLF CART

FOYER
7'-0" X 5'-0"

10' CEILING

BEDROOM 3 / STUDY
12'-0" X 11'-4"

GARAGE
19'-0" X 27'-2"

PRCH
7'-0" X 5'-0"

10' CEILING

BOOK SHELVES

© 1998 NELSON DESIGN GROUP, LLC

At the heart of this Nelson Design Group home is an impressive great room with ten foot ceilings and peninsula fireplace. Off the great room, your family will enjoy meals together any time of day in the expansive kitchen. With an island, eat-at open bar, and breakfast nook complete with bay windows, you won't hear any excuses for not finding time to eat. A secluded private entrance with french doors from the master suite to a rear covered porch allows you the opportunity to "get away" from it all.

Width: 39' 4"
Depth: 63' 2"
Total Living: 1,480 sq. ft.
Main Ceiling: 9 ft.
Price Tier: A

Bedrooms: 3
Baths: 2
Foundation: Crawl, Slab

278 Sage Meadows

COVERED PORCH
16'-0" X 8'-0"

GAS FIREPLACE

GREAT RM.
15'-8" X 14'-0"
10' BOXED CEILING

BED RM. 2 / STUDY
10'-0" X 13'-8"

OPTIONAL FRENCH DOORS

MASTER SUITE
12'-0" X 14'-0"
10' BOXED CEILING

DINING
15'-8" X 9'-0"

LIN

BATH

M.BATH

LIN

KIT.

DW
PAN.
RG.
REF.

8" COLUMNS

BED RM. 3
9'-8" X 9'-10"

FOYER

W. LAU. D

BREAKFAST RM.
11'-4" X 8'-5"

WH

STORAGE

ENTRY PORCH

GOLF CART

GARAGE
19'-4" X 29'-0"

© 1998 NELSON DESIGN GROUP, LLC

Feel the French Country flair as you step onto the covered entry porch of this Nelson Design Group home complete with traditional columns and fluid entry into a formal foyer. Enjoy cozy nights at home in your spacious great room or entertain friends on warm summer evenings on your covered rear porch. Early morning breakfasts are a delight with an eat-at kitchen bar opening to a quiet breakfast nook.

Width: 39' 0"
Depth: 73' 10"
Total Living: 1,487 sq. ft.
Main Ceiling: 9 ft.
Price Tier: A

Bedrooms: 3
Baths: 2
Foundation: Crawl, Slab, Optional Basement, Optional Daylight Basement

284 Sage Meadows

As you enter this Nelson Design Group home, you are welcomed onto a lovely covered porch with ten foot ceilings and led directly into the traditional foyer. From there you'll enjoy a combination great room and dining area divided only by magnificent wooden columns. An easily accessible kitchen is accented by a breakfast nook complete with ample windows and entry to a rear covered grilling porch. Spend hours delighting friends and family with your grilling expertise.

Width: 39' 6"

Depth: 72' 5"

Total Living: 1,504 sq. ft.

Main Ceiling: 9 ft.

Price Tier: B

Bedrooms: 3

Baths: 2

Foundation: Crawl, Slab, Optional Basement, Optional Daylight Basement

280 Sage Meadows

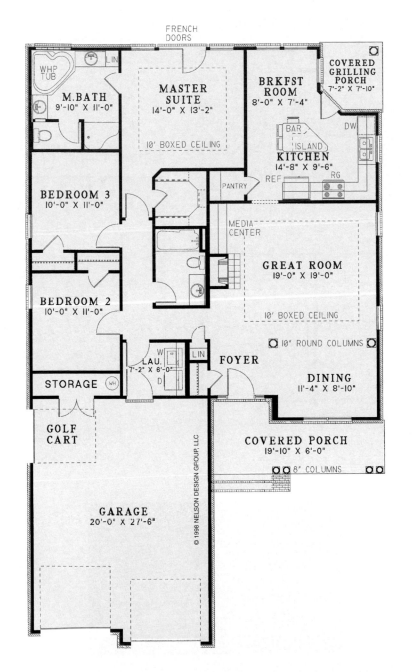

FRENCH DOORS

WHP TUB

LIN

M. BATH
9'-10" X 11'-0"

MASTER SUITE
14'-0" X 13'-2"

10' BOXED CEILING

BRKFST ROOM
8'-0" X 7'-4"

COVERED GRILLING PORCH
7'-2" X 7'-10"

DW

BAR ISLAND

KITCHEN
14'-8" X 9'-6"

REF · RG

BEDROOM 3
10'-0" X 11'-0"

PANTRY

MEDIA CENTER

GREAT ROOM
19'-0" X 19'-0"

10' BOXED CEILING

BEDROOM 2
10'-0" X 11'-0"

10" ROUND COLUMNS

W · D

LAU.
7'-2" X 6'-0"

LIN

FOYER

DINING
11'-4" X 8'-10"

STORAGE
WH

GOLF CART

COVERED PORCH
19'-10" X 6'-0"

8" COLUMNS

© 1998 NELSON DESIGN GROUP, LLC

GARAGE
20'-0" X 27'-6"

Entering this French Country Nelson Design Group home, you come upon a long covered porch enhanced by beautifully crafted columns. A quaint foyer leads you to a marvelous dining area with wooden columns and the great room with a ten foot boxed ceiling. Enjoy many hours of food and laughter with friends and family year-round when utilizing the convenience of your covered grilling porch.

Width: 40' 0"	**Main Ceiling:** 9 ft.
Depth: 67' 4"	**Bedrooms:** 3
Total Living: 1,535 sq. ft.	**Baths:** 2
Price Tier: B	**Foundation:** Crawl, Slab

Entering this French Country Nelson Design Group home, you are led through a traditional foyer enhanced by wooden columns and into a spacious great room – perfect for family get-togethers. Enjoy the privacy of your master suite complete with atrium doors and windows opening into the back yard. Delight your friends with your famous hamburgers any time of year on your convenient grilling porch located right off the kitchen. As you travel upstairs, you'll find two spacious bedrooms with a walk-through bath – a wonderful solution for the kids.

Main Floor

Upper Floor

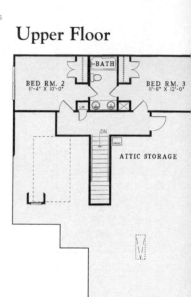

Width: 34' 0"
Depth: 66' 8"
Main Floor: 1,131 sq. ft.
Upper Floor: 443 sq. ft.
Total Living: 1,574 sq. ft.
Price Tier: B

Main Ceiling: 9 ft.
Upper Ceiling: 8 ft.
Bedrooms: 3
Baths: 2 1/2
Foundation: Crawl, Slab, Optional Basement, Optional Daylight Basement

277 Sage Meadows

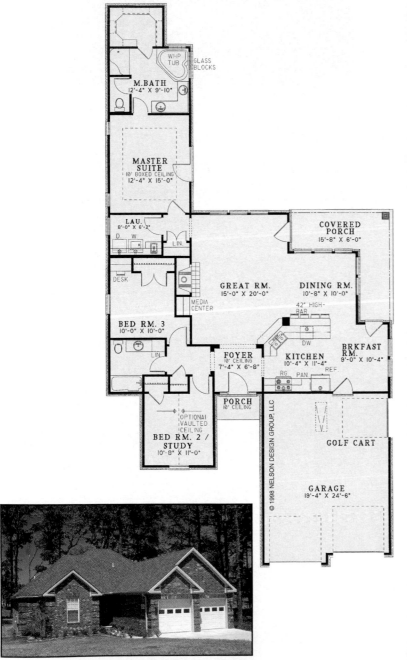

MASTER SUITE
10' BOXED CEILING
12'-4" X 15'-0"

M.BATH
12'-4" X 9'-10"

WHP TUB

GLASS BLOCKS

LAU.
8'-0" X 6'-2"

D W

LIN

DESK

MEDIA CENTER

GREAT RM.
15'-0" X 20'-0"

DINING RM.
10'-8" X 10'-0"

COVERED PORCH
15'-8" X 6'-0"

BED RM. 3
10'-0" X 10'-0"

LIN

FOYER
10' CEILING
7'-4" X 6'-8"

KITCHEN
10'-4" X 11'-4"

42" HIGH-BAR

DW

BRKFAST RM.
9'-0" X 10'-4"

RG PAN REF

OPTIONAL VAULTED CEILING

BED RM. 2 / STUDY
10'-8" X 11'-0"

PORCH
10' CEILING

GOLF CART

GARAGE
19'-4" X 24'-6"

© 1998 NELSON DESIGN GROUP, LLC

Step inside this Nelson Design Group home and enter a beautiful formal foyer with a ten foot ceiling. The foyer opens into a wonderfully spacious family area, perfect for special quality time. Visit with family or entertain friends on the timeless covered porch overlooking a calming lake or rolling golf course. Accessibility to both the great room and a cozy breakfast nook makes this porch both relaxing and convenient. Finally, enjoy your secluded master suite and bath complete with corner whirlpool tub and privacy glass block windows.

Width: 44' 0"	**Main Ceiling:** 9 ft.
Depth: 86' 2"	**Bedrooms:** 3
Total Living: 1,601 sq. ft.	**Baths:** 2
Price Tier: B	**Foundation:** Crawl, Slab

RENAISSANCE
A FRENCH COUNTRY NEIGHBORHOOD

A "rebirth" of the small country cottage and stone house combining grace, comfort and warmth describes the Renaissance Collection. This collection of French Country plans range in square footage from 1,800 to 2,200. Country living entails pure enjoyment and love for the countryside, so we've added grilling porches and an abundance of windows to bring the outside in to the home. Distinctive elements of boxed ceilings and columns grace these six French Country designs. Enjoy the return of a simple yet elegant life style.

Nelson Design Group LLC

RESIDENTIAL PLANNERS - DESIGNERS

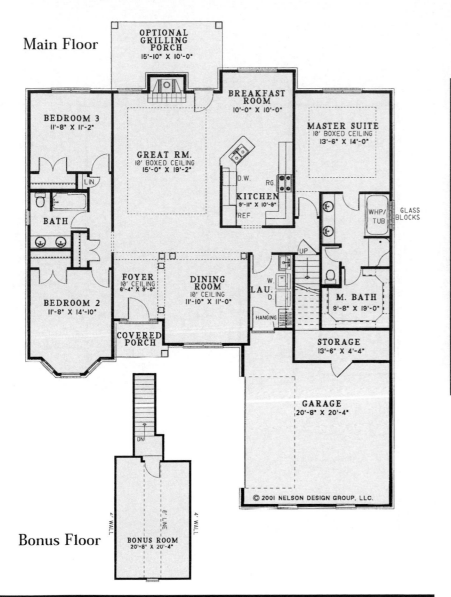

Main Floor

OPTIONAL GRILLING PORCH
15'-10" X 10'-0"

BREAKFAST ROOM
10'-0" X 10'-0"

BEDROOM 3
11'-8" X 11'-2"

MASTER SUITE
10' BOXED CEILING
13'-6" X 14'-0"

GREAT RM.
10' BOXED CEILING
15'-0" X 19'-2"

D.W.   RG

KITCHEN
9'-11" X 10'-9"

REF.

BATH

LIN

WHP/TUB   GLASS BLOCKS

FOYER
10' CEILING
6'-4" X 9'-6"

DINING ROOM
10' CEILING
11'-10" X 11'-0"

LAU.

W.

UP

BEDROOM 2
11'-8" X 14'-10"

M. BATH
9'-8" X 19'-0"

W. D.

HANGING

COVERED PORCH

STORAGE
13'-6" X 4'-4"

GARAGE
20'-8" X 20'-4"

© 2001 NELSON DESIGN GROUP, LLC.

DN

Bonus Floor

4' WALL   6' LINE   4' WALL

BONUS ROOM
20'-8" X 20'-4"

Width: 52' 0"

Depth: 69' 6"

Total Living: 1,869 sq. ft.*

*Optional Bonus: 288 sq. ft.

Price Tier: B

Main Ceiling: 9 ft.

Bonus Ceiling: 8 ft.

Bedrooms: 3

Baths: 2

Foundation: Crawl, Slab, Optional Basement, Optional Daylight Basement

545 Calais Drive

Beautiful stone and siding give warmth to this French Country design. Elegance is achieved in our Nelson Design Group home by using boxed columns and ten foot ceilings. The foyer and dining rooms are lined with columns and adjoin the great room, all with high ceilings. The kitchen and breakfast room are great for entertaining and have access to the grilling porch. This split bedroom plan has a master suite with large walk-in closet, whirlpool tub, shower and private area. A bonus room above the garage, is available with stair access near the master suite. Two bedrooms and a large bathroom are located on the other side of the great room giving privacy to the entire family.

523 Fontenay Drive

Upon entering the foyer of this Nelson Design Group home, you'll notice the magnificent boxed columns surrounding the Dining room. Ten foot ceilings enhance the foyer, dining and great rooms giving this split bedroom plan a very open effect. Entertaining becomes simple for the grill master on the grilling porch accessible to the great room. As night falls, retreat to your master bath by relaxing in your whirlpool tub. The courtyard entry garage enhances the street appeal of this beautiful French country home.

Width: 52' 0"

Depth: 69' 6"

Total Living: 1,882 sq. ft.

Main Ceiling: 9 ft.

Price Tier: B

Bedrooms: 3

Baths: 2

Foundation: Crawl, Slab, Optional Basement, Optional Daylight Basement

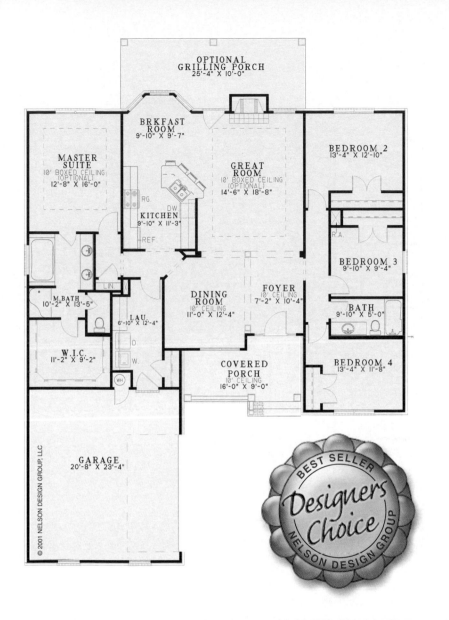

OPTIONAL
GRILLING PORCH
25'-4" X 10'-0"

BRKFAST
ROOM
9'-10" X 9'-7"

MASTER
SUITE
10' BOXED CEILING
(OPTIONAL)
12'-8" X 16'-0"

GREAT
ROOM
10' BOXED CEILING
(OPTIONAL)
14'-6" X 18'-8"

BEDROOM 2
13'-4" X 12'-10"

RG

DW

KITCHEN
9'-10" X 11'-3"

REF.

R.A.

BEDROOM 3
9'-10" X 9'-4"

M.BATH
10'-2" X 13'-5"

LIN

DINING
ROOM
10' CEILING
11'-0" X 12'-4"

FOYER
10' CEILING
7'-2" X 10'-4"

BATH
9'-10" X 5'-0"

LAU.
6'-10" X 12'-4"

D

W.I.C.
11'-2" X 9'-2"

W

WH

COVERED
PORCH
10' CEILING
16'-0" X 9'-0"

BEDROOM 4
13'-4" X 11'-8"

GARAGE
20'-8" X 23'-4"

© 2001 NELSON DESIGN GROUP, LLC

BEST SELLER
Designers Choice
NELSON DESIGN GROUP

522 Calais Drive

Width: 52' 0"
Depth: 71' 6"
Total Living: 1,930 sq. ft.
Main Ceiling: 8 ft.
Price Tier: B

Bedrooms: 4
Baths: 2
Foundation: Crawl, Slab,
Optional Basement,
Optional Daylight Basement

This enchanting Nelson Design Group home incorporates the best in floor planning all in one level. The great room - which is convenient for those family gatherings that need extra room, is highlighted by a fireplace and a ten foot boxed ceiling. Easy access from the kitchen to the dining room makes hosting a dinner party more convenient. Entertain friends and family during the summer on the rear grilling porch. As evening approaches, retreat to your master bath complete with large walk-in closet, double vanities and whirlpool bath.

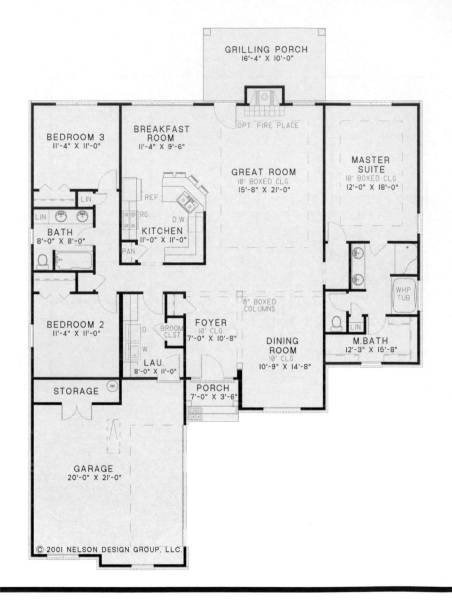

519 Chantilly Circle

Welcome your dinner guests into this elegant Nelson Design Group home enhanced by ten foot ceilings and an open floor plan. Once in the foyer, notice the boxed columns separating the dining room and great room. The great room has a fireplace and door accessing the rear grilling porch which makes for entertaining ease. Two bedrooms and a full bath are located on one side of the house, allowing the master suite total privacy. This large master bedroom has plenty of wall space for large furniture and a master bathroom with whirlpool tub, double vanity, separate shower with seat, toilet room and a walk-in closet. Enjoy this beautiful home with plenty of room for your family.

Width: 52' 0"	Bedrooms: 3
Depth: 71' 2"	Baths: 2
Total Living: 1,973 sq. ft.	Foundation: Crawl, Slab,
Main Ceiling: 9 ft.	Optional Basement,
Price Tier: B	Optional Daylight Basement

Main Floor

GRILLING PORCH
9'-8" X 9'-6"

BREAKFAST ROOM
11'-0" X 11'-4"

WHP TUB

MASTER BATH
12'-8" X 11'-4"

GREAT ROOM
16'-4" X 18'-0"

PANTRY

KITCHEN
15'-8" X 12'-0"

DW

REF. RG

FOYER
10' CLNG

DINING
10'-6" X 11'-0"

MASTER SUITE
10' BOX CEILING
12'-8" X 16'-0"

PORCH
10' CLNG

UP

D W LAU.
10'-4" X 6'-6"

GARAGE
20'-0" X 21'-10"

© 2001 NELSON DESIGN GROUP, LLC.

Upper Floor

BEDROOM 2
9'-9" X 10'-6"

BEDROOM 3
9'-9" X 10'-6"

BATH

BONUS AREA

BEDROOM 4
10'-8" X 13'-0"

DN

HVAC

ATTIC STORAGE

520 Fontenay Drive

Width: 50' 6"
Depth: 54' 8"
Main Floor: 1,495 sq. ft.
Upper Floor: 546 sq. ft.
Total Living: 2,041 sq. ft.
Price Tier: C

Main Ceiling: 9 ft.
Upper Ceiling: 8 ft.
Bedrooms: 4
Baths: 2 1/2
Foundation: Crawl, Slab, Optional Basement, Optional Daylight Basement

Drive into a courtyard entry garage and retreat to your French Country home. Nelson Design Group has designed a beautiful floor plan that is very family oriented beginning with a porch and foyer with ten foot ceilings. Enter the foyer and travel into a massive great room adjoining the breakfast room with access to a grilling porch. The kitchen bar area makes grilling easy and provides extra seating for large family gatherings. The master suite enhanced by a ten foot ceiling, is located on the main level and has 'his and her' closets leading to the master bathroom full of amenities. As you travel upstairs, you'll find three bedrooms and a full bath with optional bonus area.

Upper Floor

536 Chantilly Circle

The focal point of this French Country plan is a large stone wrapped window extending a feeling of warmth in the neighborhood. This lovely Nelson Design Group home has a great room with fireplace and access to a rear grilling porch. The kitchen has a pass thru to the great room and adjoins a large breakfast room with a bar counter. The master suite is on the main floor and has a large bathroom with walk-in closet and all the amenities. Travel upstairs and find three bedrooms and a full bathroom. Attic storage is easily accessed for seasonal usage.

Width: 50' 2"	Main Ceiling: 9 ft.
Depth: 52' 0"	Upper Ceiling: 8 ft.
Main Floor: 1,563 sq. ft.	Bedrooms: 4
Upper Floor: 727 sq. ft.	Baths: 2 1/2
Total Living: 2,290 sq. ft.	Foundation: Crawl, Slab
Price Tier: C	

To order call 1.800.590.2423 or to view similar plans visit www.nelsondesigngroup.com

The Duplex Collection
Series 1

The Duplex Collection Series 1 features over forty designs with a variety of exterior styles including Traditional, French Country, Southern Traditional and European Traditional. With a combined living space of 2,000 to 4,500 square feet, every family is easily accommodated. These creations of modular units were originally designed as individual homes that had the possibility of being built as one unit. The collaboration of smaller homes into duplexes was designed to convey the true feelings and emotions of buying a starter home or retirement home. A Traditional home environment is truly exemplified with front porches, rear grilling porches and garages. The Duplex Collection Series 1 offers all the accommodations and amenities of a single home with the benefits and savings afforded from a consolidated, low-maintenance environment.

Nelson Design Group
LLC
RESIDENTIAL PLANNERS - DESIGNERS

489 Carriage Hill

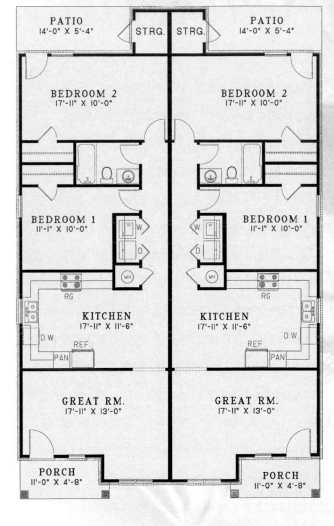

This contemporary duplex plan by Nelson Design Group will add class to any neighborhood. Brick columns and a hip roof enhance this two-bedroom plan complete with a large kitchen and small laundry closet. The great room is spacious and has a small sitting area by the front window. On the rear patio you'll be able to have a drink with friends and watch the sun set.

Width: 37' 0"
Depth: 56' 10"
Total Living: 1,844 sq. ft.
Main Ceiling: 8 ft.

Bedrooms: 4
Baths: 2
Foundation: Crawl, Slab
Price Tier: B

Home 1 *Home 2*

To order call 1.800.590.2423 or to view the rest of this collection visit www.nelsondesigngroup.com

411 Cabe Court

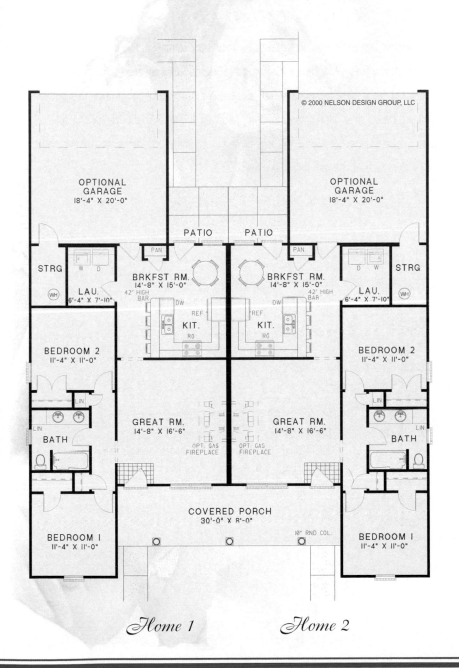

© 2000 NELSON DESIGN GROUP, LLC

OPTIONAL GARAGE
18'-4" X 20'-0"

OPTIONAL GARAGE
18'-4" X 20'-0"

PATIO

PATIO

STRG

PAN.

PAN.

STRG

LAU.
6'-4" X 7'-10"

BRKFST RM.
14'-8" X 15'-0"

BRKFST RM.
14'-8" X 15'-0"

LAU.
6'-4" X 7'-10"

42" HIGH BAR

42" HIGH BAR

DW

REF.

REF.

DW

KIT.

KIT.

RG

RG

BEDROOM 2
11'-4" X 11'-0"

BEDROOM 2
11'-4" X 11'-0"

LIN

LIN

BATH

GREAT RM.
14'-8" X 16'-6"

GREAT RM.
14'-8" X 16'-6"

BATH

OPT. GAS FIREPLACE

OPT. GAS FIREPLACE

COVERED PORCH
30'-0" X 8'-0"

10" RND COL.

BEDROOM 1
11'-4" X 11'-0"

BEDROOM 1
11'-4" X 11'-0"

Home 1

Home 2

Imagine yourself rocking away the tensions of life on the front covered porch of this southern style Nelson Design Group home. You'll be welcomed by the tiled entrance leading into the comfortable great room with fireplace. Start family traditions in the cozy kitchen with eat-at bar and breakfast room with access to rear patio. Both bedrooms have ample closet space and share a bath with 'his and her' vanities. This traditional neighborhood design will accommodate you and your family.

Width: 54' 0"	Bedrooms: 4
Depth: 65' 2"	Baths: 2
Total Living: 1,970 sq. ft.	Foundation: Crawl, Slab
Main Ceiling: 9 ft.	Price Tier: B

426 Wilshire Circle

Nelson Design Group has created a duplex by beautifully combining two homes for cost efficiency. These homes feature ten-foot boxed ceilings in the great rooms and master suite bedrooms giving a more formal effect while allowing more natural light to flow throughout. The dining rooms have a boxed column entry and view the great room fireplace for the utmost in atmosphere. Step saver kitchens have a large pantry, additional bar seating and enjoy a front view of the well-manicured lawn.

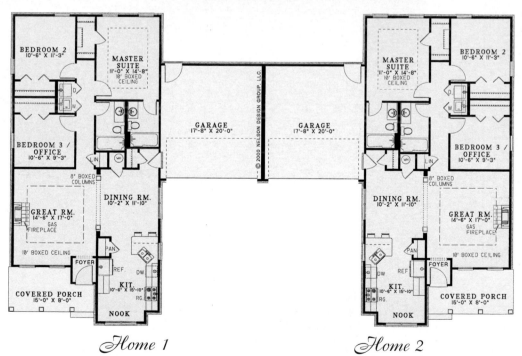

Home 1   *Home 2*

Width:	88' 0"	Bedrooms:	6
Depth:	54' 8"	Baths:	4
Total Living:	2,558 sq. ft.	Foundation:	Crawl, Slab
Main Ceiling:	9 ft.	Price Tier:	D

428 Centre Grove Circle

Tiered gables and covered porches give this Nelson Design Group duplex a warm welcome. Each home has a large great room with optional fireplace opening to a large dining area with additional seating at the shared kitchen bar counter. The kitchen views the dining and great rooms allowing for great entertaining options while a small breakfast nook is gently tucked in the rear of the kitchen providing a view of the back yard and corner-grilling porch. A roomy master suite is privately separated from the additional bedrooms and is enhanced with a ten-foot boxed ceiling and walk-in closet.

Width: 92' 0"
Depth: 54' 10"
Total Living: 2,636 sq. ft.
Main Ceiling: 9 ft.

Bedrooms: 6
Baths: 4
Foundation: Crawl, Slab
Price Tier: D

Home 1   Home 2

453 *Heather Ridge*

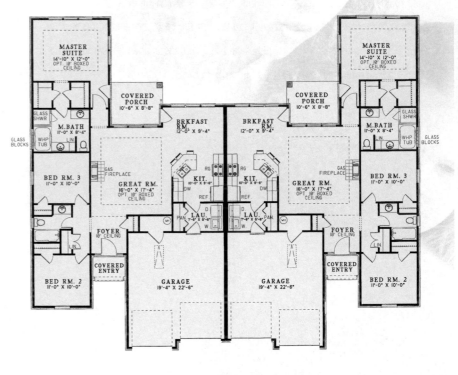

Home 1   Home 2

This duplex by Nelson Design Group incorporates living areas at the rear of the home along with a covered porch making this perfect for a lake or golf course community. The foyer has a ten foot ceiling giving a feeling of spaciousness as well as ten foot boxed ceilings in both the great room and master suite. The kitchen has bar seating and immediate access to a large pantry and laundry room for convenience. The master suite includes 'his and her' closets that separate the master bathroom from a spacious master suite full of windows for plenty of natural lighting.

Width: 76' 8"   Bedrooms: 6
Depth: 65' 6"   Baths: 4
Total Living: 2,758 sq. ft.   Foundation: Crawl, Slab
Main Ceiling: 9 ft.   Price Tier: D

429 Ivy Green

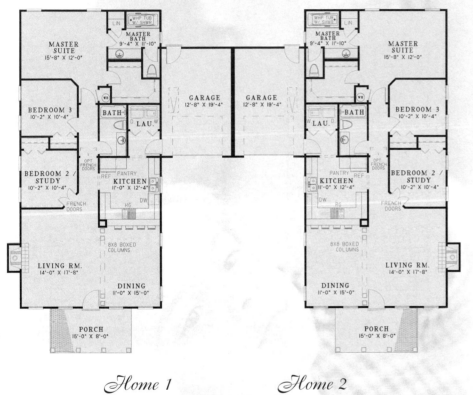

Home 1   *Home 2*

The street appeal of this Nelson Design Group duplex beautifully reflects southern charm with a centered gable and a lovely porch with columns. A spacious living room with fireplace opens to the formal dining room enhanced with a column-lined entry and views the kitchen. One of the bedrooms has french doors and will make the perfect study or home office. The master suite is placed at the rear of the home and has a large walk-in closet and luxurious bathroom with a whirlpool tub/shower. A laundry room is conveniently placed just steps from the kitchen and accesses the single garage.

Width: 82' 8"	Bedrooms: 6
Depth: 62' 0"	Baths: 4
Total Living: 2,808 sq. ft.	Foundation: Crawl, Slab
Main Ceiling: 9 ft.	Price Tier: D

408-1 Heather Ridge

Home 1   Home 2

Picture yourself hosting a dinner party surrounded by family in this Nelson Design Group Traditional Neighborhood home. After greeting guests on the covered porch, guide them into the spacious great room. Here, mingling can begin and maybe drinks around the romantic gas fireplace. Conveniently accessible to the kitchen, you can slip away to check on the excellent cuisine you are preparing. A connecting breakfast room can serve as more space for guests or a quiet place just for you. A door opening to a grilling porch allows you to prepare grilled meals with ease. When all the excitement is over, enjoy the privacy of the master suite or relax in the whirlpool bath.

Width: 80' 8"
Depth: 63' 4"
Total Living: 2,910 sq. ft.
Main Ceiling: 9 ft.

Bedrooms: 6
Baths: 4
Foundation: Crawl, Slab
Price Tier: D

454 Cabe Court

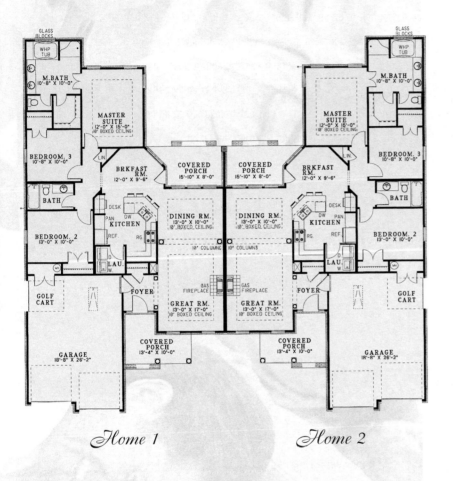

Home 1   *Home 2*

This Nelson Design Group duplex plan has the family in mind. Front and rear porches allow for outside enjoyment during the warm seasons while the great room fireplace takes the chill out of cold evenings. Ten foot-boxed ceilings are used in the formal dining room, great room and luxurious master suite for added elegance. Family time will be enjoyable in the large kitchen and breakfast room combination complete with a built in desk, bar seating and door to the grilling porch. The double garage has a golf cart bay and storage area.

Width:	79' 0"	Bedrooms:	6
Depth:	72' 5"	Baths:	4
Total Living:	3,008 sq. ft.	Foundation:	Crawl, Slab
Main Ceiling:	9 ft.	Price Tier:	E

458 Carriage Hill

This Nelson Design Group duplex is adorned with rock, siding and shutters giving a cozy European flair to an elegant interior. Beginning in the foyer enhanced with a ten foot ceiling, the front bedroom includes built in bookshelves making a wonderful study or home office. The great room and breakfast/hearth rooms share an island fireplace and access a grilling porch right outside – perfect for family gatherings! The spacious master suite bedroom is detailed with a ten foot boxed ceiling and adjoins the master bathroom featuring a corner whirlpool tub, separate shower, private toilet room and large walk in closet. A double car garage is spacious enough for additional storage.

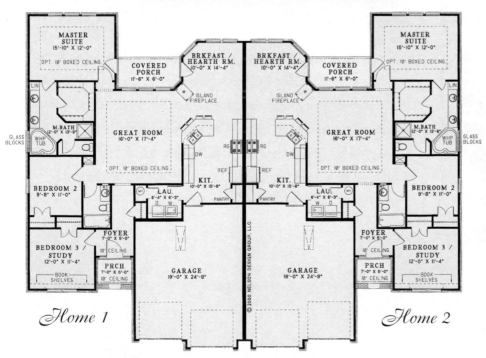

Home 1   *Home 2*

Width: 81' 0"	Bedrooms: 6
Depth: 63' 2"	Baths: 4
Total Living: 3,040 sq. ft.	Foundation: Crawl, Slab
Main Ceiling: 9 ft.	Price Tier: E

425 Cambridge Court

The ultimate family home by Nelson Design Group times two! This duplex offers the most luxurious family areas and separates the master suite from the other bedrooms for privacy. The massive great room has a nine foot boxed ceiling, large fireplace, access to the rear-covered porch and opens to a large kitchen and dining area for the ultimate in entertaining options. One of the two front bedrooms will be conveniently suited for a study or home office, for the 'work at home' professional. A master bedroom suite with nine foot boxed ceiling and a master bath with all the amenities complete this design.

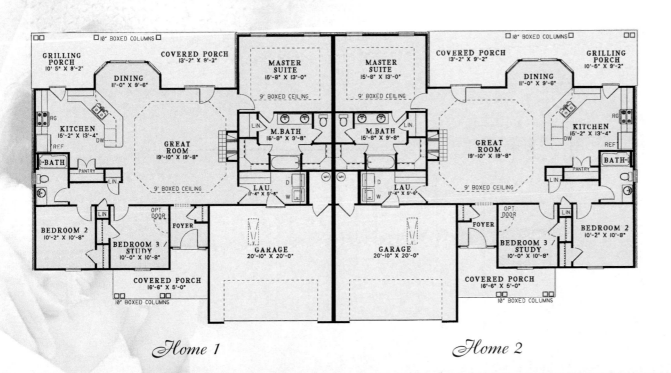

Home 1   *Home 2*

Width: 103' 0"	Bedrooms: 6
Depth: 49' 10"	Baths: 4
Total Living: 3,050 sq. ft.	Foundation: Crawl, Slab
Main Ceiling: 8 ft.	Price Tier: E

432 Brookshire

From the street this Nelson Design Group duplex appears to be two large homes sitting closely together. A large covered porch with ten inch columns and dormers enhance this traditional design. The great room has a large fireplace and gently accesses the kitchen for ease in entertaining. A family oriented kitchen has a counter with bar seating and is totally open to the breakfast room, which leads to a grilling porch. For privacy, the master suite is on the main floor and has double vanities, a separate shower and 'his and her' walk-in closets surrounding a luxurious whirlpool tub. Upstairs you'll find a full bathroom and two bedrooms each with built-in desks for quiet study time.

Width: 80' 0"	Main Ceiling: 9 ft.
Depth: 55' 2"	Upper Ceiling: 8 ft.
Main Floor: 1,960 sq. ft.	Bedrooms: 6
Upper Floor: 1,122 sq. ft.	Baths: 4
Total Living: 3,082 sq. ft.	Foundation: Crawl, Slab
Price Tier: E	

Home 1   *Home 2*

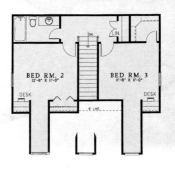

Upper 1   *Upper 2*

To order call 1.800.590.2423 or to view the rest of this collection visit www.nelsondesigngroup.com

409 Auburn Place

Home 1   Home 2

Floor plan labels (Home 1):
NOOK 9'-0" X 7'-0", LAU. 8'-8" X 5'-6", MASTER SUITE 10'-0" BOXED CEILING 12'-0" X 13'-8", KITCHEN 14'-8" X 12'-4", PANTRY, REF, DW, GARAGE 13'-0" X 20'-0", M.BATH 12'-0" X 11'-6", LIN, WHP TUB, SHWR, GLASS BLOCKS, DINING RM. 10'-8" X 10'-0", 8" COLUMNS, BED RM. 3 12'-0" X 10'-8", GREAT RM. 10'-0" BOXED CEILING 14'-8" X 20'-0", BATH, LIN, FOYER, SITTING AREA 9'-0" X 4'-0", BED RM. 2 12'-0" X 10'-4", PRCH

Floor plan labels (Home 2):
NOOK 9'-0" X 7'-0", LAU. 8'-8" X 5'-6", MASTER SUITE 10'-0" BOXED CEILING 12'-0" X 13'-8", KITCHEN 14'-8" X 12'-4", PANTRY, REF, DW, GARAGE 13'-0" X 20'-0", M.BATH 12'-0" X 11'-6", LIN, WHP TUB, SHWR, GLASS BLOCKS, DINING RM. 10'-8" X 10'-0", 8" COLUMNS, BED RM. 3 12'-0" X 10'-8", GREAT RM. 10'-0" BOXED CEILING 14'-8" X 20'-0", BATH, LIN, FOYER, SITTING AREA 9'-0" X 4'-0", BED RM. 2 12'-0" X 10'-4", PRCH

This Nelson Design Group duplex has a conservative exterior, but features an elegant interior layout. An open great room with a cozy fireplace is enhanced by a ten foot boxed ceiling and adjoins a formal dining room lined with columns. Two spacious bedrooms and a full bath are located at the front of this plan leaving convenience and privacy for the master suite at the rear of the home. The kitchen includes a large island counter with bar seating and enjoys a bay window view from the breakfast nook. A single car garage is centered between the units for sound proofing and added privacy.

Width: 82' 0"	Bedrooms: 6
Depth: 60' 4"	Baths: 4
Total Living: 3,238 sq. ft.	Foundation: Crawl, Slab
Main Ceiling: 9 ft.	Price Tier: E

406 Ivy Green

Nelson Design Group has created a brick duplex with the warmth of a single family home. Upon entering the foyer, a great room with an eleven-foot ceiling, built in media center and cozy fireplace awaits you. Travel through the foyer to the kitchen open to a hearth and dining room with optional fireplace accessing a rear covered porch. The laundry room with a built in ironing board center is centrally located and just steps away from the kitchen. For the utmost in privacy, the master suite is located away from the two additional bedrooms and full bath. The luxurious master bathroom has a corner whirlpool tub with glass block windows, a separate shower, private toilet area, large walk-in closet and private access to the rear porch. A double car garage with storage room completes this lovely design.

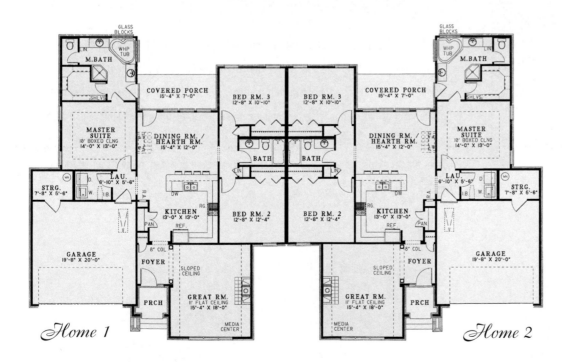

Width:	98' 0"	Bedrooms:	6
Depth:	58' 6"	Baths:	4
Total Living:	3,308 sq. ft.	Foundation:	Crawl, Slab
Main Ceiling:	9 ft.	Price Tier:	E

438 Cabe Court

MASTER SUITE
10' BOXED CEILING
21'-0" X 12'-0"

M. BATH
16'-10" X 13'-0"

LANAI
17'-4" X 8'-0"

LANAI
17'-4" X 8'-0"

MASTER SUITE
10' BOXED CEILING
21'-0" X 12'-0"

M. BATH
16'-10" X 13'-0"

GLASS BLOCKS
WHP TUB
GLASS SHWR
LIN

GAS FIREPLACE

BREAKFAST ROOM
10'-0" X 9'-0"

BREAKFAST ROOM
10'-0" X 9'-0"

GAS FIREPLACE

LIN
WHP TUB
GLASS SHWR
GLASS BLOCKS

BEDROOM 2
12'-8" X 11'-8"

GREAT ROOM
17'-2" X 15'-6"

BAR

BAR

GREAT ROOM
17'-2" X 15'-6"

BEDROOM 2
12'-8" X 11'-8"

BATH

8' COLUMNS

REF

REF

8' COLUMNS

BATH

DINING ROOM
10'-6" X 12'-0"

KIT.
9'-6" X 15'-2"

KIT.
9'-6" X 15'-2"

DINING ROOM
10'-6" X 12'-0"

FOYER

FOYER

BEDROOM 3
11' CEILING
12'-8" X 11'-8"

LAU.
9'-4" X 5'-8"

LAU.
9'-4" X 5'-8"

BEDROOM 3
11' CEILING
12'-8" X 11'-8"

PORCH

SLOPE CEILING

PORCH

SLOPE CEILING

GARAGE
20'-0" X 21'-4"

GARAGE
20'-0" X 20'-0"

Home 1   *Home 2*

This spacious Nelson Design Group duplex features round top windows and tiered gables for great street appeal. A small porch welcomes you into an open plan well designed for ultimate entertaining. The formal dining room has columns to separate it from the large great room while a spacious breakfast room opens to the kitchen enjoying a view of the great room fireplace as well as the rear lanai. The master suite is privately placed at the rear of the house and enhanced with a ten-foot boxed ceiling and luxurious bathroom. This master suite bedroom has French door access to the bathroom containing a corner whirlpool tub with glass blocks above, separate shower, private toilet area and a huge walk-in closet.

Width: 78' 0"		Bedrooms: 6	
Depth: 73' 8"		Baths: 4	
Total Living: 3,500 sq. ft.		Foundation: Crawl, Slab	
Main Ceiling: 9 ft.		Price Tier: F	

410 Cabe Court

This elegant Nelson Design Group duplex features large round top windows and tiered gables for great street appeal. An arched porch welcomes you into a well designed split bedroom floor plan offering several family areas. The breakfast and formal dining rooms are at the front of the house leaving the great room and master suite much appreciated privacy in the rear. A large laundry room is centrally located for added convenience. Upstairs you'll find a full bathroom and two additional bedrooms with creative ceilings heights.

Width:	96' 0"	Main Ceiling:	9 ft.
Depth:	43' 0"	Upper Ceiling:	8 ft.
Main Floor:	2,738 sq. ft.	Bedrooms:	6
Upper Floor:	882 sq. ft.	Baths:	4, 2 - 1/2
Total Living:	3,620 sq. ft.	Foundation:	Crawl, Slab
Price Tier:	F		

Home 1   *Home 2*

Upper 1

Upper 2

To order call 1.800.590.2423 or to view the rest of this collection visit www.nelsondesigngroup.com

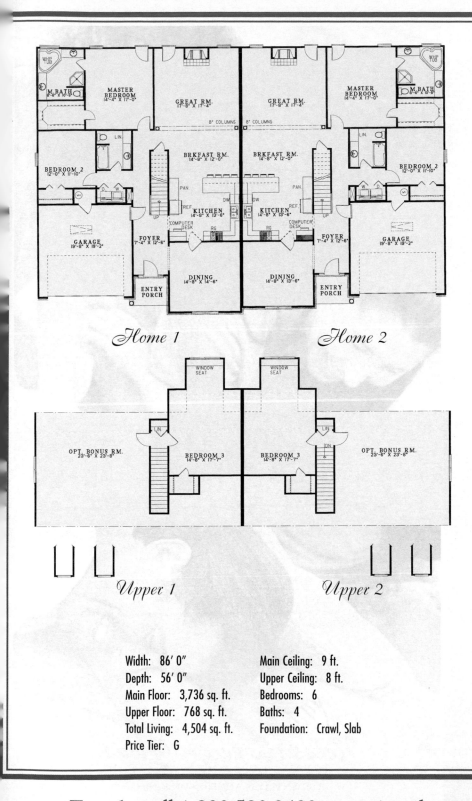

Home 1   *Home 2*

Upper 1   *Upper 2*

Width: 86' 0"
Depth: 56' 0"
Main Floor: 3,736 sq. ft.
Upper Floor: 768 sq. ft.
Total Living: 4,504 sq. ft.
Price Tier: G

Main Ceiling: 9 ft.
Upper Ceiling: 8 ft.
Bedrooms: 6
Baths: 4
Foundation: Crawl, Slab

442 Carriage Hill

This Nelson Design Group duplex design features a spacious great room with columns, a cozy fireplace and access to a well-manicured backyard. Also opening to the great room is a large breakfast room with additional seating at the kitchen bar counter. A built-in computer desk in the kitchen will be great for study time and monitoring children on the computer. The master suite is located on the main floor and has a large walk-in closet, private bathroom with corner whirlpool tub, separate shower and double vanities. The upstairs has an optional bonus room and a huge bedroom with window seat and walk-in closet.

The Waterfront Collection

Eleven beautiful designs that emphasize the rear view of the plan. Enjoy a waterfront or lake view through large windows with vaulted ceilings providing ample natural lighting. These plans range between 1,200 to 6,500 square feet and include beautiful fireplaces, loft areas and massive decks, perfect for entertaining. These designs are family oriented and luxurious while allowing full enjoyment of your natural setting.

Nelson Design Group LLC

RESIDENTIAL PLANNERS - DESIGNERS

Main Floor

COVERED PORCH
16'-10" X 5'-0"

FOYER

KITCHEN
10'-7" X 11'-10"

FRENCH DOORS

STACKED W/D

GRILLING PORCH
11'-0" X 5'-0"

BALCONY LINE

MASTER SUITE
11'-6" X 17'-0"

FRENCH DOORS

GREAT RM.
16'-2" X 17'-8"
OPEN TO ABOVE

STONE FIREPLACE

FRENCH DOORS   FRENCH DOORS

DECK

Upper Floor

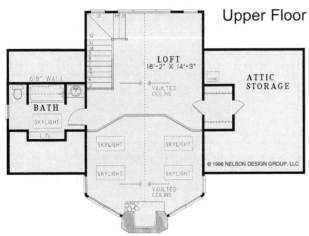

6'8" WALL

BATH
SKYLIGHT

LIN.

LOFT
16'-2" X 14'-3"

VAULTED CEILING

ATTIC STORAGE

HVAC

SKYLIGHT   SKYLIGHT

SKYLIGHT   SKYLIGHT

VAULTED CEILING

© 1998 NELSON DESIGN GROUP, LLC

Width: 42' 0"	**Main Ceiling:** 9 ft.
Depth: 36' 2"	**Upper Ceiling:** 8 ft.
Main Floor: 862 sq. ft.	**Bedrooms:** 2
Upper Floor: 332 sq. ft.	**Baths:** 2
Total Living: 1,194 sq. ft.	**Foundation:** Crawl, Slab, Basement, Daylight Basement
Price Tier: A	

Front Elevation

Rear Elevation

174 Waterfront Cove

This charming romantic Nelson Design Group home has the master suite on the main floor with french door access to the rear deck, perfect overlooking a calming lake. Lead your guests through the foyer and entertain in the spacious great room with skylights and stone fireplace - perfect after a day on the lake. Mornings can begin in your kitchen with french door access to the rear deck for morning coffee. After a long day, retreat to the master suite with full master bath. The upstairs loft features vaulted ceilings and large closet accessing attic storage. A full bath with skylight completes this plan.

Front Elevation

Rear Elevation

Main Floor

© 1998 NELSON DESIGN GROUP, LLC

DECK 26'-8" X 8'-0"

MASTER SUITE 15'-8" X 14'-6"

MASTER BATH 10'-6" X 21'-8"

SEAT GLASS SHWR

LIN

KNEE SPACE

WHIRL TUB

PANTRY REF.

VAULTED CEILING

KITCHEN 12'-4" X 11'-0"

DW TC

UP

DINING 12'-0" X 12'-0"

GREAT ROOM 26'-0" X 20'-0"

MEDIA CENTER

8' DECK

Upper Floor

BEDROOM 2 9'-10" X 14'-0"

BEDROOM 3 9'-10" X 14'-0"

BATH

LOFT 26'-0" X 8'-8"

OPEN TO BELOW

VAULTED CEILING

BEST SELLER
Designers Choice
NELSON DESIGN GROUP

231 Waterfront Cove

Vacation throughout the year in this Nelson Design Group home. You will be delighted with the open great room with vaulted ceiling and full window view of the lake or mountains. A media center and fireplace add efficiency as well as enjoyment. Enjoy cozy evenings locked away in your secluded master suite and bath which include double vanities, glass shower and large whirlpool tub. The loft area features two bedrooms which share a full bath. This home is heavenly for a family and weekend guests.

Width: 47' 0"	**Main Ceiling:** 8 ft.
Depth: 63' 0"	**Upper Ceiling:** 8 ft.
Main Floor: 1,413 sq. ft.	**Bedrooms:** 3
Upper Floor: 641 sq. ft.	**Baths:** 2 1/2
Total Living: 2,054 sq. ft.	**Foundation:** Crawl, Slab, Basement, Daylight Basement
Price Tier: C	

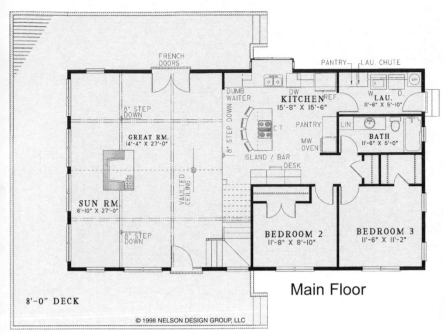

Main Floor

8'-0" DECK

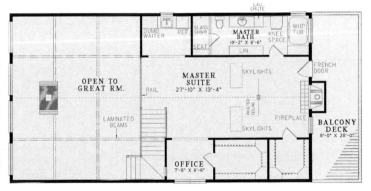

Upper Floor

Rear Elevation

173 Waterfront Cove

A vacation home with the master suite upstairs makes this Nelson Design Group home desirable. The eight foot wrap around deck with access to both sides of the great room is perfect for entertaining weekend guests. Breakfast is made easy with an island bar, ideal for big breakfasts outdoors people enjoy. The master suite comes complete with skylights, vaulted ceilings and a fireplace, just right for those romantic evenings for the two of you. You also have a private access to the rear balcony deck through French doors.

Width: 50' 0"	**Main Ceiling:** 8 ft.
Depth: 28' 0"	**Upper Ceiling:** 8 ft.
Main Floor: 1,400 sq. ft.	**Bedrooms:** 3
Upper Floor: 743 sq. ft.	**Baths:** 2
Total Living: 2,143 sq. ft.	**Foundation:** Crawl, Slab,
Price Tier: C	Optional Basement,
	Optional Daylight Basement

332 Waterfront Cove

This premier Nelson Design Group vacation home is perfect for entertaining out-of-town guests. Your friends will enjoy remembering old times in the vaulted great room which includes wet bar, media center, built-ins and access to the rear deck through a sliding door. Begin the morning with a big breakfast in your kitchen and breakfast room before heading to the lake. Evenings can begin with an elegant cuisine in the formal dining room, before making your way upstairs to the game room for a round of pool. Next, relax and unwind in the outdoor hot tub.

Main Floor

Upper Floor

© 1994 Nelson Design Group, LLC.

Width: 75' 0"	Main Ceiling: 9 ft.
Depth: 100' 0"	Upper Ceiling: 8 ft.
Total Living: 2,611 sq. ft.*	Bedrooms: 3
*Optional Bonus: 424 sq. ft.	Baths: 2 1/2
Price Tier: D	Foundation: Crawl, Slab, Basement, Daylight Basement

Main Floor

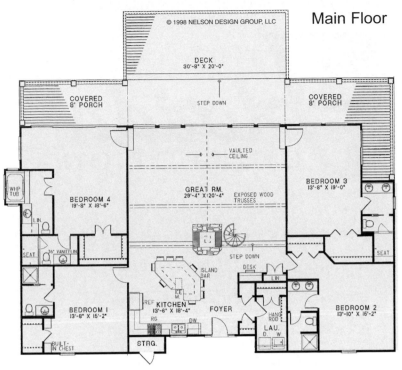

© 1998 NELSON DESIGN GROUP, LLC

DECK
30'-8" X 20'-0"

COVERED
8' PORCH

COVERED
8' PORCH

STEP DOWN

WHP
TUB

VAULTED
CEILING

BEDROOM 4
19'-8" X 18'-6"

GREAT RM.
29'-4" X 20'-4"

EXPOSED WOOD
TRUSSES

BEDROOM 3
13'-8" X 19'-0"

SEAT

36" VANITY LIN

SEAT

STEP DOWN

DESK

ISLAND
BAR

LIN

BEDROOM I
13'-8" X 15'-2"

REF

KITCHEN
13'-6" X 18'-4"

FOYER

HANG
ROD

BEDROOM 2
13'-10" X 15'-2"

BUILT-
IN CHEST

RG

DW

LAU.
D W

STRG.

Upper Floor

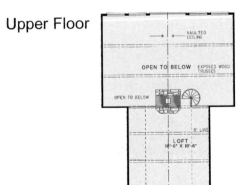

VAULTED
CEILING

OPEN TO BELOW

EXPOSED WOOD
TRUSSES

OPEN TO BELOW

6' LINE

LOFT
18'-0" X 18'-6"

226 Waterfront Cove

This Nelson Design Group plan is a vacation dream home come true. As you enter the foyer, you are exposed to the spacious great room with large rock fireplace - perfect for entertaining family and friends. If more room is needed for the party, lead them into your kitchen with large island bar. Your guests will enjoy climbing the spiral staircase to the loft above with a great view of the lake. You□ll find plenty of space and privacy in all of your bedrooms, complete with their own baths. The fourth bedroom and bath includes a whirlpool bath and glass shower for relaxing comfort.

Width: 73' 0"	**Main Ceiling:** 8 ft.
Depth: 69' 4"	**Upper Ceiling:** 8 ft.
Main Floor: 2,687 sq. ft.	**Bedrooms:** 4
Upper Floor: 342 sq. ft.	**Baths:** 5
Total Living: 3,029 sq. ft.	**Foundation:** Crawl, Slab,
Price Tier: E	Opt. Basement,
	Opt. Daylight Basement

THE *Florida* COLLECTION

An oasis of amenities in twelve designs created for a warm climate. These designs range between 1,800 to 3,600 square feet and include open spacious living areas, luxurious master suites and lanais perfect for entertaining. High ceilings and columns are used throughout giving a grand effect while arched openings and a plenitude of windows allow natural light to shine throughout.

Nelson Design Group LLC

RESIDENTIAL PLANNERS - DESIGNERS

The Evandale

BATH

BEDROOM 4
11'-2" X 15'-4"

LIN.

PORCH
13'-6" X 4'-8"

BREAKFAST AREA
12" CEILING
9'-8" X 10'-8"

LANAI
18'-4" X 11'-8"

SITTING ROOM
11'-0" X 8'-6"

BEDROOM 3
13'-2" X 13'-2"

BUILT-INS

GREAT ROOM
12" CEILING
18'-6" X 19'-6"

42" HIGH BAR

KITCHEN
12'-8" X 16'-6"

DW

REF

CT

ISLAND

MASTER SUITE
14'-2" X 18'-8"

OPTIONAL FIREPLACE

BEDROOM 2
13'-2" X 14'-10"

BATH

WET BAR

12' CEILING

BUTLER'S PANTRY PAN

OVEN MW

LIVING ROOM
12' CEILING
13'-0" X 19'-10"

OPTIONAL FIREPLACE

LAU.
10'-4" X 8'-6"

8' COLUMNS

FOYER
12' CEILING
8'-6" X 6'-2"

ARCHED OPENING

DINING
10' BOXED CLNG
16'-10" X 12'-2"

PORCH
8'-6" X 11'-6"

M.BATH
16'-0" X 21'-4"

LIN.

KNEE SPACE

LIN.

GLASS SHWR. SEAT

3 CAR GARAGE
22'-4" X 31'-8"

2X4 BOXED COLUMNS

WHP TUB

© 2001 NELSON DESIGN GROUP LLC

NDG552

$\mathcal{T}$his sprawling four-bedroom plan from Nelson Design Group centers on an ultra-functional kitchen accessing all living areas with ease. A handy eat-at bar and island help make this kitchen any gourmet's dream reality. Separate living and great rooms each flaunt gas fireplaces and lots of open space. All three secondary bedrooms feature private bath accesses. The exquisite master suite presents a radiant fireplace, large sitting area, private entrance to the lanai and a massive bath that includes his and her walk in closets and an oversized whirlpool bath.

Width: 74' 2"

Depth: 81' 2"

Total Living: 3,021 sq. ft.

Main Ceiling: 9' 4" ft.

Bedrooms: 4

Baths: 3

Foundation: Slab

Price Tier: E

THE RiverBend™ COLLECTION

The River Bend Collection™ of cottage cabins, designed by Nelson Design Group, includes ten unique designs perfect for second residences and relaxing getaways. Each River Bend Collection™ design has a living space of 1,200 to 1,500 square feet. There's a River Bend home perfect for your favorite setting. Enjoy fly fishing for rainbows, casting for lunker bass, hunting for deer or a secluded weekend. Our spacious, feature-filled designs allow you to enjoy the great outdoors with all the comforts of home. Make memories that last a lifetime from your River Bend cottage cabin hideaway.

Nelson Design Group LLC

RESIDENTIAL PLANNERS · DESIGNERS

RIVER VIEW

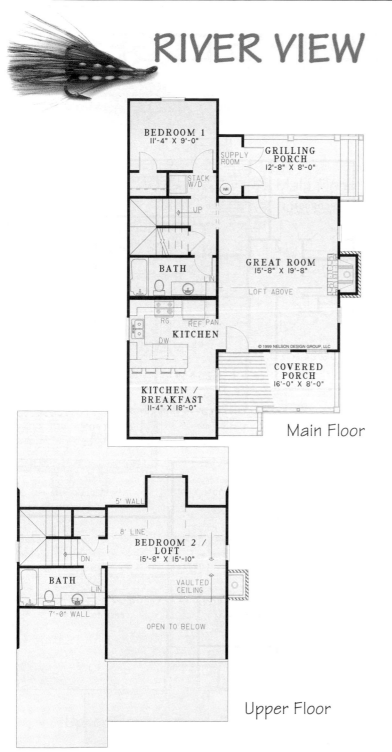

BEDROOM 1
11'-4" X 9'-0"

SUPPLY ROOM

GRILLING PORCH
12'-8" X 8'-0"

STACK W/D

WH

UP

BATH

GREAT ROOM
15'-8" X 19'-8"

LOFT ABOVE

LIN

RG.   REF   PAN.

KITCHEN

DW

© 1999 NELSON DESIGN GROUP, LLC

KITCHEN / BREAKFAST
11'-4" X 18'-0"

COVERED PORCH
16'-0" X 8'-0"

Main Floor

5' WALL

8' LINE

BEDROOM 2 / LOFT
15'-8" X 15'-10"

DN

BATH

LIN

VAULTED CEILING

7'-0" WALL

OPEN TO BELOW

Upper Floor

NDG421

Width: 30' 4"	Main Ceiling: 8 ft.
Depth: 44' 6"	Upper Ceiling: 8 ft.
Main Floor: 859 sq. ft.	Bedrooms: 2
Upper Floor: 319 sq. ft.	Baths: 2
Total Living: 1,178 sq. ft.	Foundation: Crawl, Slab,
Price Tier: A	Optional Basement,
	Optional Daylight Basement

Mom and Dad waved from the front porch as the children splashed in the water. It was always so wonderful coming to their vacation spot on the River Bend. The mornings were composed of gathering flowers that sprang up along the banks of the river and important trout fishing lessons from Dad. Afternoons consisted of picnics on the riverbank and long walks in the woods. Evenings were spent beside the fireplace where each family member shared stories of the day's adventures. This was the view of life that they enjoyed...the one that took place at River View.

NDG416

HUNTER'S DEN

Main Floor

- GRILLING PORCH 11'-8" X 6'-0"
- REF. PANTRY
- KITCHEN 9'-4" X 10'-10"
- RG
- DW
- DINING 10'-0" X 13'-6"
- SUPPLY ROOM
- WH
- BATH
- STACK W/D
- DEN 15'-6" X 18'-10"
- UP
- BEDROOM 1 11'-4" X 11'-0"
- 8' COVERED PORCH
- © 1999 NELSON DESIGN GROUP LLC

Upper Floor

- BATH
- LIN
- 5' WALL
- 8' LINE
- DN
- BEDROOM 3 11'-4" X 12'-8"
- BEDROOM 2 13'-4" X 14'-6"
- 8' LINE
- 5' WALL
- 4' WALL

Width: 39' 8"
Depth: 38' 4"
Main Floor: 890 sq. ft.
Upper Floor: 507 sq. ft.
Total Living: 1,397 sq. ft.
Price Tier: A

Main Ceiling: 8 ft.
Upper Ceiling: 8 ft.
Bedrooms: 3
Baths: 2
Foundation: Crawl, Slab, Optional Basement, Optional Daylight Basement

After a brisk fall day, hunters gather here to reminisce over the day's events. Each brother has his own rendition of how big the deer, that they encountered, really was. The days at Hunter's Den are like the leaves on a breeze, floating by with such peacefulness. As the men exchange stories on the front porch, their minds recall a time of when their parents had first built their getaway. Each brother remembered the hikes in the woods and exciting hunting trips with dad that all began here...at Hunter's Den.

To order call 1.800.590.2423 or to view similar plans visit www.nelsondesigngroup.com

PINEY CREEK

Main Floor

GRILLING PORCH
15'-8" X 8'-0"

BEDROOM 1
12'-4" X 11'-4"

© 1999 NELSON DESIGN GROUP, LLC

KITCHEN
15'-4" X 11'-10"

STACKED
W/D

BATH

PAN

BALCONY LINE

GREAT RM.
17'-0" X 16'-2"

DINING
10'-6" X 13'-6"

VAULTED CEILING
OPEN TO ABOVE

UP

10'-9" WALL

COVERED PORCH
32'-0" X 8'-0"

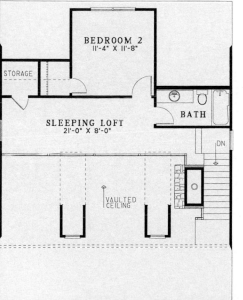

BEDROOM 2
11'-4" X 11'-8"

STORAGE

BATH

SLEEPING LOFT
21'-0" X 8'-0"

DN

VAULTED
CEILING

Upper Floor

NDG420

Width: 32' 0"   Main Ceiling: 8 ft.
Depth: 42' 0"   Upper Ceiling: 8 ft.
Main Floor: 948 sq. ft.   Bedrooms: 2
Upper Floor: 452 sq. ft.   Baths: 2
Total Living: 1,400 sq. ft. Foundation: Crawl, Slab, Opt. Basement,
Price Tier: A   Opt. Daylight Basement

As he helped her up to the steps of the cabin, the couple began reminiscing about the many summers they had spent there. The summer afternoons when their children and grandchildren came to visit were undeniably the most treasured. Watching as they caught their first fish, floated on intertubes and picked flowers in the field always brought a smile to their faces. As they looked out across River Bend, they imagined many generations of their family spending their summers here...at Piney Creek.

STONE BROOK

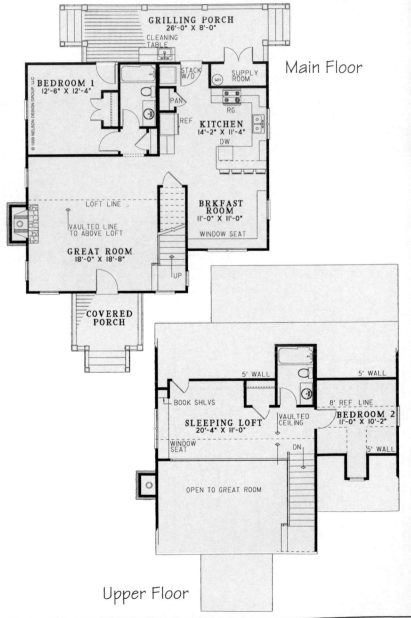

Main Floor

Upper Floor

NDG422

Width: 36' 2"
Depth: 48' 0"
Main Floor: 1,016 sq. ft.
Upper Floor: 409 sq. ft.
Total Living: 1,425 sq. ft.
Price Tier: A

Main Ceiling: 8 ft.
Upper Ceiling: 8 ft.
Bedrooms: 2
Baths: 2
Foundation: Crawl, Slab,
Optional Basement,
Optional Daylight Basement

As she walked down the stairs from the loft, she could see the sun rising like a fire. Across the horizon, when she sat on the window seat and stared out into the dawning of a new day, she could see the water rippling onto the shore to greet the stones for the first time that day. Catching a glimpse of movement, her eyes focused on her husband displaying the stringer of fish caught that morning in River Bend. This would be the first of many memorable weekends and vacations...at Stone Brook.

CANOE POINT

Main Floor

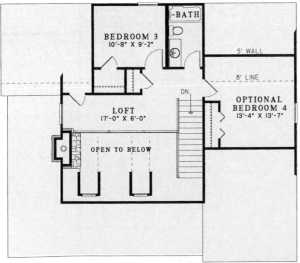

Upper Floor

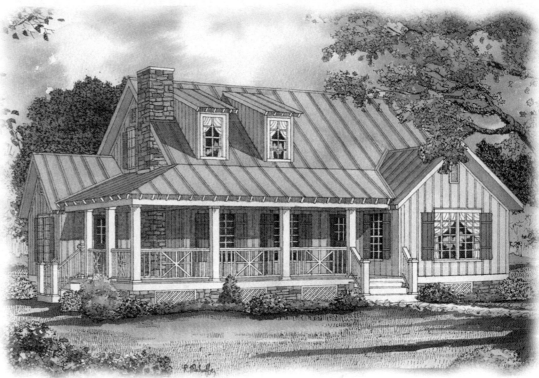

NDG418

Width: 44' 2"	Main Ceiling: 8 ft.
Depth: 39' 0"	Upper Ceiling: 8 ft.
Main Floor: 1,140 sq. ft.	Bedrooms: 4
Upper Floor: 332 sq. ft.	Baths: 2
Total Living: 1,472 sq. ft.*	Foundation: Crawl, Slab,
*Bonus: 199 sq. ft.	Optional Basement,
Price Tier: A	Optional Daylight Basement

They sat on the front porch and watched as the canoes floated by. People always enjoyed canoeing at this point of River Bend because of its thrilling rapids. Watching the canoes was a family event because of the variety of expressions on the canoeists faces and the screams of excitement as they battled the rapids. Mom would make scorecards for everyone to hold up to rate the thrill-seekers on their skills. Canoe Point was a memorable place that was familiar to all.

TABLE ROCK

NDG423

Width: 37' 2"
Depth: 45' 0"
Main Floor: 1,159 sq. ft.
Upper Floor: 383 sq. ft.
Total Living: 1,542 sq. ft.
Price Tier: B

Main Ceiling: 8 ft.
Upper Ceiling: 8 ft.
Bedrooms: 2
Baths: 2
Foundation: Crawl, Slab,
Optional Basement,
Optional Daylight Basement

They giggled with delight as the fish began to nibble on their toes as they dipped their feet into the water. The children always loved the lazy summers at Grandma's and Grandpa's cabin. They loved the early morning swims in River Bend's cool waters and the lemonade that Grandma served in the afternoons. What they especially enjoyed, was laying on the large flat rock that allowed the rivers water to gently splash over its surface providing cool relief from the summer's heat. The days here at Table Rock would always be home to their fondest memories.

Main Floor

Upper Floor

To order call 1.800.590.2423 or to view similar plans visit www.nelsondesigngroup.com

CREEK SIDE

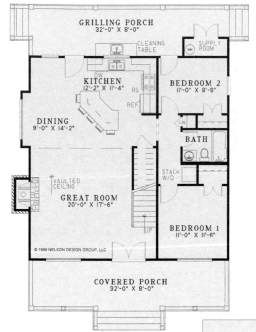

Main Floor

NDG415

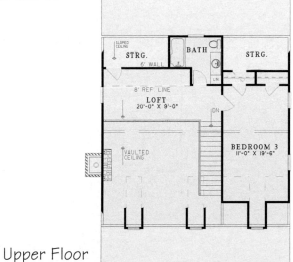

Upper Floor

Width: 34' 4"
Depth: 48' 4"
Main Floor: 1,031 sq. ft.
Upper Floor: 513 sq. ft.
Total Living: 1,544 sq. ft.
Price Tier: B

Main Ceiling: 8 ft.
Upper Ceiling: 8 ft.
Bedrooms: 3
Baths: 2
Foundation: Crawl, Slab,
               Optional Basement,
               Optional Daylight Basement

He began thinking where he was as he cast the fly rod upstream. A dream world. Not just any ole' dream world, but his dream world. Everything was as he had always imagined and hoped for. The cold, crisp waters of River Bend tickled his legs with its voice. Across the river, a trout leaped to an unknown destination. The porch of the cabin beckoned him to come and relax in the cool shade. The sun showered it's rays onto the water causing him to catch a glimpse of his own reflection. He was always a happy man when he was at his dream getaway called Creek Side.

NDG417

LAKE SIDE

Main Floor

Width: 50' 4"
Depth: 48' 0"
Main Floor: 1,440 sq. ft.
Upper Floor: 530 sq. ft.
Total Living: 1,970 sq. ft.
Price Tier: B

Main Ceiling: 8 ft.
Upper Ceiling: 8 ft.
Bedrooms: 4
Baths: 4
Foundation: Crawl, Slab,
   Optional Basement,
   Optional Daylight Basement

They woke up early that summer morning to watch the sun rise over the mountains. As they sat on the porch drinking coffee, they began talking about the future. This was only the first of many vacations at their new retreat. They began dreaming of the fishing lessons with their children and the nighttime storytelling beside the fireplace. This was a place in which to build traditions. Traditions that would last throughout the generations. Traditions that would begin here...at Lake Side.

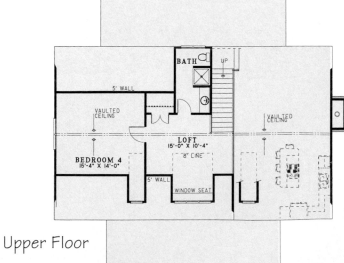

Upper Floor

Every day, in communities across the country, more and more homebuyers are leaving conventional 'cookie-cutter' developments in search of something special. In increasing numbers, discerning buyers are choosing log homes for their warmth, beauty and natural charm.

When they choose a Jim Barna log home, they get much more – a builder friendly, well engineered building system, low maintenance, energy efficient with a lifetime warranty on all log elements. They also get personalized service, access to experienced log builders and special prices on major home items from financing to fixtures. Maybe that's why BUILDER magazine ranked Jim Barna Log Systems as the #1 log home company in America.*

DESIGNS BY NELSON

Jim Barna is proud to offer plans and design services through Nelson Design Group by exclusive arrangement. The next 12 pages of plans, plus the other plans included on our websites, represent the latest concepts in comfortable living. For the full collection of collaborative plans and ideas, visit nelsondesigngroup.com or jimbarna.com.

* (Builder Magazine, May 2002)

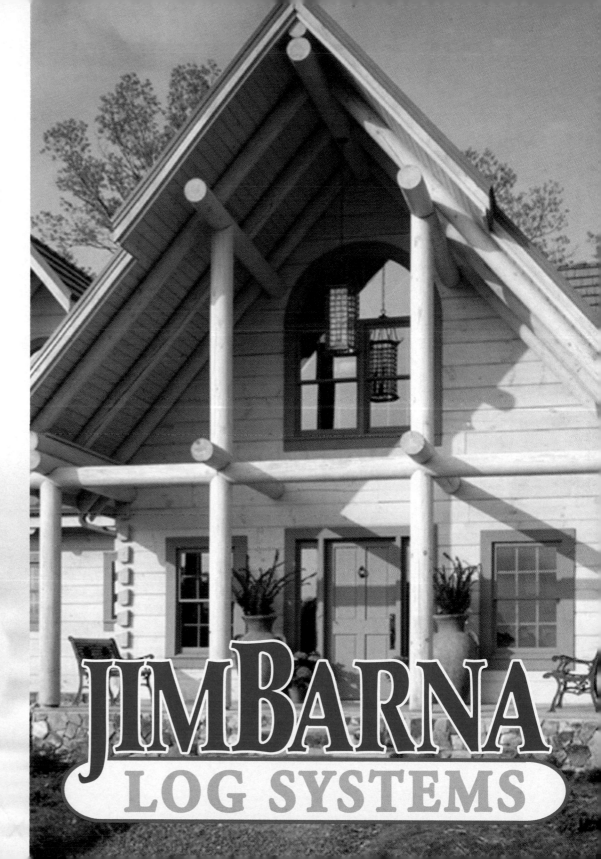

JIMBARNA
LOG SYSTEMS

LOG HOMES TODAY'S CHOICE FOR COMFORTABLE LIVING

No longer mere 'cabins,' today's log homes are built around today's families. Using modern milling techniques and specialized construction methods, solid log homes offer unparalleled structural integrity, keeping your family warm, safe and secure in any climate. And, by featuring all natural elements, from log walls to timber beams and trusses and knotty pine ceilings, Jim Barna log homes are the perfect 'stress relief' for today's busy lifestyle. It's no wonder that log homes are one of the fastest growing trends in the current housing market.

LET THE LIGHT SHINE IN

Cabins used to be small, dark and dreary. Not so today. Homes from Jim Barna Log Systems tend to feature open, spacious rooms, often with vaulted ceilings and lots of glass. Large kitchens, great rooms, porches and decks make our homes great for entertaining friends or just enjoying family, and the perfect choice for "indoor/outdoor living." And the large master suites can be as lavish as you like!

SOUND INVESTMENT

Even with all the features we build into our homes, they are more affordable than one might think. In fact, with infinite choices in styles and amenities, we can offer homes in every price point and budget, from vacation cottages and starter homes for growing families to high-end executive and retirement homes. According to a study done by the National Association of Home Builders, log homes are an excellent investment, appreciating in value at nearly twice the rate of conventional 'stick-built' homes. Plus, Jim Barna helps protect your investment with the strongest warranty in the industry - a lifetime warranty on all log elements, and an available 10-year structural warranty from Bonded Builders Home Warranty Association on all other building materials we supply.

Contact your Jim Barna representative for specific details.

NDG1028

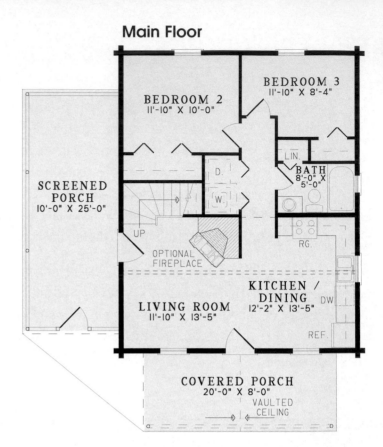

SCREENED PORCH
10'-0" X 25'-0"

BEDROOM 2
11'-10" X 10'-0"

BEDROOM 3
11'-10" X 8'-4"

LIN.

BATH
8'-0" X 5'-0"

D.

W.

UP

RG.

OPTIONAL FIREPLACE

KITCHEN / DINING
12'-2" X 13'-5"

DW

LIVING ROOM
11'-10" X 13'-5"

REF.

COVERED PORCH
20'-0" X 8'-0"

VAULTED CEILING

Upper Floor

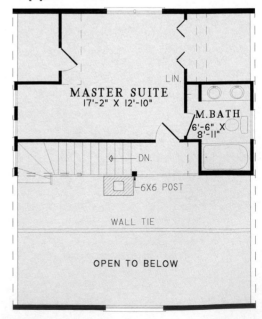

LIN.

MASTER SUITE
17'-2" X 12'-10"

M.BATH
6'-6" X 8'-11"

DN.

6X6 POST

WALL TIE

OPEN TO BELOW

The Spruce Creek

Width: 35' 0"

Depth: 39' 0"

Main Floor: 775 sq. ft. (72 sq. meters)

Upper Floor: 347 sq. ft. (32 sq. meters)

Total Living: 1,122 sq. ft. (104 sq. meters)

Foundation: Crawl, Optional Basement,
             Optional Daylight Basement

Price Tier: A

Main Floor

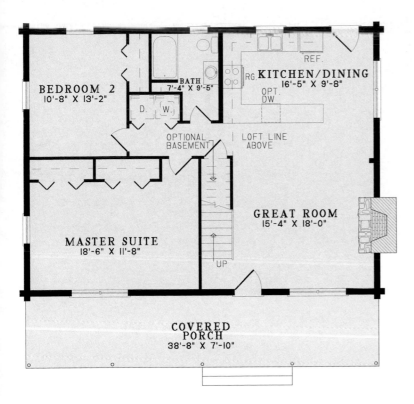

BEDROOM 2
10'-8" X 13'-2"

BATH
7'-4" X 9'-5"

REF.

RG. KITCHEN/DINING
16'-5" X 9'-8"

OPT.
DW

D W

OPTIONAL
BASEMENT

LOFT LINE
ABOVE

GREAT ROOM
15'-4" X 18'-0"

MASTER SUITE
18'-6" X 11'-8"

UP

COVERED
PORCH
38'-8" X 7'-10"

NDG1003

Upper Floor

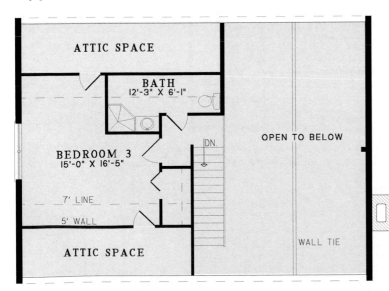

ATTIC SPACE

BATH
12'-3" X 6'-1"

OPEN TO BELOW

DN.

BEDROOM 3
15'-0" X 16'-5"

7' LINE

5' WALL

ATTIC SPACE

WALL TIE

The LaFollette

Width: 39' 0"

Depth: 36' 10"

Main Floor: 1,131 sq. ft. (105 sq. meters)

Upper Floor: 346 sq. ft. (32 sq. meters)

Total Living: 1,477 sq. ft. (137 sq. meters)

Foundation: Crawl, Optional Basement,
Optional Daylight Basement

Price Tier: A

NDG1015

The Blue Ridge

Width: 40' 0"

Depth: 36' 0"

Main Floor: 1,120 sq. ft. (104 sq. meters)

Upper Floor: 605 sq. ft. (56 sq. meters)

Total Living: 1,725 sq. ft. (160 sq. meters)

Foundation: Crawl, Optional Basement,
Optional Daylight Basement

Price Tier: B

Main Floor

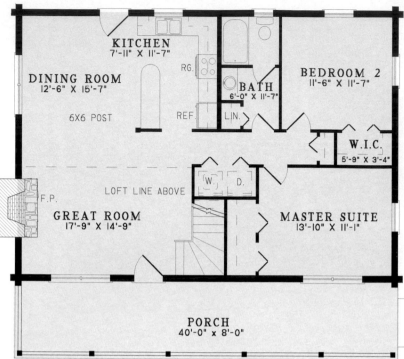

Upper Floor

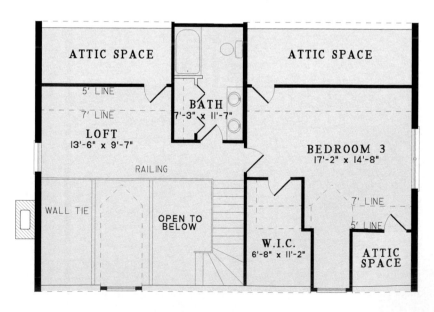

The Twin Cove

Width: 74' 0"

Depth: 41' 8"

Main Floor: 1,140 sq. ft. (106 sq. meters)

Upper Floor: 690 sq. ft. (64 sq. meters)

Total Living: 1,830 sq. ft. (170 sq. meters)

Foundation: Crawl, Optional Basement, Optional Daylight Basement

Price Tier: B

NDG1062

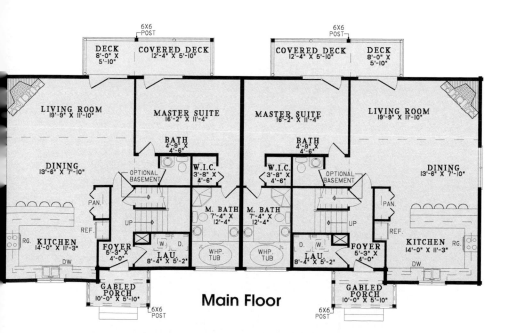

Main Floor

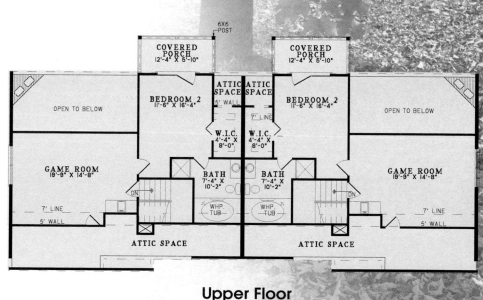

Upper Floor

To order call 1.800.590.2423 or to view similar plans visit www.nelsondesigngroup.com

NDG1030

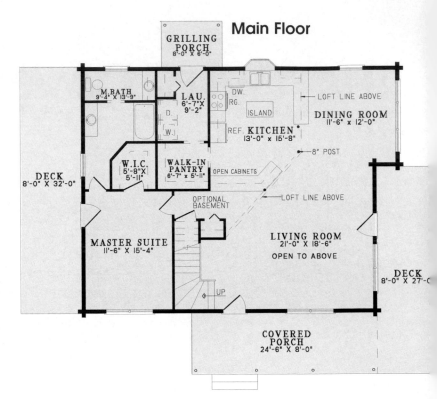

Main Floor

GRILLING PORCH 8'-0" X 6'-0"

M.BATH 9'-4" X 13'-9"

LAU. 6'-7" X 9'-2"

DW RG

ISLAND

REF. KITCHEN 13'-0" X 15'-8"

DINING ROOM 11'-6" x 12'-0"

LOFT LINE ABOVE

8" POST

W.I.C. 5'-8" X 5'-11"

WALK-IN PANTRY 6'-7" x 5'-11"

OPEN CABINETS

LOFT LINE ABOVE

DECK 8'-0" X 32'-0"

OPTIONAL BASEMENT

MASTER SUITE 11'-6" X 15'-4"

LIVING ROOM 21'-0" X 18'-6"

OPEN TO ABOVE

UP

DECK 8'-0" X 27'-0"

COVERED PORCH 24'-6" X 8'-0"

The Etowah

Width: 50' 0"

Depth: 46' 0"

Main Floor: 1,287 sq. ft. (120 sq. meters)

Upper Floor: 653 sq. ft. (61 sq. meters)

Total Living: 1,940 sq. ft. (181 sq. meters)

Foundation: Crawl, Optional Basement, Optional Daylight Basement

Price Tier: B

Upper Floor

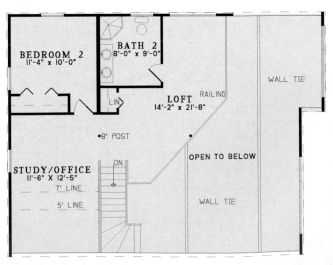

BEDROOM 2 11'-4" x 10'-0"

BATH 2 8'-0" x 9'-0"

WALL TIE

LIN

LOFT 14'-2" x 21'-8"

RAILING

8' POST

OPEN TO BELOW

STUDY/OFFICE 11'-6" X 12'-5"

DN

7' LINE

5' LINE

WALL TIE

Main Floor

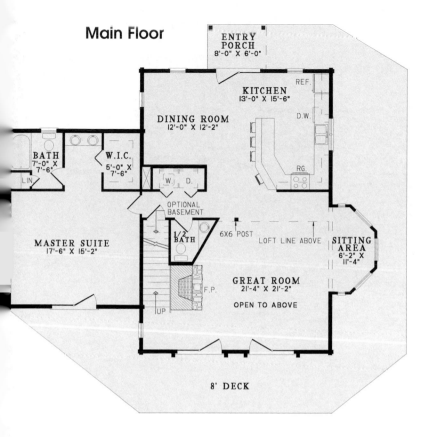

ENTRY PORCH
8'-0" X 6'-0"

KITCHEN
13'-0" X 15'-6"

REF.

D.W.

RG.

DINING ROOM
12'-0" X 12'-2"

BATH
7'-0" X 7'-6"

LIN

W.I.C.
5'-0" X 7'-6"

W. D.

OPTIONAL BASEMENT

1/2 BATH

6X6 POST

LOFT LINE ABOVE

SITTING AREA
6'-2" X 11'-4"

MASTER SUITE
17'-6" X 15'-2"

GREAT ROOM
21'-4" X 21'-2"

OPEN TO ABOVE

F.P.

UP

8' DECK

Upper Floor

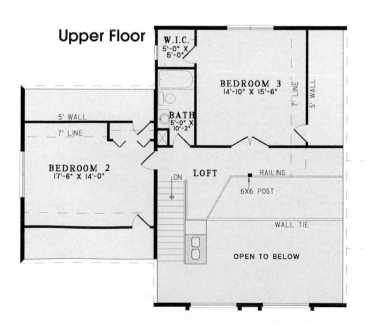

W.I.C.
5'-0" X 5'-0"

BEDROOM 3
14'-10" X 15'-6"

7' LINE

5' WALL

BATH
5'-0" X 10'-2"

5' WALL

7' LINE

BEDROOM 2
17'-6" X 14'-0"

DN

LOFT

RAILING

6X6 POST

WALL TIE

OPEN TO BELOW

NDG1013

The Eagle Ridge

Width: 54' 0"

Depth: 52' 0"

Main Floor: 1,556 sq. ft. (145 sq. meters)

Upper Floor: 581 sq. ft. (54 sq. meters)

Total Living: 2,137 sq. ft. (199 sq. meters)

Foundation: Crawl, Optional Basement, Optional Daylight Basement

Price Tier: C

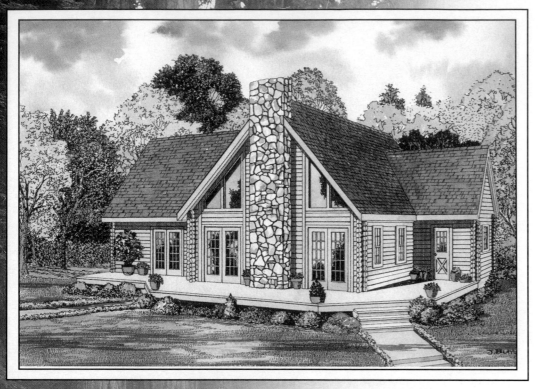

NDG1014

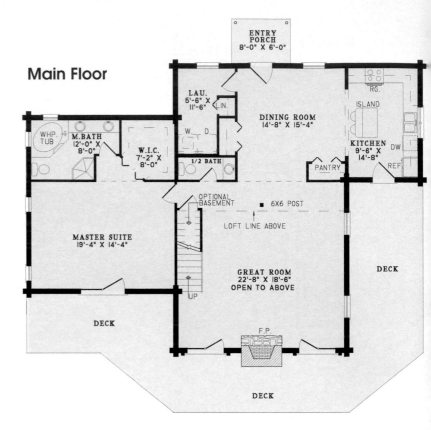

Main Floor

ENTRY PORCH 8'-0" X 6'-0"

LAU. 5'-6" X 11'-6"

DINING ROOM 14'-8" X 15'-4"

RG.

ISLAND

KITCHEN 9'-6" X 14'-8"

DW

WHP. TUB

M.BATH 12'-0" X 8'-0"

W.I.C. 7'-2" X 8'-0"

W. D.

1/2 BATH

LIN.

PANTRY

REF

MASTER SUITE 19'-4" X 14'-4"

OPTIONAL BASEMENT

6X6 POST

LOFT LINE ABOVE

DECK

UP

GREAT ROOM 22'-8" X 18'-6" OPEN TO ABOVE

DECK

F.P.

DECK

DECK

The Monterey

Width: 54' 0"

Depth: 53' 0"

Main Floor: 1,576 sq. ft. (146 sq. meters)

Upper Floor: 630 sq. ft. (59 sq. meters)

Total Living: 2,206 sq. ft. (205 sq. meters)

Foundation: Crawl, Optional Basement, Optional Daylight Basement

Price Tier: C

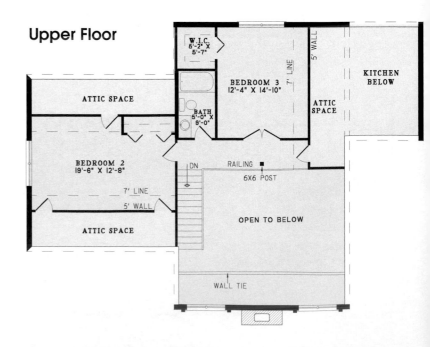

Upper Floor

W.I.C. 5'-2" X 5'-7"

BEDROOM 3 12'-4" X 14'-10"

7' LINE

5' WALL

KITCHEN BELOW

ATTIC SPACE

BATH 5'-0" X 9'-0"

ATTIC SPACE

BEDROOM 2 19'-6" X 12'-8"

DN

RAILING

6X6 POST

7' LINE

5' WALL

ATTIC SPACE

OPEN TO BELOW

WALL TIE

The Montara

Width: 64' 0"

Depth: 51' 0"

Main Floor: 1,892 sq. ft. (176 sq. meters)

Upper Floor: 520 sq. ft. (48 sq. meters)

Total Living: 2,412 sq. ft. (224 sq. meters)

Foundation: Crawl, Optional Basement,
Optional Daylight Basement

Price Tier: C

NDG1011

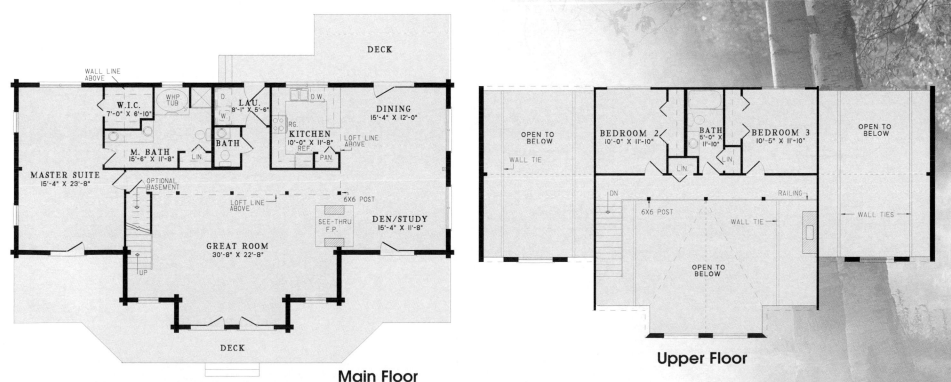

Main Floor

Upper Floor

To order call 1.800.590.2423 or to view similar plans visit www.nelsondesigngroup.com

the Savannah

Width: 66' 0"

Depth: 48' 0"

Main Floor: 1,600 sq. ft. (149 sq. meters)

Upper Floor: 1,141 sq. ft. (106 sq. meters)

Total Living: 2,741 sq. ft. (255 sq. meters)

Foundation: Crawl, Optional Basement, Optional Daylight Basement

Price Tier: D

NDG1049

Main Floor

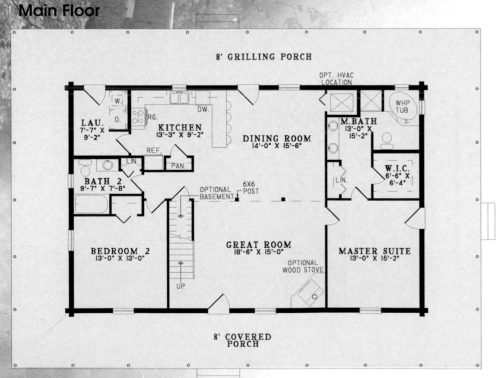

Upper Floor

Main Floor

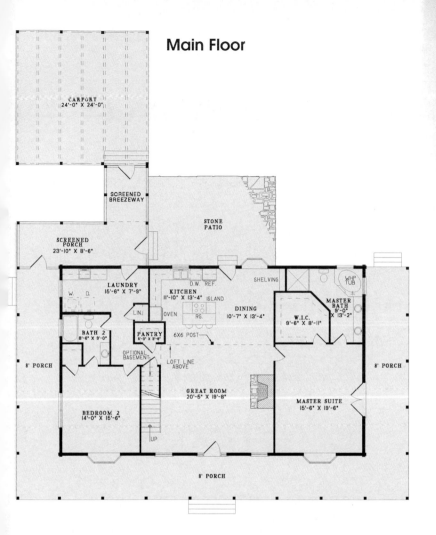

CARPORT
24'-0" X 24'-0"

SCREENED
BREEZEWAY

STONE
PATIO

SCREENED
PORCH
23'-10" X 8'-6"

LAUNDRY
15'-6" X 7'-9"

KITCHEN
11'-10" X 13'-4"

D.W. REF.
ISLAND

SHELVING

DINING
10'-7" X 13'-4"

WHP
TUB

MASTER
BATH
9'-0"
X 13'-2"

OVEN

RG.

W.I.C.
9'-6" X 8'-11"

LIN.

BATH 2
8'-6" X 9'-0"

PANTRY
6'-3" X 9'-6"

6X6 POST

8' PORCH

OPTIONAL
BASEMENT

LOFT LINE
ABOVE

8' PORCH

BEDROOM 2
14'-0" X 15'-6"

GREAT ROOM
20'-5" X 19'-8"

MASTER SUITE
15'-6" X 19'-6"

UP

8' PORCH

NDG1016

Upper Floor

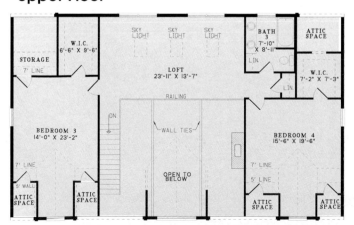

STORAGE
7' LINE

W.I.C.
6'-6" X 9'-6"

SKY
LIGHT

SKY
LIGHT

SKY
LIGHT

BATH
3
7'-10"
X 8'-11"

ATTIC
SPACE

LOFT
23'-11" X 13'-7"

LIN.

W.I.C.
7'-2" X 7'-3"

RAILING

LIN.

DN

BEDROOM 3
14'-0" X 23'-2"

WALL TIES

BEDROOM 4
15'-6" X 19'-6"

7' LINE

OPEN TO
BELOW

7' LINE

5' WALL

5' LINE

ATTIC
SPACE

ATTIC
SPACE

ATTIC
SPACE

ATTIC
SPACE

The Emerson

Width: 70' 10"

Depth: 83' 8"

Main Floor: 1,870 sq. ft. (174 sq. meters)

Upper Floor: 1,228 sq. ft. (114 sq. meters)

Total Living: 3,098 sq. ft. (288 sq. meters)

Foundation: Crawl, Optional Basement,
Optional Daylight Basement

Price Tier: E

NDG1010

The Westwind IV

Width: 68' 0"

Depth: 45' 5"

Main Floor: 2,126 sq. ft. (197 sq. meters)

Upper Floor: 1,215 sq. ft. (113 sq. meters)

Total Living: 3,341 sq. ft. (310 sq. meters)

Foundation: Crawl, Optional Basement, Optional Daylight Basement

Price Tier: E

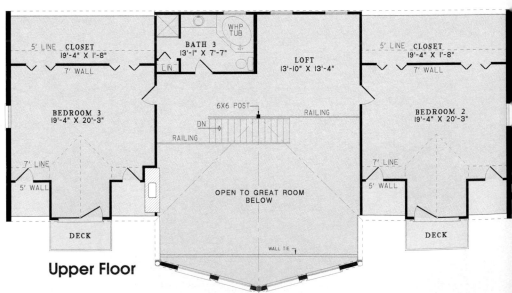

Main Floor

DECK

MASTER BATH
13'-3" X 7'-5"

WHP TUB

FAMILY ROOM
13'-8" X 13'-2"

PANTRY
6'-2" X 5'-11"

REF. DW

KITCHEN
13'-10" X 13'-4"

1/2 BATH

RG

ISLAND

MASTER SUITE
19'-4" X 26'-8"

W.I.C.
11'-0" X 5'-6"

OPTIONAL BASEMENT

UP

LOFT LINE ABOVE

LOFT LINE ABOVE

DINING ROOM
19'-4" X 13'-2"

F.P.

GREAT ROOM
26'-8" X 22'-8"

DECK ABOVE

DECK

DECK ABOVE

Upper Floor

5' LINE CLOSET
19'-4" X 1'-8"

7' WALL

BATH 3
13'-1" X 7'-7"

WHP TUB

LIN

LOFT
13'-10" X 13'-4"

5' LINE CLOSET
19'-4" X 1'-8"

7' WALL

BEDROOM 3
19'-4" X 20'-3"

6X6 POST

RAILING

DN

RAILING

BEDROOM 2
19'-4" X 20'-3"

7' LINE

5' WALL

OPEN TO GREAT ROOM BELOW

7' LINE

5' WALL

DECK

WALL TIE

DECK

To order call 1.800.590.2423 or to view similar plans visit www.nelsondesigngroup.com

The Bradford

Width: 111' 0"

Depth: 73' 0"

Main Floor: 2,775 sq. ft. (258 sq. meters)

Upper Floor: 1,767 sq. ft. (164 sq. meters)

Total Living: 4,542 sq. ft. (422 sq. meters)

Foundation: Crawl, Optional Basement, Optional Daylight Basement

Price Tier: G

NDG1047

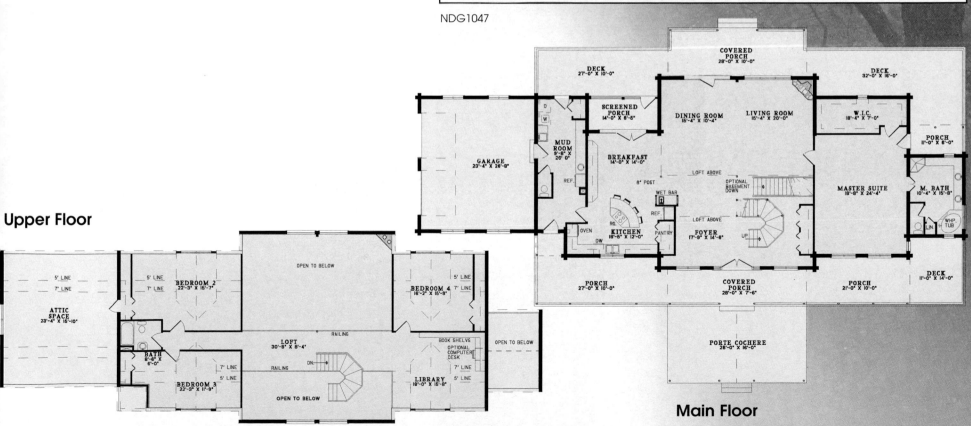

Upper Floor

Main Floor

Stock Plans

For more than 15 years, Nelson Design Group, LLC has been designing *superior* homes for builders and custom plans for clients throughout the country. As a certified member of the American Institute of Building Designers (AIBD), we are nationally known and have been recognized and *highlighted* in publications such as *HomeStyles Publishing, Home Design Alternatives, Builder Magazine* (the official publication of the National Association of Home Builders), *Home Planners, Architectural Designs, Garlinghouse, Good Housekeeping, Old House Journal, House Beautiful, Southern Living, Better Homes and Gardens*, and others.

A successful and *innovative* company is created by providing the best possible product with creative and knowledgeable people to carry each project to completion. Nelson Design Group, LLC Residential Planners-Designers is one such success.

Our staff of designers offers the qualities a consumer searching for a home desires — experience, creativity and efficiency. We offer *unique* and diversified designs, as well as Southern Traditionals, Lake Houses, Country Styles and Modern Classics. We can modify any of our plans to suit your needs — saving time and guaranteeing customer *satisfaction*.

The next pages will reflect stock plans from our portfolio. Visit our web site at www.nelsondesigngroup.com for additional plans.

106 Maple Street

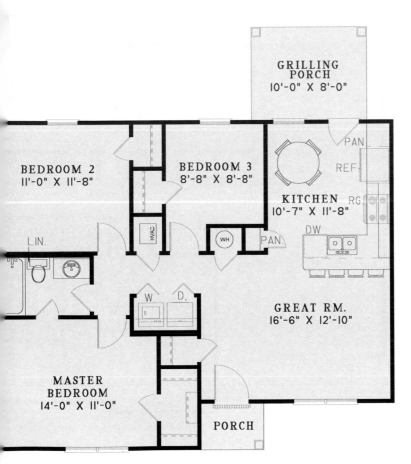

GRILLING PORCH
10'-0" X 8'-0"

BEDROOM 2
11'-0" X 11'-8"

BEDROOM 3
8'-8" X 8'-8"

KITCHEN
10'-7" X 11'-8"

PAN

REF

RG

DW

PAN

HVAC

WH

LIN.

W. D.

GREAT RM.
16'-6" X 12'-10"

MASTER BEDROOM
14'-0" X 11'-0"

PORCH

This Nelson Design Group economical design is perfect for the couple just starting out. An eight inch boxed column adorns the quaint covered porch. As you enter the home you'll feel openness created in the great room which flows through to the kitchen with eat-at bar and access to the rear grilling porch. Bedroom two can easily be converted into a study for those that work at home. The master bedroom will provide the privacy needed at the end of the day with private access to the bath and ample closet space.

Width: 35' 0"
Depth: 36' 6"
Total Living: 930 sq. ft.

Main Ceiling: 8 ft.
Bedrooms: 3
Baths: 1
Foundation: Crawl, Slab

Price Tier: A

207 Maple Street

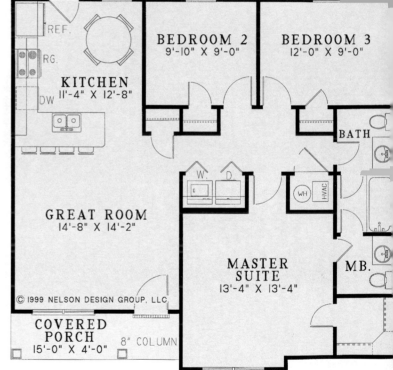

This charming Nelson Design Group country home is the perfect starter plan. Visit with neighbors on your front porch as the children ride their bikes. Upon entering, you'll feel all the comforts of home in your spacious great room which provides a comfortable atmosphere with an open view to the kitchen. Your master suite features a walk-in closet with a private access to the bath. Listening for that newborn baby is made easier with the nursery close by.

Width: 34' 6"
Depth: 32' 6"
Total Living: 1,029 sq. ft.

Price Tier: A

Main Ceiling: 8 ft.
Bedrooms: 3
Baths: 1 1/2
Foundation: Crawl, Slab

To order call 1.800.590.2423 or to view similar plans visit www.nelsondesigngroup.com

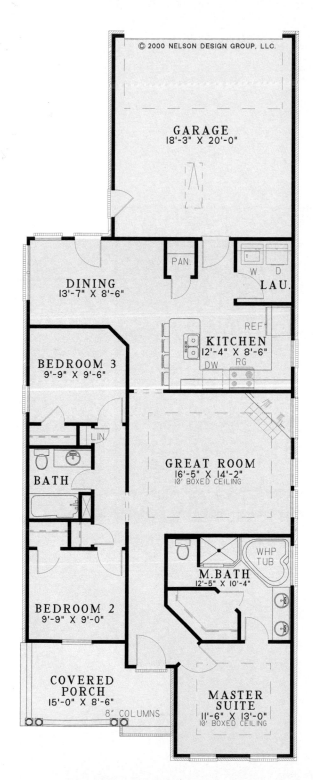

© 2000 NELSON DESIGN GROUP, LLC.

GARAGE
18'-3" X 20'-0"

DINING
13'-7" X 8'-6"

PAN.

W. D
LAU.

REF

KITCHEN
12'-4" X 8'-6"

DW   RG

BEDROOM 3
9'-9" X 9'-6"

LIN

BATH

GREAT ROOM
16'-5" X 14'-2"
10' BOXED CEILING

WHP TUB

M. BATH
12'-5" X 10'-4"

BEDROOM 2
9'-9" X 9'-0"

COVERED PORCH
15'-0" X 8'-6"

8" COLUMNS

MASTER SUITE
11'-6" X 13'-0"
10' BOXED CEILING

499 Fir Street

This delightful home plan by Nelson Design Group has a roomy interior but well suited for a narrow lot. A cozy covered porch with columns is the perfect place to enjoy a cup of tea and visit with neighbors. Separate from the other bedrooms is the master suite enhanced with a ten foot boxed ceiling and a private bath including a corner whirlpool tub, separate shower, double vanity and walk-in closet. Centrally located is the great room with an angled fireplace, boxed ceiling and plenty of wall space. Follow through to a wonderfully designed kitchen with bar seating, a dining area with access to the rear and a convenient laundry room.

Width: 27' 2"
Depth: 72' 10"
Total Living: 1,263 sq. ft.

Price Tier: A

Main Ceiling: 9 ft.
Bedrooms: 3
Baths: 2
Foundation: Crawl, Slab

533 Maple Street

M. BATH
12'-6" X 5'-0"

W.I.C.

W
D

MASTER
SUITE
OPT. 9' BOXED
CEILING
13'-4" X 11'-4"

W.I.C.

STORAGE
15'-0" X 3'-0"

DINING
10'-0" X 12'-0"

GREAT ROOM
OPT. 9' BOXED
CEILING
17'-4" X 13'-0"

KITCHEN
10'-0" X 10'-2"

PAN.
REF.
D.W.
RG.

GARAGE
20'-0" X 19'-8"

© 2000 NELSON DESIGN GROUP, LLC.

BATH

FOYER
7'-0" X 6'-6"

BEDROOM 2
10'-0" X 9'-6"

BEDROOM 3
10'-0" X 10'-8"

COVERED
PORCH
8'-0" X 6'-0"

This beautiful country Nelson Design Group home invites you onto the covered front porch. As you receive your guests into the foyer, lead them into the cozy great room for drinks about the fireplace. The culinary expert of the home may take advantage of the open kitchen design. As your guests begin their retreat and the children are tucked away in their rooms, you can retreat into the master suite offering 'his and her' walk-in closets, and full bath amenities.

Width: 51' 0"
Depth: 49' 0"
Total Living: 1,324 sq. ft.

Price Tier: A

Main Ceiling: 8 ft.
Bedrooms: 3
Baths: 2
Foundation: Crawl, Slab,
Optional Basement,
Optional Daylight Basement

593 Hannah Lane

This beautiful and economic Nelson Design Group home affords opportunities for encompassing quality time. The kitchen offers a snack bar for breakfast. The family can gather around the fireplace accenting the great room on wintry evenings or travel out to the rear-grilling porch for summer barbecues. At the days end you retreat to the comfort of your suite knowing that your children are safely just down the hall in their private rooms separated by a full bath.

Width: 45' 0"
Depth: 56' 0"
Total Living: 1,344 sq. ft.

Main Ceiling: 8 ft.
Bedrooms: 3
Baths: 2
Foundation: Crawl, Slab

Price Tier: A

150-1 Spruce Street

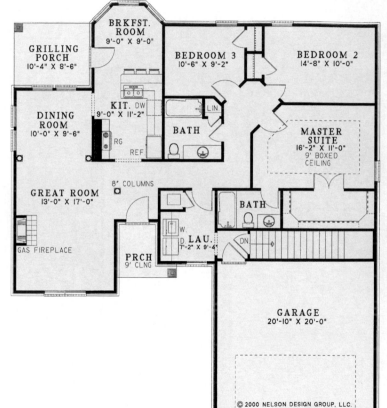

© 2000 NELSON DESIGN GROUP, LLC.

If you are looking for elegance and warmth you'll find both in this French Traditional Nelson Design Group home. Upon entering this design you'll feel the openness created by the expansive great room with optional fireplace adjoined by the formal dining room with eight inch columns. Meal preparation is made easy in the convenient kitchen and breakfast room with access to a lovely covered porch, perfect for morning coffee and paper. Bedroom two could be utilized as an office for the young professional. Nine foot boxed ceilings, full bath and large walk-in closet accent the master bedroom. This open floor plan design has everything suitable for the families of today.

Width: 48' 2"
Depth: 53' 10"
Total Living: 1,353 sq. ft.

Price Tier: A

Main Ceiling: 8 ft.
Bedrooms: 3
Baths: 2
Foundation: Crawl, Slab, Basement, Daylight Basement

200 Spruce Street

Elevation A

8" COLUMN

COVERED PORCH
12'-0" X 4'-0"

BEDROOM 3
12'-0" X 11'-2"

BEDROOM 2
11'-4" X 9'-6"

HVAC

BATH

GREAT ROOM
9' BOX CEILING
17'-2" X 15'-2"

LIN   WH

MASTER SUITE
9' BOX CEILING
15'-0" X 11'-6"

PAN.

KITCHEN
10'-0" X 11'-2"

RG.

FOYER
7'-0" X 8'-8"

LAU.

D

W

M. BATH
14'-6" X 5'-6"

DW   REF

PORCH
7'-0" X 5'-0"

GARAGE
20'-10" X 20'-0"

8" COLUMNS

DINING ROOM
10'-0" X 10'-6"

VAULTED CEILING

© 1999 NELSON DESIGN GROUP, LLC.

Elevation B

Entertaining will be easy in this Nelson Design Group home. The vaulted ceiling in the dining room creates a feeling of grandeur for your dinner party guests. Afterwards, lead your guests into the spacious great room and around the fire for dessert, coffee and conversation. Preparation of dinner is easy in your open kitchen with fluid access to the dining room. After your guests leave, retire for the evening to your master suite, enhanced by a nine foot boxed ceiling. But don't worry about the children, they will be nestled in their own bedrooms with plenty of space.

Width: 41' 6"
Depth: 53' 6"
Total Living: 1,355 sq. ft.

Price Tier: A

Main Ceiling: 8 ft.
Bedrooms: 3
Baths: 2
Foundation: Crawl, Slab,
Optional Basement,
Optional Daylight Basement

498 Fir Street

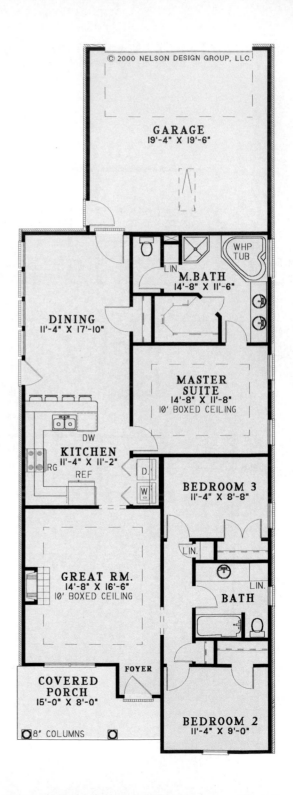

Charming and comfortable describe this Nelson Design Group narrow lot home. An eight-foot porch leads into a foyer open to the great room detailed with a ten foot boxed ceiling and cozy fireplace. The kitchen has a bar counter adjoining the dining room spacious enough for a large family gathering. Privacy will be appreciated in the elegant master suite also enhanced with a boxed ceiling and complete with a large walk-in closet, corner whirlpool tub, separate shower and double vanity.

Width: 27' 0"
Depth: 75' 10"
Total Living: 1,370 sq. ft.

Price Tier: A

Main Ceiling: 9 ft.
Bedrooms: 3
Baths: 2
Foundation: Crawl, Slab

102 Spruce Street

MASTER SUITE
13'-6" X 13'-6"

9' BOXED CEILING

GREAT ROOM
17'-0" X 13'-6"

9' BOXED CEILING

GAS FIREPLACE

BEDROOM 3
11'-4" X 11'-8"

BATH

LIN

BATH

KITCHEN

DW. REF.

DINING
11'-2" X 13'-8"

FOYER

HVAC

W

D

STRG.

WH

PRCH

BEDROOM 2
11'-4" X 11'-6"

VAULTED CEILING

GARAGE
19'-4" X 21'-6"

T his adorable Nelson Design Group home is perfect for family gatherings and unexpected visits from friends. The comfortable great room accommodates everyone. Your spacious kitchen will be most convenient when preparing those last minute details. And the added peninsula allows you to serve breakfast for the children quickly. One bedroom offers a spacious walk-in closet and the other features a vaulted ceiling. The master suite provides distance from the children for retreat and relaxtion when things get too hectic.

Width: 48' 0"
Depth: 48' 0"
Total Living: 1,381 sq. ft.

Main Ceiling: 8 ft.
Bedrooms: 3
Baths: 2
Foundation: Crawl, Slab, Basement Daylight Basement

Price Tier: A

To order call 1.800.590.2423 or to view similar plans visit www.nelsondesigngroup.com

473 Hannah Lane

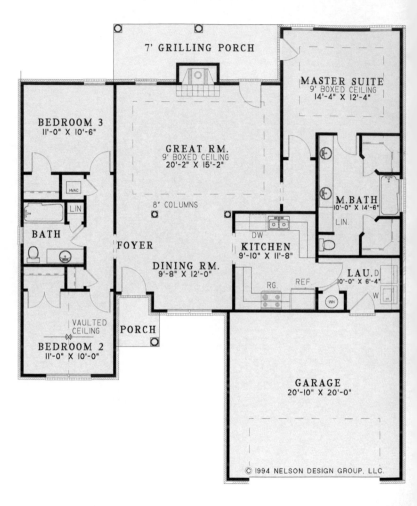

7' GRILLING PORCH

MASTER SUITE
9' BOXED CEILING
14'-4" X 12'-4"

BEDROOM 3
11'-0" X 10'-6"

GREAT RM.
9' BOXED CEILING
20'-2" X 15'-2"

HVAC

LIN

BATH

8" COLUMNS

M.BATH
10'-0" X 14'-6"

LIN

FOYER

KITCHEN
9'-10" X 11'-8"

DW

DINING RM.
9'-8" X 12'-0"

LAU.D
10'-0" X 6'-4"

RG.

REF.

VAULTED
CEILING

PORCH

BEDROOM 2
11'-0" X 10'-0"

GARAGE
20'-10" X 20'-0"

© 1994 NELSON DESIGN GROUP, LLC.

This Nelson Design Group home features a charming roundtop window focal point for great street appeal. An expansive great room combines with the formal dining room allowing for the ultimate in entertaining. A well-designed kitchen has abundant storage and a conveniently located laundry room with garage access. The master suite has private access to the rear porch and a private bathroom with his and her walk-in closets.

Width: 46' 10"
Depth: 54' 10"
Total Living: 1,485 sq. ft.

Price Tier: A

Main Ceiling: 8 ft.
Bedrooms: 3
Baths: 2
Foundation: Crawl, Slab,
Optional Basement,
Optional Daylight Basement

115 Spruce Street

GLASS SHWR

LIN

WHP TUB

M.BATH
8'-0" X 18'-0"

MASTER SUITE
9' PAN CEILING
13'-0" X 14'-0"

DINING
11'-6" X 10'-6"

GREAT ROOM
15'-4" X 19'-8"
9' BOXED CEILING

BAR

BEDROOM 3
12'-4" X 10'-8"

BATH

KIT.
10'-6" X 10'-0"

RG

REF

DW

LAU.
9'-4" X 5'-6"

D

W

HVAC

WH

PAN.

PRCH

BEDROOM 2
10'-8" X 12'-0"

VAULTED CEILING

GARAGE
20'-10" X 20'-0"

©1998 NELSON DESIGN GROUP, LLC.

Picture yourself in this Nelson Design Group home. Walking through the foyer, you'll enter the spacious great room with fireplace. A convenient bar located in the kitchen makes snack time a breeze. If you're hosting a dinner party, the open dining room with fluid access to the kitchen makes entertaining your guests easy. When night falls, retire to your master suite bathroom, which comes complete with double vanities, whirlpool tub and glass shower. Bedrooms two and three feature individual walk-in closets.

Width: 48' 6"
Depth: 48' 4"
Total Living: 1,500 sq. ft.

Price Tier: B

Main Ceiling: 8 ft.
Bedrooms: 3
Baths: 2
Foundation: Crawl, Slab, Basement, Daylight Basement

476 Olive Street

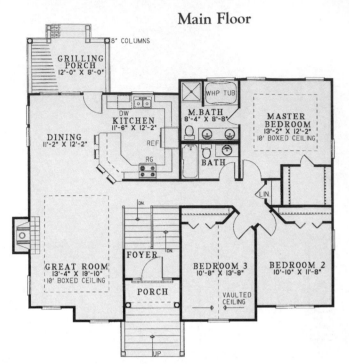

Main Floor

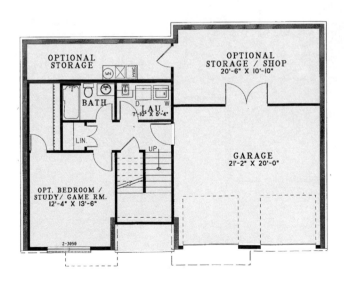

Lower Floor

An impressive front entrance is achieved by the interesting gable roof line of this livable three bedroom Nelson Design Group home. Once inside, you'll enjoy an open floor plan with access to the kitchen, which makes entertaining friends very rewarding. Or spend the evenings alone with your family outside on the rear grilling porch. In the evening, you'll find enjoyment as you retreat to your master bath, relaxing in the whirlpool tub. Unexpected guests can be easily accommodated by the optional bedroom downstairs, or convert it to a family game room.

Width: 44' 4"
Depth: 41' 0"
Main Floor: 1,425 sq. ft.
Lower Floor: 89 sq. ft.
Total Living: 1,514 sq. ft.*
*Optional Bonus: 336 sq. ft.

Main Ceiling: 9 ft.
Lower Ceiling: 8 ft.
Bedrooms: 3
Baths: 3
Foundation: Basement, Daylight Basement

Price Tier: B

To order call 1.800.590.2423 or to view similar plans visit www.nelsondesigngroup.com

113-1-1 Chestnut Lane

Front Elevation

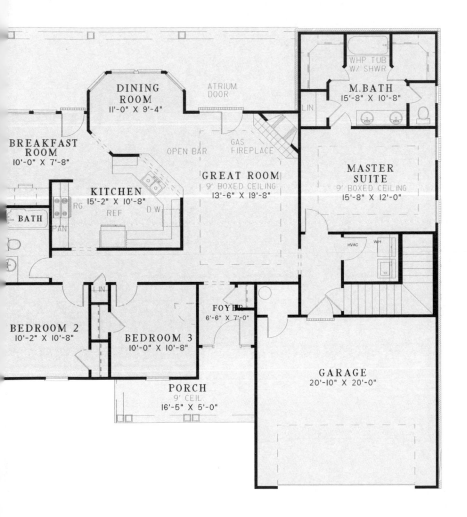

DINING ROOM
11'-0" X 9'-4"

ATRIUM DOOR

WHP TUB W/ SHWR

M.BATH
15'-8" X 10'-8"

BREAKFAST ROOM
10'-0" X 7'-8"

OPEN BAR

GAS FIREPLACE

LIN

KITCHEN
15'-2" X 10'-8"

GREAT ROOM
9' BOXED CEILING
13'-6" X 19'-8"

MASTER SUITE
9' BOXED CEILING
15'-8" X 12'-0"

RG   REF   D W

BATH

PAN

HVAC   WH

LIN

BEDROOM 2
10'-2" X 10'-8"

BEDROOM 3
10'-0" X 10'-8"

FOYER
6'-6" X 7'-0"

GARAGE
20'-10" X 20'-0"

PORCH
9' CEIL
16'-5" X 5'-0"

Rear Elevation

Numerous amenities within this Nelson Design Group traditional home create an attractive design. The great room, complete with fireplace, is the central entertaining area of your home. In your spacious kitchen you will be able to prepare anything your guests desire. Complete with french door access to the great room, you'll find a rear grilling porch - just right for summer barbeques. A convenient computer nook just off the kitchen allows you to monitor the children's activity. You may choose to spend a day lounging in your private master suite complete with whirlpool tub, separate shower and 'his and her' walk-in closets.

Width: 51' 6"
Depth: 53' 4"
Total Living: 1,525 sq. ft.

Price Tier: B

Main Ceiling: 8 ft.
Bedrooms: 3
Baths: 2
Foundation: Crawl, Slab, Basement, Daylight Basement

159

114-1 Spruce Street

Welcome friends and neighbors on the cozy front porch of this Nelson Design Group home. Leading your guests through the foyer, you'll enter a spacious great room with a nine foot boxed ceiling, corner fireplace and access to a wonderful dining room bay area. The kitchen is well planned with an open bar to the great room, cozy breakfast room and convenient laundry area. As the night falls and your guests leave, retreat to your master suite enhanced with a boxed ceiling and luxurious private bath.

Width: 51' 6"
Depth: 49' 10"
Total Living: 1,525 sq. ft.

Price Tier: B

Main Ceiling: 8 ft.
Bedrooms: 3
Baths: 2
Foundation: Crawl, Slab, Basement,
Daylight Basement

148 Spruce Street

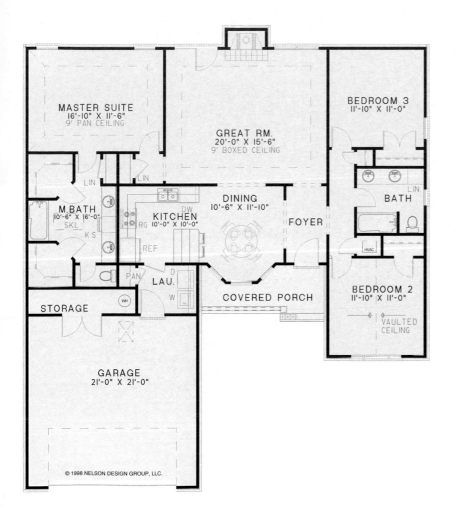

MASTER SUITE
16'-10" X 11'-6"
9' PAN CEILING

GREAT RM.
20'-0" X 15'-6"
9' BOXED CEILING

BEDROOM 3
11'-10" X 11'-0"

LIN

LIN

M.BATH
10'-6" X 6'-0"
SKL

KITCHEN
10'-0" X 10'-0"

DINING
10'-6" X 11'-10"

FOYER

BATH

LIN

KS

DW

RG

REF

PAN

LAU.

D

W

HVAC

STORAGE

WH

COVERED PORCH

BEDROOM 2
11'-10" X 11'-0"

VAULTED
CEILING

GARAGE
21'-0" X 21'-0"

© 1998 NELSON DESIGN GROUP, LLC.

Welcome your friends and neighbors on the cozy front porch of this Nelson Design Group home. Leading your guests through the foyer, you'll enter the spacious great room which will prove to be a convenient gathering place with its inviting fireplace. Preparing meals is easy with the ample counter space in the open kitchen with view to the dining room. As evening approaches and your guests depart, retreat to your master bath, complete with whirlpool tub, skylights, and 'his and her' walk-in closets. But don't worry about the children, they have their own bedrooms with shared bath.

Width: 50' 0"
Depth: 56' 0"
Total Living: 1,538 sq. ft.

Price Tier: B

Main Ceiling: 8 ft.
Bedrooms: 3
Baths: 2
Foundation: Crawl, Slab, Basement, Daylight Basement

497 Cottonwood Drive

© 2000 NELSON DESIGN GROUP, LLC.

GARAGE
17'-9" X 19'-8"

GRILLING PORCH

DINING
12'-6" X 10'-0"

LAU.

DESK

WHP TUB

KITCHEN
12'-6" X 11'-6"

DW

RG

REF

PAN

M.BATH
15'-6" X 11'-6"

GREAT RM.
12'-6" X 15'-0"

MASTER SUITE
11'-8" X 15'-0"

UP

COVERED PORCH
29'-0" X 8'-0"

8" COLUMNS

Upper Floor

BATH

DN.

LIN

BEDROOM 2
12'-10" X 11'-0"

BEDROOM 3
12'-0" X 11'-0"

DESK

DESK

Round columns on a lovely covered porch enhance this old-fashioned Nelson Design Group plan. An expansive great room with fireplace and staircase separate the family quarters from a glorious master suite. A family oriented kitchen is centrally located and has a dining area, laundry room and grilling porch. The large master suite has a private bath with his and her walk-in closets separated by a whirlpool tub, separate shower and private toilet area. A full bath, two additional bedrooms both with dormer windows and built-in study desks are on the second level allowing family their own space.

Width: 29' 0"
Depth: 68' 8"
Main Floor: 982 sq. ft.
Upper Floor: 561 sq. ft.
Total Living: 1,543 sq. ft.

Main Ceiling: 9 ft.
Upper Ceiling: 8 ft.
Bedrooms: 3
Baths: 2
Foundation: Crawl, Slab

Price Tier: B

To order call 1.800.590.2423 or to view similar plans visit www.nelsondesigngroup.com

570 Quail Drive

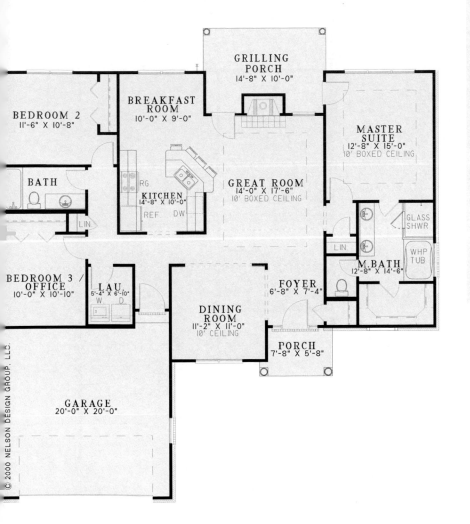

Floor plan:

- **BEDROOM 2** 11'-6" X 10'-8"
- **BATH**
- **BEDROOM 3 / OFFICE** 10'-0" X 10'-10"
- **LAU.** 5'-4" X 6'-10" W D
- **BREAKFAST ROOM** 10'-0" X 9'-0"
- **KITCHEN** 14'-8" X 10'-0" REF DW
- **GRILLING PORCH** 14'-8" X 10'-0"
- **GREAT ROOM** 14'-0" X 17'-6" 10' BOXED CEILING
- **MASTER SUITE** 12'-8" X 15'-0" 10' BOXED CEILING
- **GLASS SHWR**
- **WHP TUB**
- **M.BATH** 12'-8" X 14'-6"
- **FOYER** 6'-8" X 7'-4"
- **DINING ROOM** 11'-2" X 11'-0" 10' CEILING
- **PORCH** 7'-8" X 5'-8"
- **GARAGE** 20'-0" X 20'-0"

© 2000 NELSON DESIGN GROUP, LLC.

Cedar shake and brick are a wonderful combination for this Nelson Design Group home. The arched entry porch welcomes guests into an open great room viewing a formal dining room and accessing a large kitchen with breakfast room. The laundry room is located just steps from the kitchen for added convenience. Two bedrooms, one perfect for a home office, are located on the opposite side of the home and share a full bathroom. This split plan offers an elegant master suite with private access to the rear-grilling porch perfect for enjoying starlit evenings.

Width: 52' 2"
Depth: 55' 8"
Total Living: 1,560 sq. ft.

Price Tier: B

Main Ceiling: 9 ft.
Bedrooms: 3
Baths: 2
Foundation: Crawl, Slab, Optional Basement, Optional Daylight Basement

456 Fir Street

Nelson Design Group offers optimum value for the first time homebuyers. From the covered front porch you enter a beautiful great room with fireplace and sitting area. The kitchen affords an island bar and nook. The master suite opens to the bath showcasing a large walk-in closet, whirlpool tub and shower. The children share full bath access between their rooms. Additional storage space in the garage completes this design.

Width: 27' 8"
Depth: 76' 4"
Total Living: 1,574 sq. ft.

Price Tier: B

Main Ceiling: 9 ft.
Bedrooms: 3
Baths: 2
Foundation: Crawl, Slab

513 Hannah Lane

Elevation A

GRILLING PORCH
16'-0" X 8'-0"

OPT. FIREPLACE

DINING RM.
10'-6" X 10'-6"

MASTER SUITE
9' BOX CEILING
13'-0" X 18'-0"

GREAT RM.
9' BOXED CEILING
13'-0" X 18'-0"

M. BATH
8' X 11'-8"

LIN

W.I.C.

KIT.
10'-6" X 11'

DW

RG

REF

OPTIONAL COMPUTER CENTER

BEDROOM 3
12'-4" X 10'-8"

LAU.
13'-6" X 5'-6"

D

W

BATH

WH

PAN.

PORCH

BEDROOM 2
10'-8" X 13'-8"

VAULTED CEILING

GARAGE
20'-10" X 20'-0"

© 2001 NELSON DESIGN GROUP, LLC.

Elevation B

Comfortable living and a spacious interior are available in this Nelson Design Group home. Boxed ceilings are used in the great room and master suite allowing natural light to flow throughout. An optional computer center and fireplace in the great room allows family to enjoy quiet time together while doing homework or simply reading. The dining room is open to the kitchen and both can enjoy a view of the great room fireplace if desired. Also available in the kitchen is a walk-in pantry and laundry room. All bedrooms have walk-in closets and close proximity to a bathroom. A vaulted ceiling is used in the front bedroom making the perfect study or home office.

Width: 48' 6"
Depth: 56' 8"
Total Living   1,574 sq. ft.

Price Tier: B

Main Ceiling: 8 ft.
Bedrooms: 3
Baths: 2
Foundation: Crawl, Slab,
Optional Basement,
Optional Daylight Basement

569 Thomas Road

© 2001 NELSON DESIGN GROUP, LLC.

GARAGE
22'-0" X 22'-0"

STORAGE
11'-4" X 6'-0"

GRILLING PORCH
24'-8" X 8'-0"

WH

BEDROOM 3
11'-10" X 10'-0"

DINING
9'-0" X 10'-4"

KITCHEN
7'-8" X 10'-0"

LAU.

DW

RG. REF.

W.

D.

WHP TUB

M.BATH
15'-8" X 12'-2"

BATH

LIN.

VAULTED
CEILING

BEDROOM 2
11'-10" X 10'-6"

LIVING ROOM
20'-0" X 19'-4"

MASTER
SUITE
15'-8" X 17'-2"

COVERED
PORCH
20'-8" X 8'-0"

This country home from Nelson Design Group offers a covered front porch with columns begging to be adorned with garland at Christmas. The vaulted ceiling living room hosts a bountiful tree beside the fireplace where stockings are carefully hung. The kitchen provides for a luscious dinner lovingly served in the dining room amidst family and friends. The children lay nestled in their rooms with walk-in closet and shared full bath access. The master bath invites you into the whirlpool tub to relax as you await the arrival of Christmas morn.

Width: 59' 0"
Depth: 67' 0"
Total Living: 1,597 sq. ft.

Main Ceiling: 9 ft.
Bedrooms: 3
Baths: 2
Foundation: Crawl, Slab

Price Tier: B

GLASS BLOCKS

WHP TUB

M.BATH
16'-4" X 10'-8"

KNEE SPACE

MASTER SUITE
10' BOX CEILING
16'-4" X 12'-0"

LANAI
22'-0" X 8'-0"

GAS FIREPLACE

BREAKFAST ROOM
10'-0" X 9'-0"

BAR

BEDROOM 2
12'-8" X 11'-8"

GREAT ROOM
17'-2" X 15'-6"

REF

8" COLUMNS

DW

BATH

RG

LIN

DINING ROOM
10'-6" X 12'-0"

KIT.
9'-6" X 15'-2"

FOYER

LAU.
9'-6" X 5'-6"

LIN

D

W

WH

PAN

BEDROOM 3
11' CEILING
12'-8" X 11'-8"

PORCH

SLOPE CEILING

GARAGE
20'-0" X 20'-0"

©1998 NELSON DESIGN GROUP, LLC.

101 Brighton Court

Passersby will marvel at the lavish window accents and gabled roofline of this Nelson Design Group home. Walking through the foyer affords a stunning view of an immense open plan that begs to entertain. The vast great room merges with all living areas providing instant access and convenience. The walk-through kitchen features an angled bar and entry to the utility room and garage. Isolated at the rear of the house is the master suite with a ten foot boxed ceiling and corner whirlpool tub with a glass block window for natural lighting.

Width: 39' 0"
Depth: 70' 0"
Total Living: 1,608 sq. ft.

Price Tier: B

Main Ceiling: 9 ft.
Bedrooms: 3
Baths: 2
Foundation: Crawl, Slab, Basement, Daylight Basement

To order call 1.800.590.2423 or to view similar plans visit www.nelsondesigngroup.com

165 Willow Lane

© 1996 NELSON DESIGN GROUP, LLC.

This Nelson Design Group home features all the amenities you've come to expect in your future home. Enjoy hours of quality time in front of the fireplace in the great room with access to the formal dining room with eight inch columns. The kitchen features a snack bar open to the breakfast room with easy access to the rear grilling porch for summer barbecues. The master bath affords the convenience of an expansive walk-in closet and double vanities. The whirlpool tub offers solace from the day's worries as the steam envelops you. The children have the privacy of bedrooms located on the opposite side of the home with a full bath between.

Width: 53' 0"
Depth: 59' 10"
Total Living: 1,636 sq. ft.

Price Tier: B

Main Ceiling: 8 ft.
Bedrooms: 3
Baths: 2
Foundation: Crawl, Slab

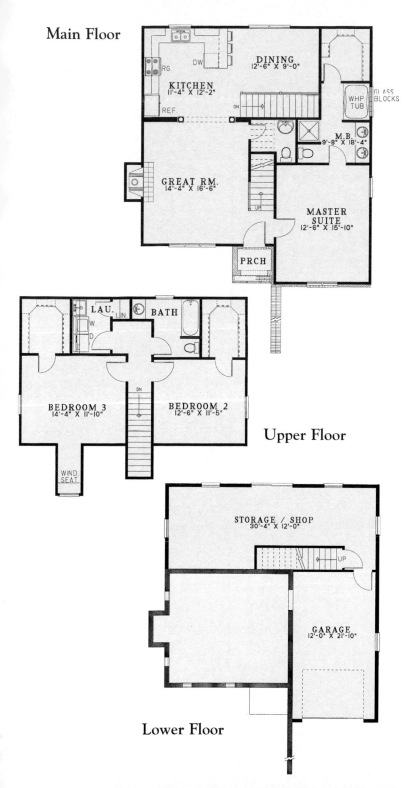

Main Floor

DINING
12'-6" X 9'-0"

KITCHEN
11'-4" X 12'-2"

GLASS BLOCKS

WHP TUB

M.B.
9'-8" X 18'-4"

GREAT RM.
14'-4" X 16'-6"

MASTER SUITE
12'-6" X 15'-10"

PRCH

LAU.   BATH

BEDROOM 3
14'-4" X 11'-10"

BEDROOM 2
12'-6" X 11'-5"

Upper Floor

WIND. SEAT

STORAGE / SHOP
30'-4" X 12'-0"

GARAGE
12'-0" X 21'-10"

Lower Floor

451 Aspen Heights

This split level has all the amenities you'll need to call it home. As you enter this Nelson Design Group home, a spacious great room with fireplace and column lined entry to the kitchen give an elegant flair to this traditional plan. Dinner parties are sure to be successful with the convenience of the kitchen open to the dining room. A set of stairs lead you to a full bathroom, laundry room with sink, and two bedrooms with large walk-in closets. One room features a lovely window seat allowing for natural light. The master suite is sure to capture your heart with its large bedroom and master bath.

Width: 33' 8"	Main Ceiling: 9 ft.
Depth: 35' 2"	Upper Ceiling: 9 ft.
Main Floor: 1,008 sq. ft.	Bedrooms: 3
Upper Floor 637 sq. ft.	Baths: 2 1/2
Total Living: 1,645 sq. ft.*	Foundation: Basement, Daylight Basement
*Optional Lower: 391 sq. ft.	

Price Tier: B

268 Walnut Lane

© 1998 NELSON DESIGN GROUP, LLC.

GARAGE
19'-6" X 20'-0"

M. BATH
13'-4" X 12'-6"

GLASS SHWR

WHP TUB

LIN

MASTER SUITE
13'-4" X 18'-4"
10' BOXED CEILING

BED RM. 3
11'-10" X 13'-10"

WH

BATH

BED RM. 2
11'-0" X 12'-0"

COURT YARD

GREAT RM.
16'-0" X 17'-8"
10' BOXED CEILING

DINING RM.
13'-4" X 12'-6"

PORCH
16'-4" X 8'-0"

PAN.

RG

KITCHEN
13'-4" X 12'-6"

REF.

DW

This Nelson Design Group home is wonderful for raising children. The gorgeous courtyard is certain to be a favorite for family cookouts and is viewed by several rooms. Your spacious kitchen, with fluid access to the dining room, makes preparing meals a breeze. The open great room, complete with fireplace, allows get-togethers and family time all the more simple. If you're concerned about room for the kids, don't worry. They'll have abundant space in the two extra bedrooms- one with walk-in closet. Your master suite includes a corner whirlpool bath, a separate shower and double vanities.

Width: 33' 10"
Depth: 69' 6"
Total Living: 1,660 sq. ft.

Price Tier: B

Main Ceiling: 9 ft.
Bedrooms: 3
Baths: 2
Foundation: Crawl, Slab

219 Tyler Street

Floor plan labels:

- GLASS BLOCKS
- WHP TUB
- M. BATH 12'-4" X 12'-10"
- LIN.
- MASTER SUITE 12'-4" X 13'-0" 9' BOXED CEILING
- BATH
- LIN.
- DINING 9'-6" X 11'-0" 9' CEILING
- GRILLING PORCH 10'-0" X 7'-6"
- GREAT RM. 15'-4" X 19'-6" 10' BOXED CEILING
- 8" COLUMNS
- BRKFAST RM. 9'-6" X 12'-6"
- RG.
- DW
- OPTIONAL COMPUTER CENTER
- KITCHEN 10'-8" X 13'-8"
- FOYER 9' CEILING
- PAN. REF.
- LAU. 5'-6" X 6'-4"
- W. D.
- BEDROOM 3 10'-0" X 13'-0"
- BEDROOM 2 / STUDY 10'-0" X 12'-0"
- ENTRY PORCH
- WH
- STRG.
- OPTIONAL BASEMENT STAIRS
- GARAGE 20'-10" X 20'-0"
- © 1992 NELSON DESIGN GROUP, LLC.

Nelson Design Group features this lovely home accented with angled walls, columns and boxed ceilings. The foyer has a nine-foot ceiling and leads to an open great room/dining room separated by eight-inch columns. Nearby is a step saver kitchen and breakfast room with bar counter seating and plenty of windows for natural lighting. On the opposite side of this well planned home are the bedrooms including a private master suite enhanced by a nine foot boxed ceiling. The private bathroom includes a large walk-in closet, double vanity and a corner whirlpool tub with obscure glass blocks above.

Width: 49' 2"
Depth: 67' 2"
Total Living: 1,679 sq. ft.

Main Ceiling: 8 ft.
Bedrooms: 3
Baths: 2
Foundation: Crawl, Slab,
Optional Basement,
Optional Daylight Basement

Price Tier: B

379 Spruce Street

Elevation A

Elevation B

PORCH 29'-8" X 8'-0"

8" COLUMNS

FRENCH DOOR

MASTER SUITE 9' PAN CEILING 16'-2" X 12'-6"

BEDROOM 3 10'-10" X 11'-8"

FRENCH DOOR

BREAKFAST ROOM 12'-10" X 9'-0"

COMP CENTER

M.BATH 12'-4" X 16'-8"

WHP TUB

GREAT ROOM 9' CEILING 16'-6" X 18'-4"

KITCHEN 12'-10" X 9'-4"

ISLAND

LAU. 6'-0" X 7'-0"

HVAC

LIN

RG

REF

DW

W D

LIN

BATH

8" COLUMN

FOYER 10' CEILING 6'-10" X 6'-6"

DN

OPTIONAL BASEMENT PLAN

BEDROOM 2 13'-6" X 10'-8"

PORCH 6'-6" X 5'-10"

DINING 10' CEILING 11'-8" X 12'-2"

GARAGE 22'-4" X 20'-8"

8" COLUMNS

© 1999 NELSON DESIGN GROUP, LLC.

An open feeling is created in this Nelson Design Group home by use of high ceilings in several rooms. Preparing meals for your family is easy with your spacious kitchen, complete with center island. You may also entertain on your rear covered porch with french door access from the breakfast room as well as your master suite. Get lost in your expansive master bath, which includes double vanities, whirlpool tub and 'his and her' walk-in closets. You'll find the extra two bedrooms in this design just right for children, a home office or weekend guests.

Width: 58' 0"
Depth: 53' 6"
Total Living: 1,722 sq. ft.

Price Tier: B

Main Ceiling: 8 ft.
Bedrooms: 3
Baths: 2
Foundation: Crawl, Slab, Basement, Daylight Basement

153 Tyler Street

Floor Plan Labels:

- MASTER SUITE 15'-4" X 13'-4" 9' BOXED CEILING
- GRILLING PORCH 19'-6" X 5'-6"
- BEDROOM 3 12'-0" X 11'-6"
- GREAT RM. 19'-2" X 17'-6" 9' BOXED CEILING
- M. BATH 14'-8" X 10'-0"
- LAU. 7'-4" X 7'-9"
- BATH
- FOYER
- GARAGE 20'-10" X 20'-0"
- DINING RM. 10'-6" X 12'-6"
- KIT. 10'-8" X 11'-4"
- BEDROOM 2 12'-0" X 11'-6"
- PORCH
- BREAKFAST ROOM 10'-8" X 8'-2"

© 1995 NELSON DESIGN GROUP, LLC.

Nelson Design Group has created this delightful plan to fill the needs of a growing family. Use the formal dining room as a study if a formal setting isn't your cup of tea and invite guests over for a cozy evening of grilling on the rear porch and fireside conversation in the great room. In the morning you can enjoy coffee and the paper in the breakfast room adjoining a well-designed kitchen. At the end of a long day, retreat to your master suite with a private bath containing his and her closets, private toilet area and double vanities. On the other side of the home are two spacious bedrooms and a full bath allowing teens and guests their own private space.

Width: 61' 0"
Depth: 54' 0"
Total Living: 1,734 sq. ft.

Main Ceiling: 8 ft.
Bedrooms: 3
Baths: 2
Foundation: Crawl, Slab

Price Tier: B

220 Chestnut Lane

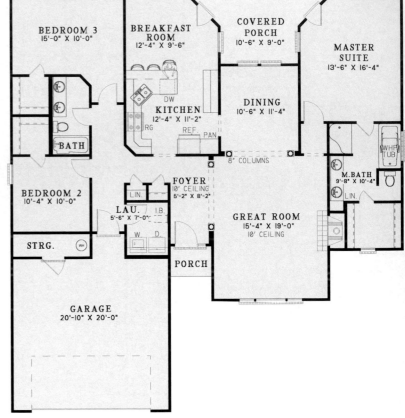

BEDROOM 3
15'-0" X 10'-0"

BREAKFAST ROOM
12'-4" X 9'-6"

COVERED PORCH
10'-6" X 9'-0"

MASTER SUITE
13'-6" X 16'-4"

KITCHEN
12'-4" X 11'-2"

DINING
10'-6" X 11'-4"

DW

REF. PAN

BATH

8" COLUMNS

WHP TUB

M.BATH
9'-8" X 10'-4"

BEDROOM 2
10'-4" X 10'-0"

LIN.

FOYER
10' CEILING
5'-2" X 8'-2"

LAU.
5'-6" X 7'-0"

I.B.

LIN.

GREAT ROOM
15'-4" X 19'-0"
10' CEILING

STRG.

W D

PORCH

GARAGE
20'-10" X 20'-0"

Nelson Design Group has created an ideal split bedroom home with privacy for everyone. An inviting great room will certainly draw the entire family together as you enjoy the fireplace's glow. Your functional kitchen allows you to entertain easily at large parties in the dining room or family night dinners in the cozy breakfast room. The rear covered porch provides the ideal place for grilling steaks. The children and yourself will find the secluded bedrooms perfect as the long day ends.

Width: 53' 0"
Depth: 55' 4"
Total Living: 1,764 sq. ft.

Price Tier: B

Main Ceiling: 9 ft.
Bedrooms: 3
Baths: 2
Foundation: Crawl, Slab, Basement, Daylight Basement

142 Olive Street

Main Floor

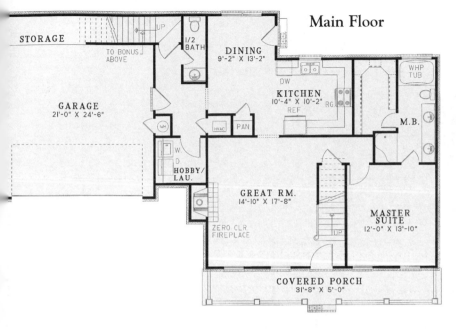

STORAGE

UP

1/2 BATH

TO BONUS ABOVE

DINING
9'-2" X 13'-2"

DW

KITCHEN
10'-4" X 10'-2"

REF

RG

WHP TUB

M.B.

GARAGE
21'-0" X 24'-6"

WH

HVAC

PAN

W
D

HOBBY/
LAU.

GREAT RM.
14'-10" X 17'-8"

ZERO CLR. FIREPLACE

UP

MASTER SUITE
12'-0" X 13'-10"

COVERED PORCH
31'-8" X 5'-0"

Upper Floor

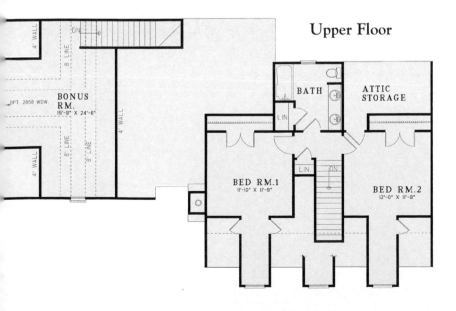

DN

4' WALL

8' LINE

OPT. 2850 WDW.

BONUS RM.
15'-8" X 24'-6"

4' WALL

8' LINE

8' LINE

4' WALL

4' WALL

BATH

LIN

ATTIC STORAGE

LIN

DN

BED RM.1
11'-10" X 11'-8"

BED RM.2
12'-0" X 11'-8"

A rocking chair on the front porch of this Nelson Design Group home awaits you. Entering this home, you'll encounter the spacious great room with a romantic fireplace for special occasions or everyday winter enjoyment. Preparing meals for the family will be easy with fluid access to the open kitchen. At the end of the day, relax in your master bath with soothing whirlpool tub. On the upper floor, the children will discover innovative ways to utilize the nook created by their windows. Maximize the bonus area over the garage as a future game room or home office.

Width: 60' 2"
Depth: 39' 10"
Main Floor: 1,124 sq. ft.
Upper Floor: 659 sq. ft.
Total Living: 1,783 sq. ft.*
*Optional Bonus: 324 sq. ft.

Main Ceiling: 8 ft.
Upper Ceiling: 8 ft.
Bedrooms: 3
Baths: 2 1/2
Foundation: Crawl, Slab, Basement, Daylight Basement

Price Tier: B

567 Thomas Road

This beautiful Nelson Design Group home envelops you with southern charm. Imagine welcoming your guests onto the front porch of this traditional country home. The great room with vaulted ceilings and easy access to the kitchen and grilling porch is an excellent place for family gatherings. After the guests leave and the children are in their bedrooms with shared bath and ample closet space, you and your loved one can find solitude in the master suite with ten foot boxed ceiling and master bath complete with whirlpool tub, glass shower, and 'his and her' vanities.

Width: 65' 8"
Depth: 57' 0"
Total Living: 1,813 sq. ft.

Price Tier: B

Main Ceiling: 9 ft.
Bedrooms: 3
Baths: 2
Foundation: Crawl, Slab,
Optional Basement,
Optional Daylight Basement

548 Tyler Street

This traditional Nelson Design Group home welcomes you into a world of entertaining options. Family gatherings are a breeze in an expansive great room with fireplace and access to the rear-grilling porch. The kitchen has an angled bar counter and an abundance of storage allowing ease in meal preparation. Teens and overnight guests will have plenty of privacy on one side of the house while the heads of household have peace and quiet in their master suite. This master bedroom has built-in bookshelves, private access to the rear porch, a nine-foot boxed ceiling, and a private bathroom including 'his and her' walk-in closets, whirlpool bath and double vanity.

Width: 50' 8"
Depth: 62' 4"
Total Living: 1,832 sq. ft.

Price Tier: B

Main Ceiling: 8 ft.
Bedrooms: 4
Baths: 2
Foundation: Crawl, Slab,
Optional Basement,
Optional Daylight Basement

To order call 1.800.590.2423 or to view similar plans visit www.nelsondesigngroup.com

613 William Court

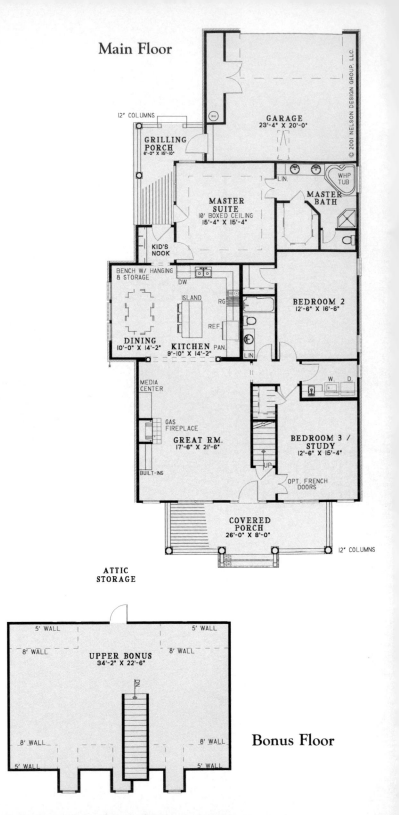

Main Floor

12" COLUMNS

GRILLING PORCH
6'-0" X 15'-10"

GARAGE
23'-4" X 20'-0"

MASTER SUITE
10' BOXED CEILING
15'-4" X 15'-4"

MASTER BATH

WHP TUB

LIN.

KID'S NOOK

BENCH W/ HANGING & STORAGE

DW

ISLAND

RG

REF.

PAN.

LIN

BEDROOM 2
12'-6" X 16'-6"

DINING
10'-0" X 14'-2"

KITCHEN
9'-10" X 14'-2"

MEDIA CENTER

GAS FIREPLACE

GREAT RM.
17'-6" X 21'-6"

BUILT-INS

W. D.

UP

BEDROOM 3 / STUDY
12'-6" X 15'-4"

OPT. FRENCH DOORS

COVERED PORCH
26'-0" X 8'-0"

12" COLUMNS

ATTIC STORAGE

UPPER BONUS
34'-2" X 22'-6"

5' WALL   5' WALL
8' WALL   8' WALL
8' WALL   8' WALL
5' WALL   5' WALL

DN

Bonus Floor

T his Nelson Design Group plan has true southern flair, great street appeal and a cozy welcome for guests. The main level has a large great room with a fireplace nestled between built-ins and views the kitchen through a cased opening with columns. This spacious kitchen adjoins the dining area and has a wall of windows for plenty of natural light. A kid's nook helps keep clutter at a minimum and leads to the grilling porch. Luxury, privacy and convenience best describe the master suite with French doors, a ten-foot boxed ceiling and an impressive private bathroom. Stairs lead to an upper bonus area with varied ceiling heights and a world of options, present or future.

Width: 39' 0"
Depth: 81' 0"
Total Living: 1,832 sq. ft.*
*Optional Bonus: 790 sq. t.

Price Tier: B

Main Ceiling: 9 ft.
Bonus Ceiling: 8 ft.
Bedrooms: 3
Baths: 2
Foundation: Crawl, Slab

516 Belmont Avenue

Elevation A

Elevation B

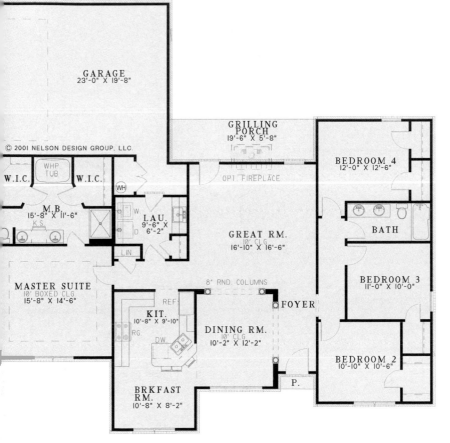

© 2001 NELSON DESIGN GROUP, LLC.

GARAGE
23'-0" X 19'-8"

GRILLING PORCH
19'-6" X 5'-8"

OPT. FIREPLACE

WHP TUB

W.I.C.   W.I.C.

WH

M.B.
15'-8" X 11'-6"

KS

LAU.
9'-6" X 6'-2"

W
D

LIN

GREAT RM.
10' CLG
16'-10" X 16'-6"

BEDROOM 4
12'-0" X 12'-6"

BATH

MASTER SUITE
10' BOXED CLG
15'-8" X 14'-6"

8" RND. COLUMNS

REF

KIT.
10'-8" X 9'-10"

RG

DW

DINING RM.
10' CLG
10'-2" X 12'-2"

FOYER

BEDROOM 3
11'-0" X 10'-0"

BRKFAST RM.
10'-8" X 8'-2"

P.

BEDROOM 2
10'-10" X 10'-6"

T wo wonderful exteriors are available for this Nelson Design Group split bedroom plan. Enter a lovely foyer separating the column-lined formal dining room from three additional bedrooms and full bathroom. As this dining room gently accesses the kitchen it has a view of the great room fireplace for a cozy atmosphere while dining. Near the kitchen is a large laundry room with storage and access to the garage. And just steps away is the master suite bedroom with a ten foot boxed ceiling and private bath with walk-in closets, whirlpool tub, separate shower and double vanity with knee space.

Width: 58' 8"
Depth: 56' 6"
Total Living: 1,841 sq. ft.

Price Tier: B

Main Ceiling: 9 ft.
Bedrooms: 4
Baths: 2
Foundation: Crawl, Slab

To order call 1.800.590.2423 or to view similar plans visit www.nelsondesigngroup.com

365 Spruce Street

Elevation A

Elevation B

The entry of this split bedroom Nelson Design Group home shows off the sensational columns which frame the dining room. Romance the one you love by the fireplace in the comfortable great room with beautiful french doors accessing the rear porch. Afterwards, retreat to your master suite and bath, complete with 'his and her' walk-in closets, double vanities and a wonderful whirlpool bath. Don't worry about the children, they will be having dreams of their own in the bedrooms located on the opposite side of this home.

Width: 58' 8"
Depth: 58' 6"
Total Living: 1,854 sq. ft.

Price Tier: B

Main Ceiling: 9 ft.
Bedrooms: 4
Baths: 2
Foundation: Crawl, Slab,
Optional Basement,
Optional Daylight Basement

© 1999 NELSON DESIGN GROUP, LLC.

GARAGE
23'-0" X 21'-8"

PORCH
19'-6" X 5'-8"

FRENCH DOOR   FRENCH DOOR

WHP TUB

HVAC   WH

BEDROOM 4
12'-0" X 10'-6"

KNEE SPACE

M.BATH
15'-8" X 11'-6"

W   D

LAU.
8'-2" X 9'-8"

GREAT ROOM
10' CEILING
16'-10" X 16'-6"

LIN

BATH

PAN   LIN

MASTER SUITE
15'-8" X 14'-6"

REF

KIT.
10'-8" X 9'-10"

RG.   DW

DINING ROOM
10' CEILING
10'-6" X 12'-6"

FOYER
10' CEIL
5'-0" X 10'-10"

BEDROOM 3
11'-0" X 10'-0"

BREAKFAST ROOM
10'-8" X 5'-6"

PRCH

BEDROOM 2
11'-0" X 10'-6"

Main Floor

GRILLING PORCH
10'-10" X 8'-0"

GARAGE
20'-0" X 20'-4"

© 2001 NELSON DESIGN GROUP, LLC.

BRKFAST NOOK / DINING
12'-8" X 10'-6"

PAN

LAU.
6'-6" X 7'-4"

D

W

UP

W.I.C.

KITCHEN
13'-0" X 9'-8"

DW

RG

REF

LIN

M.BATH
14'-0" X 16'-4"

WHP TUB.

W.I.C.

COMPUTER CENTER

GREAT ROOM
16'-0" X 13'-0"

FOYER

MASTER SUITE
14'-0" X 16'-2"

COVERED PORCH
21'-0" X 6'-0"

Upper Floor

ATTIC STORAGE

HVAC

DN

BATH

LIN

BEDROOM 2
14'-4" X 13'-0"

LOFT
10'-6" X 13'-0"

BALCONY
21'-0" X 6'-0"

BEDROOM 3
14'-0" X 13'-0"

605 William Drive

This Nelson Design Group split bedroom plan issues both privacy and convenience. The foyer leads into a cozy great room with fireplace and an optional built-in computer center. Nearby is a swinging door leading to the kitchen complete with bar seating, a spacious dining nook and accessing the rear grilling porch. This main level has a large master suite with private bath including walk-in closets, whirlpool tub, separate shower and a double vanity. Upstairs are two additional bedrooms, full bath and a door leading to the front balcony for enjoying starlit evenings.

Width: 36' 4"
Depth: 61' 6"
Main Floor: 1,268 sq. ft.
Upper Floor: 602 sq. ft.
Total Living: 1,870 sq. ft.

Main Ceiling: 9 ft.
Upper Ceiling: 8 ft.
Bedrooms: 3
Baths: 2 1/2
Foundation: Crawl, Slab,
Optional Basement,
Optional Daylight Basement

Price Tier: B

136 Spruce Street

Main Floor

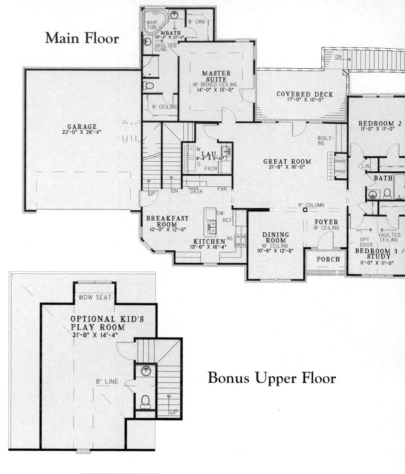

Bonus Upper Floor

Bonus Lower Floor

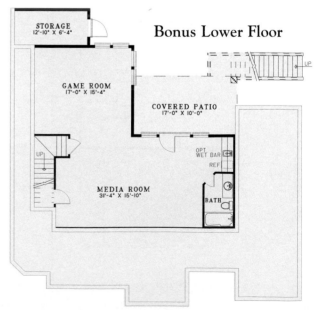

Nelson Design Group has created a French traditional home with an astonishing exterior. Walk through the brick arched entry and discover an equally impressive interior design. Entering through the foyer, you'll feel the openness in the great room that will prove to be the heart of the home. Breakfast tradition will begin in the kitchen with the kids waiting in the breakfast room for their meal. Spend evenings on the beautiful deck which is accessible from the master suite and great room. Upstairs, you'll find an optional bonus room, perfect as a playroom for the kids.

Width: 73' 4"
Depth: 51' 8"
Total Living: 1,871 sq. ft.*
*Upper Bonus: 390 sq. ft.
*Lower Bonus: 860 sq. ft.

Main Ceiling: 9 ft.
Bonus Ceilings: 8 ft.
Bedrooms: 3
Baths: 3 1/2
Foundation: Crawl, Slab, Basement
Daylight Basement

Price Tier: B

BEST SELLER
Designers Choice
NELSON DESIGN GROUP

483 Spruce Street

GRILLING PORCH
27'-0" X 10'-0"

BREAKFAST ROOM
9'-11" X 9'-7"

MASTER SUITE
13'-7" X 15'-0"
10' BOXED CEILING

GREAT ROOM
16'-0" X 17'-8"
10' BOXED CEILING

BEDROOM 2
11'-2" X 10'-6"

RG.

DW

KITCHEN
9'-11" X 14'-9"

REF. PAN.

8' COLUMNS

LIN

BEDROOM 3
10'-0" X 10'-4"

KNEE SPACE

M.BATH
13'-7" X 11'-0"

WHP TUB

W

D   LAU.

DINING ROOM
12'-6" X 12'-4"
10' CEILING

FOYER
8'-0" X 10'-4"
10' CEILING

LIN

BATH

STORAGE

7' COVERED PORCH
10' CEILING

BEDROOM 4
13'-6" X 12'-4"

DESK

OPTIONAL SIDE LOAD

GARAGE
19'-4" X 19'-6"

© 2000 NELSON DESIGN GROUP, LLC.

Multiple arches, alluring columns and a comfortable, covered porch welcome guests to this stylish Nelson Design Group home. The interior showcases an open, airy floor plan with smooth transitions and minimal wasted space. The large great room with ten foot boxed ceiling flowing into the formal dining room provides ample space for extravagant parties or casual gatherings. The secluded master suite offers a soothing, relaxing atmosphere after a long and busy day.

Width: 57' 0"
Depth: 61' 4"
Total Living: 1,880 sq. ft.

Main Ceiling: 9 ft.
Bedrooms: 4
Baths: 2
Foundation: Crawl, Slab, Basement, Daylight Basement

Price Tier: B

646 Quail Drive

Width: 76' 10"
Depth: 53' 4"
Total Living: 2,373 sq. ft.*
*Optional Bonus 1: 776 sq. ft.
*Optional Bonus 2: 896 sq. ft.
Main Ceiling: 9 ft.
Bonus Ceiling: 8 ft.
Bedrooms: 4
Baths: 3
Foundation: Crawl, Slab,
Optional Basement,
Optional Daylight Basement

Price Tier: C

— Featured Plan —

Main Floor

MASTER SUITE 17'-9" X 16'-4"
M. BATH 11'-10" X 23'-2"
LAUNDRY 8'-10" X 6'-4"
GARAGE 21'-0" X 22'-0"
STORAGE 7'-8" X 4'-4"
GRILLING PORCH 35'-10" X 10'-0"
BREAKFAST ROOM 12'-0" X 8'-0"
KITCHEN 12'-0" X 12'-0"
GREAT ROOM 19'-4" X 17'-8"
DINING 11'-10" X 12'-0"
FOYER 7'-0" X 11'-0"
BEDROOM 2/STUDY 12'-0" X 12'-0"
BEDROOM 4 12'-6" X 11'-0"
BEDROOM 3 11'-0" X 11'-0"
COVERED PORCH 33'-0" X 8'-0"

© 2002 NELSON DESIGN GROUP, LLC.

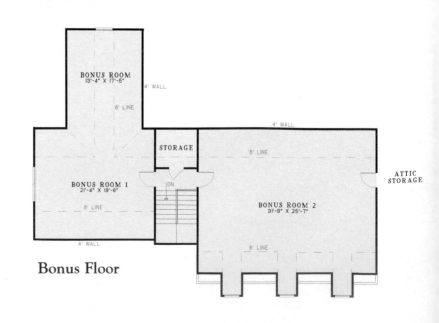

Bonus Floor

BONUS ROOM 13'-4" X 17'-5"
BONUS ROOM 1 21'-4" X 19'-6"
BONUS ROOM 2 31'-8" X 25'-7"
STORAGE
ATTIC STORAGE

Main Floor

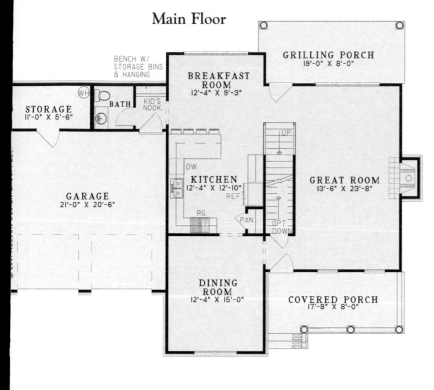

STORAGE
11'-0" X 5'-6"

BENCH W/ STORAGE BINS & HANGING

WH

BATH

KID'S NOOK

GARAGE
21'-0" X 20'-6"

BREAKFAST ROOM
12'-4" X 9'-3"

GRILLING PORCH
19'-0" X 8'-0"

DW

KITCHEN
12'-4" X 12'-10"

REF

RG.

PAN

UP

OPT DOWN

GREAT ROOM
13'-6" X 23'-8"

DINING ROOM
12'-4" X 15'-0"

COVERED PORCH
17'-8" X 8'-0"

Upper Floor

BEDROOM 3
12'-4" X 15'-0"

WHP TUB

M.BATH
12'-4" X 8'-4"

W.I.C.

LIN

D   W

BONUS ROOM
21'-0" X 13'-6"

BATH

DN

LIN

BENCH

MASTER SUITE
13'-6" X 15'-0"
9' BOXED CEILING

BEDROOM 2
12'-4" X 13'-8"

568 Cypress Drive

The quaint covered porch of this Nelson Design Group home will welcome friends and family alike. A spacious great room with fireplace accesses the rear-grilling porch perfect for entertaining. The kitchen and large breakfast room full of windows has additional bar seating and flows through to a formal dining room. For convenience, a kid's nook and half bath near the garage entry complete the main level. Traveling upstairs, you'll find a luxurious master suite, two additional bedrooms, a full bath and the laundry room. Family will love the bonus room, which can easily be converted into a TV area or game room.

Width: 54' 4"
Depth: 43' 0"
Main Floor: 998 sq. ft.
Upper Floor: 896 sq. ft.
Total Living: 1,894 sq. ft.*
*Optional Bonus: 300 sq. ft.

Main Ceiling: 9 ft.
Upper Ceiling: 8 ft.
Bedrooms: 3
Baths: 2 1/2
Foundation: Crawl, Slab,
Optional Basement,
Optional Daylight Basement

Price Tier: B

509 Mockingbird Lane

MASTER SUITE
10" BOXED CEILING
14'-0" X 15'-6"

WHP TUB

VAULTED CEILING

GLASS BLOCKS

W.I.C.
11'-8" X 5'-6"

STRG.

GARAGE
22'-10" X 20'-8"

TO OPTIONAL BASEMENT

BREAKFAST ROOM
10'-10" X 10'-7"

SCREENED PORCH
16'-0" X 12'-0"

REF.

KITCHEN
10'-10" X 11'-8"

PAN.

GREAT RM.
16'-0" X 20'-8"

DINING RM.
10' CEILING
12'-2" X 11'-4"

8" COLUMNS

FOYER
10' CEILING
7'-0" X 7'-10"

PORCH
7'-6" X 5'-2"

BEDROOM 3
12'-0" X 11'-6"

LIN

LIN

BEDROOM 2
12'-0" X 11'-10"

OPTIONAL VAULTED CEILING

© 2000 NELSON DESIGN GROUP LLC.

You'll enjoy entertaining in this elegant, open-space floor plan from Nelson Design Group. The dining room with column accents is ideal for formal dinner parties with coffee to follow in the spacious and comfortable great room where you'll find a cozy fireplace and easy access to the kitchen for snacks. When the guests have departed you can retire to your master suite for a relaxing soak in the large whirlpool tub or enjoy the privacy and comfort of the large, screened back porch.

Width: 56' 0"
Depth: 64' 4"
Total Living: 1,909 sq. ft.

Price Tier: B

Main Ceiling: 9 ft.
Bedrooms: 3
Baths: 2
Foundation: Crawl, Slab,
Optional Basement,
Optional Daylight Basement

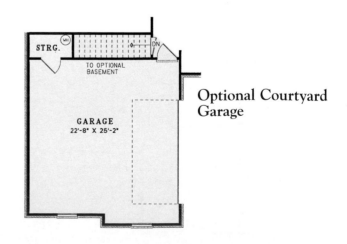

STRG.

TO OPTIONAL BASEMENT

GARAGE
22'-8" X 25'-2"

Optional Courtyard Garage

602 Olive Street

Main Floor

DECK

GRILLING PORCH
18'-0" X 12'-0"

BEDROOM 2
12'-2" X 12'-2"

DINING / HEARTH ROOM
13'-0" X 19'-6"

ATRIUM DOORS

LAU.
13'-8" X 6'-8"

W. D.

© 2002 NELSON DESIGN GROUP, LLC.

PAN.

GLASS SHWR

WHP TUB

GARAGE
23'-8" X 21'-4"

DW

KITCHEN
14'-5" X 18' 6"
RG

REF.

M.BATH
13'-8" X 13'-8"

BATH

LIN.

BEDROOM 3
12'-2" X 12'-2"

LIVING RM.
21'-0" X 16'-0"

MASTER SUITE
13'-8" X 13'-10"

MEDIA CENTER

UP

8' COVERED PORCH

Bonus Floor

4' WALL

ATTIC STORAGE

6'8" LINE

6'8" WALL

8' LINE

BATH

GAME ROOM
37'-4" X 18'-8"

8' LINE

DN.

6'8" LINE

VAULTED

4' WALL

HVAC

This low country home has a wrap around porch that everyone will fall in love with. Upon entering, the beautiful fireplace and media center make for great entertaining. The hearth room fireplace allows for more intimate gatherings. Notice the ample counter space in the kitchen as well as a convenient island bar. A large master suite provides plenty of storage space with your master bath sporting a magnificent corner whirlpool bath. Two additional bedrooms share a walk-through bathroom. Upstairs, find a full bath and large game room.

Width: 84' 0"
Depth: 55' 6"
Total Living: 1,921 sq. ft.*
*Optional Bonus: 812 sq. ft.

Price Tier: B

Main Ceiling: 8 ft.
Bonus Ceiling: 8 ft.
Bedrooms: 3
Baths: 3
Foundation: Crawl, Slab, Basement, Daylight Basement

566 Thomas Road

Main Floor

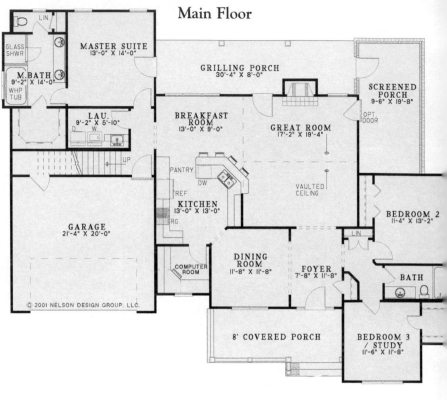

© 2001 NELSON DESIGN GROUP, LLC.

This southern traditional Nelson Design Group home has spacious family areas as well as a secluded master suite for the ultimate in privacy. Eight-foot covered porches are used on the front and rear of this lovely home in addition to a corner screened porch for pure enjoyment of the seasons. A vaulted ceiling enhances the great room, which is open to the kitchen allowing for ease in entertaining. A convenient computer room is hidden in the kitchen corner for the heads of the home to keep organized. Stairs located a few steps from the kitchen and master suite lead to a bonus room with creative ceiling heights and plenty of attic space.

Width: 67' 10"
Depth: 55' 6"
Total Living: 1,923 sq. ft.*
*Optional Bonus: 313 sq. ft.

Main Ceiling: 9 ft.
Bonus Ceiling: 8 ft.
Bedrooms: 3
Baths: 2
Foundation: Crawl, Slab,
Optional Basement,
Optional Daylight Basement

Price Tier: B

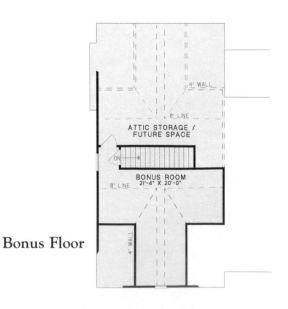

Bonus Floor

To order call 1.800.590.2423 or to view similar plans visit www.nelsondesigngroup.com

364 Cambridge Court

© 1999 NELSON DESIGN GROUP, LLC.

Entering through the foyer of this Nelson Design Group home, your guests will admire the magnificent columns which surround the dining room. Leading them into the great room, they can relax by the fireplace with conversation, while you finish preparing the evening meal in your spacious kitchen. Beautiful French doors lead your guests to the rear covered porch of your home for star gazing. As the guests leave for the evening, retreat to your master suite and bath. You'll enjoy the double vanities, 'his and her' walk-in closets and an alluring whirlpool bath.

Width: 63' 10"
Depth: 62' 10"
Total Living: 1,926 sq. ft.

Main Ceiling: 9 ft.
Bedrooms: 4
Baths: 2
Foundation: Crawl, Slab

Price Tier: B

205 Mockingbird Lane

BREAKFAST ROOM 9'-4" X 10'-11"

COVERED PORCH 18'-5" X 4'-0"

BEDROOM 4 13'-6" X 14'-6"

MASTER SUITE 15'-0" X 15'-0" 9' PAN CEILING

GREAT ROOM 9' BOX CEILING 15'-0" X 19'-6"

BUILT-INS

KITCHEN 9'-11" X 12'-7"

RG.

DW

REF.

PAN.

BATH

KNEE SPACE

M. BATH 15'-0" X 11'-8"

GLASS BLOCKS

WHP TUB

DINING ROOM 11'-6" X 9'-8"

FOYER 7'-0" X 7'-0"

BEDROOM 3 10'-0" X 10'-4"

LIN.

STORAGE

W

D

LAU.

HVAC

LIN

10" RND COL W/ BASE

4' PORCH

BEDROOM 2 12'-4" X 10'-6"

GARAGE 20'-10" X 20'-0"

© 1991 NELSON DESIGN GROUP, LLC.

Stately columns and a covered porch welcome you to this traditional Nelson Design Group four-bedroom home. The foyer ushers guests into your home with class and style. Built-in shelving in the boxed-ceiling great room takes advantage of the area next to the radiant fireplace for use as a media center or mini-library. The ample storage space provided by large walk-in closets throughout is sure to make organizing a snap. The luxuriously appointed master suite is located just off the breakfast room and features a nine foot pan ceiling.

Width: 58' 0"
Depth: 54' 10"
Total Living: 1,940 sq. ft.

Price Tier: B

Main Ceiling: 8 ft.
Bedrooms: 4
Baths: 2
Foundation: Crawl, Slab, Basement, Daylight Basement

To order call 1.800.590.2423 or to view similar plans visit www.nelsondesigngroup.com

468 Madison Drive

BRICK PRIVACY WALL

PATIO
16'-0" X 8'-0"

MASTER SUITE
9' BOXED CEILING
14'-0" X 15'-10"

BEDROOM 2
11'-0" X 12'-0"

BEDROOM 3
12'-0" X 12'-0"

WHP TUB

M.BATH
12'-0" X 15'-10"

LIN

LAU.
8'-2" X 6'-6"

W. D.

GAS BIBB

11' CEILING

LIN

HVAC

GRILLING PORCH

GREAT ROOM
12 BOXED CEILING
21'-2" X 17'-0"

BATH

STORAGE
9'-2" X 3'-6"

BEDROOM 4
12'-0" X 11'-0"

8" COLUMNS

OPTIONAL BASEMENT PLAN

BRKFAST ROOM
11'-10" X 8'-8"

DINING ROOM
11' CEILING
12'-0" X 11'-8"

FOYER
11' CEILING

GARAGE
21'-6" X 22'-4"

PAN.   REF.

KITCHEN
11'-10" X 9'-4"

RG.

DW

PORCH

© 2001 NELSON DESIGN GROUP, LLC.

This four-bedroom plan by Nelson Design Group has interior columns and high ceilings for an exceptional welcome. A formal dining room opens to the great room allowing guests to mingle before dinner or enjoy conversation on the grilling porch. The master suite features a nine foot ceiling and luxurious private bath as well as patio with a brick privacy wall for enjoying starlit evenings.

Width: 53' 0"
Depth: 53' 6"
Total Living: 1,950 sq. ft.

Price Tier: B

Main Ceiling: 8 ft.
Bedrooms: 4
Baths: 2
Foundation: Crawl, Slab,
Optional Basement,
Optional Daylight Basement

191

347 Maple Street

Best Seller · Designers Choice · Nelson Design Group

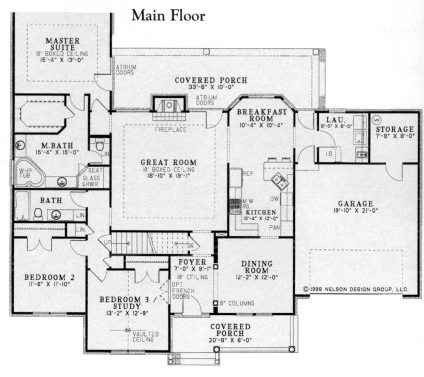

Main Floor

MASTER SUITE
10' BOXED CEILING
15'-4" X 13'-0"

COVERED PORCH
33'-8" X 10'-0"

ATRIUM DOORS

M. BATH
15'-4" X 15'-0"

WHP TUB

SEAT GLASS SHWR

BATH

FIREPLACE

GREAT ROOM
10' BOXED CEILING
18'-10" X 19'-1"

BREAKFAST ROOM
10'-4" X 10'-4"

LAU.
8'-0" X 8'-0"

STORAGE
7'-8" X 8'-0"

REF.

KITCHEN
10'-4" X 12'-0"

GARAGE
19'-10" X 21'-0"

UP

BEDROOM 2
11'-6" X 11'-10"

FOYER
7'-0" X 9'-1"
10' CEILING

DINING ROOM
12'-2" X 12'-0"

©1998 NELSON DESIGN GROUP, LLC.

BEDROOM 3 / STUDY
13'-2" X 12'-9"

OPT. FRENCH DOORS

8" COLUMNS

VAULTED CEILING

COVERED PORCH
20'-8" X 6'-0"

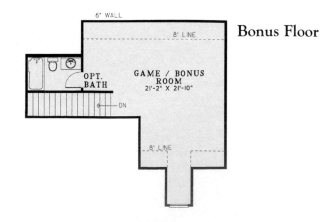

Bonus Floor

6" WALL

8' LINE

OPT. BATH

GAME / BONUS ROOM
21'-2" X 21'-10"

DN

8' LINE

If you yearn for a functional yet beautiful home, Nelson Design Group has created such a home. Once inside, eight inch columns frame the dining room entry, allowing for elegant dining. A spacious great room provides ample room and atrium door access to the rear covered porch. The third bedroom has a vaulted ceiling and optional french doors for the ultimate study. Once guests leave, your master bath with all the amenities will be the most relaxing place in your home. Upstairs, find an optional bonus room and full bath.

Width: 66' 0"
Depth: 55' 0"
Total Living: 1,957 sq. ft.*
*Optional Bonus: 479 sq. ft.

Price Tier: B

Main Ceiling: 9 ft.
Bonus Ceiling: 8 ft.
Bedrooms: 3
Baths: 3
Foundation: Crawl, Slab, Basement, Daylight Basement

To order call 1.800.590.2423 or to view similar plans visit www.nelsondesigngroup.com

544 Glendale Avenue

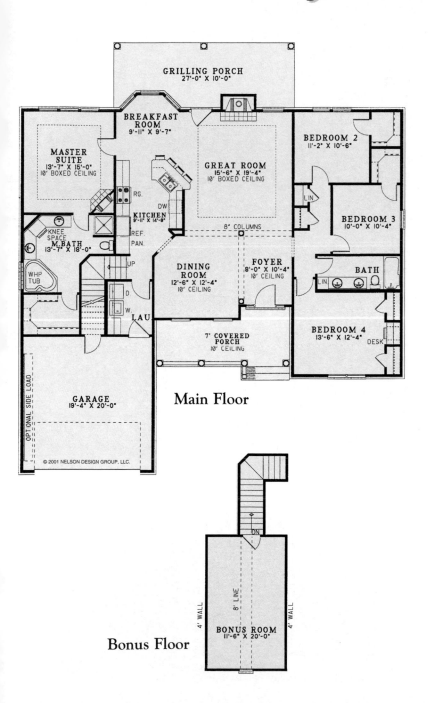

Main Floor

GRILLING PORCH
27'-0" X 10'-0"

BREAKFAST ROOM
9'-11" X 9'-7"

MASTER SUITE
13'-7" X 15'-0"
10' BOXED CEILING

GREAT ROOM
15'-6" X 19'-4"
10' BOXED CEILING

BEDROOM 2
11'-2" X 10'-6"

RG.

DW

KITCHEN
9'-11" X 14'-9"

REF. PAN.

KNEE SPACE

M.BATH
13'-7" X 18'-0"

WHP TUB

UP

8" COLUMNS

LIN

BEDROOM 3
10'-0" X 10'-4"

DINING ROOM
12'-6" X 12'-4"
10' CEILING

FOYER
8'-0" X 10'-4"
10' CEILING

BATH

LIN

D

W.

LAU

7' COVERED PORCH
10' CEILING

BEDROOM 4
13'-6" X 12'-4"

DESK

OPTIONAL SIDE LOAD

GARAGE
19'-4" X 20'-0"

© 2001 NELSON DESIGN GROUP, LLC.

Bonus Floor

DN

4' WALL

8' LINE

4' WALL

BONUS ROOM
11'-6" X 20'-0"

Elevation A

Elevation B

Tall columns and ten foot ceilings add elegance to an open floor plan in this split-bedroom Nelson Design Group home. The foyer flows effortlessly into the dining and great rooms. The bay-windowed breakfast room provides a sunny alternative to the formal dining room and affords a lively view of the back yard and grilling porch. With a large whirlpool tub, boxed ceiling and cozy corner fireplace, the master suite is truly a private sanctuary.

Width: 57' 0"
Depth: 64' 4"
Total Living: 1,965 sq. ft.*
*Optional Bonus: 251 sq. ft.

Price Tier: B

Main Ceiling: 9 ft.
Bonus Ceiling: 8 ft.
Bedrooms: 4
Baths: 2
Foundation: Crawl, Slab,
Optional Basement,
Optional Daylight Basement

381 Hickory Place

12' x 12' BRICK COLUMNS

© 1999 NELSON DESIGN GROUP, LLC.

M.BATH 14'-10" X 14'-4"

KNEE SPACE

WHP TUB

8" COLUMNS

MASTER SUITE 14'-10" X 15'-6"

COVERED PORCH 16'-2" X 9'-0"

GRILLING PORCH 12'-4" X 6'-0"

ATRIUM DOOR

LAU. 8'-10" X 5'-8"

STORAGE 11'-8" X 5'-8"

FIREPLACE

BREAKFAST ROOM 11'-8" X 10'-6"

OFFICE 14'-10" X 10'-6"

GREAT ROOM 10' CEILING 16'-2" X 20'-0"

BUILT-INS

D.W.

KITCHEN 11'-8" X 12'-6"

GARAGE 20'-10" X 20'-0"

PAN

REF

BATH

LIN

FOYER 10' CEILING 7'-0" X 9'-6"

DINING ROOM 10' CEILING 11'-8" X 11'-6"

BEDROOM 2 11'-10" X 11'-6"

BEDROOM 3 11'-10" X 11'-2"

PORCH 7'-0" X 4'-4"

VAULT   VAULT

Enter the brick arched entry of this Nelson Design Group creation and prepare for the perfect home. An inviting great room with a romantic fireplace is a comfortable gathering room while a formal dining room allows for elegant entertaining. The kitchen adjoins a large breakfast room with atrium door to the rear grilling porch. The master suite features a private office and has the ultimate master bathroom. A corner whirlpool tub is framed by columns and a large walk-in closet, shower and private toilet.

Width: 65' 2"
Depth: 63' 0"
Total Living: 1,994 sq. ft.

Price Tier: B

Main Ceiling: 9 ft.
Bedrooms: 3
Baths: 2
Foundation: Crawl, Slab, Basement, Daylight Basement

To order call 1.800.590.2423 or to view similar plans visit www.nelsondesigngroup.com

517 Belmont Avenue

BEST SELLER
Designers Choice
NELSON DESIGN GROUP

Elevation A

Elevation B

BATH

BRKFST RM.
12'-4" X 9'-6"

GRILLING PORCH
15'-0" X 10'-0"

OPT. DOOR

OPT. FIREPLACE

M.BATH
8'-10" X 21'-0"

K.S.

WHP TUB

GUEST BEDROOM/DEN/STUDY
12'-8" X 11'-6"

KIT.
12'-4" X 13'-6"

DW.

RG.

MASTER SUITE
10' BOXED CEILING
13'-4" X 15'-8"

GREAT RM.
10' CEILING
15'-0" X 18'-4"

W.I.C.

LAU.
5'-6" X 5'-10"

D W

REF.

PAN.

BATH

LIN.

LIN.

STORAGE WH

8" COLUMNS

FOYER
7'-4" X 7'-10"

GARAGE
20'-10" X 23'-0"

DINING RM.
10' BOX CEILING
12'-2" X 13'-4"

PORCH

BEDROOM 3
11'-0" X 10'-4"

VAULTED CEILING

BEDROOM 2
11'-2" X 11'-6"

© 2001 NELSON DESIGN GROUP, LLC.

This impressive Nelson Design Group home offers you two different exterior finishes. Full brick or siding will enable you to determine the overall style you want. High ceilings and a rear-grilling porch will be focal points when entertaining. The master suite has a ten foot boxed ceiling and lovely private bathroom with a whirlpool tub and large walk-in closet. If a study or home office is desired, consider the fourth bedroom, which is conveniently located next to the kitchen and breakfast room.

Width: 64' 2"
Depth: 52' 0"
Total Living: 1,989 sq. ft.

Price Tier: B

Main Ceiling: 9 ft.
Bedrooms: 4
Baths: 3
Foundation: Crawl, Slab,
Optional Basement,
Optional Daylight Basement

163 Emery Lane

Main Floor

© 1996 NELSON DESIGN GROUP, LLC.

GARAGE
20'-4" X 21'-4"

GRILLING PORCH
36'-2" X 8'-0"

LAU.

WHP. TUB

GLASS SHWR.

M.BATH
16'-6" X 12'-2"

GREAT ROOM
16'-6" X 17'-4"

KITCHEN
10'-8" X 17'-4"

REF. PAN.

RG.

D.W.

MASTER SUITE
12'-8" X 16'-10"

BREAKFAST ROOM
8'-8" X 9'-8"

DINING ROOM
12'-8" X 11'-8"

FOYER
9'-4" X 12'-0"
UP

COVERED PORCH
37'-0" X 8'-0"

This Nelson Design Group home reflects true southern charm hosting both a front covered porch and large rear-grilling porch for the ultimate in family gatherings. Upon entering the foyer, stairs will lead you to an upstairs complete with two bedrooms each with large walk-in closets and private access to a shared bath. A luxurious master suite complete with a corner whirlpool tub, glass shower and large walk-in closet is located on the main floor for both convenience and privacy. A formal dining room gently accesses the kitchen and breakfast room for ease in entertaining.

Width: 56' 8"
Depth: 65' 8"
Main Floor: 1,352 sq. ft.
Upper Floor: 673 sq. ft.
Total Living: 2,025 sq. ft.

Main Ceiling: 8 ft.
Upper Ceiling: 8 ft.
Bedrooms: 3
Baths: 2 1/2
Foundation: Crawl, Slab,
Optional Basement,
Optional Daylight Basement

Price Tier: C

Upper Floor

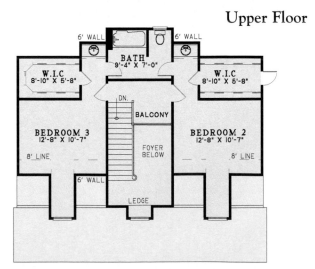

6' WALL

6' WALL

BATH
9'-4" X 7'-0"

W.I.C
8'-10" X 5'-8"

W.I.C
8'-10" X 5'-8"

DN.

BALCONY

8' LINE

BEDROOM 3
12'-8" X 10'-7"

FOYER BELOW

BEDROOM 2
12'-8" X 10'-7"

8' LINE

6' WALL

LEDGE

472-1 Mockingbird Lane

Main Floor

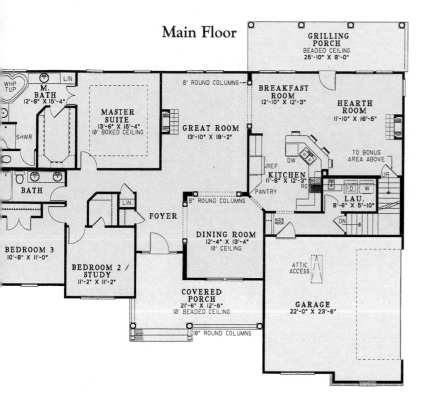

GRILLING PORCH
BEADED CEILING
25'-10" X 8'-0"

8' ROUND COLUMNS

BREAKFAST ROOM
12'-10" X 12'-3"

HEARTH ROOM
11'-10" X 16'-5"

WHP TUP

M. BATH
12'-8" X 15'-4"

LIN.

MASTER SUITE
13'-6" X 15'-4"
10' BOXED CEILING

GREAT ROOM
13'-10" X 19'-2"

TO BONUS AREA ABOVE

SHWR

REF. DW

KITCHEN
11'-8" X 12'-3"

UP

BATH

PANTRY

RG

LAU.
8'-6" X 5'-10"

LIN.

KID'S NOOK

FOYER

8' ROUND COLUMNS

DN

DINING ROOM
12'-4" X 13'-4"
10' CEILING

BEDROOM 3
10'-8" X 11'-0"

BEDROOM 2 / STUDY
11'-2" X 11'-2"

ATTIC ACCESS

COVERED PORCH
21'-6" X 12'-6"
10' BEADED CEILING

GARAGE
22'-0" X 23'-6"

10" ROUND COLUMNS

Bonus Floor

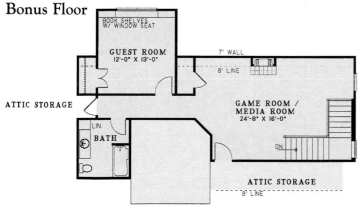

BOOK SHELVES W/ WINDOW SEAT

GUEST ROOM
12'-0" X 13'-0"

7' WALL

8' LINE

ATTIC STORAGE

LIN.

BATH

GAME ROOM / MEDIA ROOM
24'-8" X 16'-0"

DN

ATTIC STORAGE

8' LINE

Y ou'll enjoy entertaining family during those frigid winter months as holiday visitors gather around one of the three inviting fireplaces in this stunning Nelson Design Group two-story country home. The open floor plan allows everyone plenty of room to roam and the expansive kitchen allows for effortless service to all living areas. Overnight guests will enjoy the view from their window seat snuggled within an entire wall of built-in bookshelves. The luxurious master suite features a corner whirlpool bath with ample natural lighting and a ten foot boxed ceiling.

Width: 66' 4"
Depth: 58' 7"
Total Living: 2,029 sq. ft.*
*Optional Bonus: 754 sq. ft.

Main Ceiling: 9 ft.
Bonus Ceiling: 8 ft.
Bedrooms: 4
Baths: 3
Foundation: Crawl, Slab, Basement, Daylight Basement

Price Tier: C

320 Olive Street

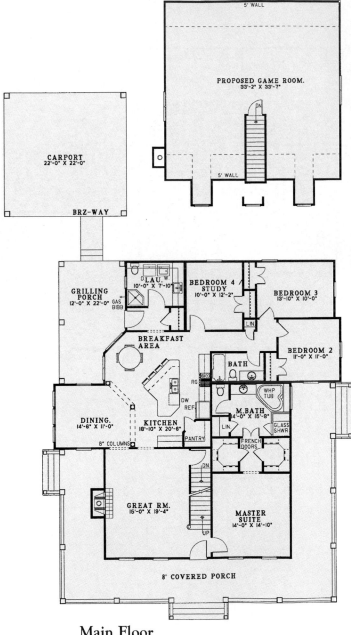

Bonus Floor

CARPORT
22'-0" X 22'-0"

BRZ-WAY

PROPOSED GAME ROOM.
33'-2" X 33'-7"

5' WALL

Main Floor

This Nelson Design Group plan showcases a deep, wraparound front porch for summer shade, panoramic views and more than enough space for comfortable outside entertaining. When the weather turns cool everyone can warm their toes in front of the great room's fireplace while hot chocolate is being prepared in the nearby walk-through kitchen. The snack bar, breakfast room and formal dining room offer several mealtime options. 'His and her' walk-in closets surround elegant french doors in the master suite leading to the well-appointed sizable bath.

Width: 60' 6"
Depth: 91' 4"
Total Living: 2,039 sq. ft. *
*Optional Bonus: 1,155 sq. ft.

Price Tier: C

Main Ceiling: 9 ft.
Bonus Ceiling: 8 ft.
Bedrooms: 4
Baths: 3
Foundation: Crawl, Slab,
Optional Basement,
Optional Daylight Basement

To order call 1.800.590.2423 or to view similar plans visit www.nelsondesigngroup.com

162 Alexander Drive

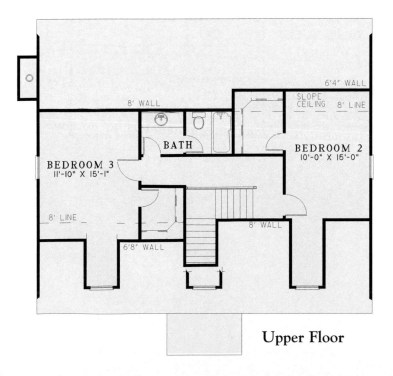

Main Floor

BUILT-IN MEDIA CENTER

DEN
21'-6" X 13'-2"

MASTER SUITE
11'-8" X 14'-7"

RAISED BAR

C.T.

KITCHEN
17'-2" X 10'-0"

DW

D   W

M.BATH
7'-10" X 8'-4"

OVEN   REF   PANTRY

SLOPE CEILING

DINING ROOM
17'-2" X 10'-6"

UP

BOOK SHELVES

LIVING RM./OFFICE
16'-0" X 10'-9"

PORCH
9'-0" X 5'-0"

10" RND COLUMNS

Upper Floor

6'4" WALL

8' WALL

SLOPE CEILING   8' LINE

BATH

BEDROOM 2
10'-0" X 15'-0"

BEDROOM 3
11'-10" X 15'-1"

8' LINE

8' WALL

6'8" WALL

This Nelson Design Group home seems to beckon to all who step upon the porch. The den welcomes your presence beside the fireplace or enjoy the built-in media center. The kitchen offers a snack bar for informal meals to be shared. The living room stands quietly ready to be your retreat for completing the day's paperwork or enjoying a book showcased upon the built-in book shelves. The master suite offers the ease of two walk-in closets while the bath provides a haven for relaxation in the whirlpool tub. The upper floor calls to the children with their own walk-in closets and shared full bath.

Width: 42' 4"
Depth: 40' 0"
Main Floor: 1,400 sq. ft.
Upper Floor: 644 sq. ft.
Total Living: 2,044 sq. ft.

Main Ceiling: 9 ft.
Upper Ceiling: 8 ft.
Bedrooms: 3
Baths: 2 1/2
Foundation: Crawl, Slab,
Optional Basement,
Optional Daylight Basement

Price Tier: C

110 Dogwood Avenue

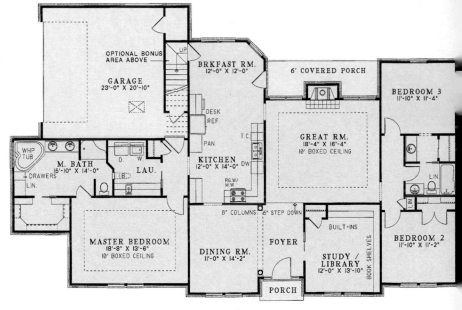

Imagine coming home to this French Classic Nelson Design Group home. Upon entering this split bedroom design you'll be enchanted by the elegance of the formal dining room with eight inch columns complete with easy access to the kitchen and breakfast room with a beautiful rear view. Spending time with family will be heart-felt in the great room with fireplace, or just spend some time alone reading in the study/library with built-ins and bookshelves. The children will have their own space and shared bath on one side of the house, while you have some privacy on the other in the master bedroom complete with master bath, huge walk-in closet and access to the laundry room. This plan is complete with all the amenities you'll need to call it home.

Width: 71' 10"
Depth: 46' 0"
Total Living: 2,092 sq. ft.

Main Ceiling: 9 ft.
Bedrooms: 3
Baths: 2
Foundation: Crawl, Slab,
Optional Basement,
Optional Daylight Basement

Price Tier: C

255 Cherry Street

Elevation B

Imagine the compliments you'll receive while hosting a dinner party in this exquisite home from Nelson Design Group. Guests will marvel at the gallery lined with built-in bookshelves and the massive great room with elegant fireplace and high ceilings throughout. A stylish French door allows the dinner party to transition outside to the vast covered grilling porch. When the party is over, you can relax in the beautiful breakfast bay before retiring to the master suite enhanced by his and her walk-in closets and oversized whirlpool bath.

Width: 69' 2"
Depth: 74' 10"
Total Living: 2,096 sq. ft.

Price Tier: C

Main Ceiling: 8 ft.
Bedrooms: 3
Baths: 2 1/2
Foundation: Crawl, Slab,
Optional Basement,
Optional Daylight Basement

190 Cherry Street

Elevation A

BEST SELLER
Designers Choice
NELSON DESIGN GROUP

Elevation B

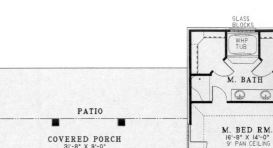

GLASS BLOCKS
WHP TUB
M. BATH
M. BED RM.
16'-8" X 14'-0"
9' PAN CEILING

PATIO

COVERED PORCH
31'-8" X 9'-0"

BED RM. 4
14'-4" X 11'-0"

BRKFST. RM.
12'-6" X 9'-6"

KITCHEN
12'-6" X 10'-0"

I.B. LAU.

LIN.

BATH

GREAT RM.
19'-6" X 17'-0"
10' CEILING

REF

PAN

1/2 B.

STOR.

HVAC

WB

BUILT-INS
(OPT. TO STUDY)

BED RM. 3
10'-6" X 12'-0"

OPT DOOR

DW

OVEN

CT

FOYER
10' CEILING

DINING RM.
11'-0" X 12'-0"
9' CEILING

GARAGE
20'-4" X 21'-0"

BED RM. 2 / STUDY
11'-0" X 12'-0"

PORCH

8' CEILING

PLANTER

© 1998 NELSON DESIGN GROUP, LLC.

Imagine welcoming guests into this Nelson Design Group split bedroom home. The spacious dining room will be superb for your formal dinner parties followed by coffee in the comfortable great room. The morning sun rays shining through the bay window of the breakfast room is a beautiful beginning to each day. As night falls, your secluded master suite has a private access to the rear porch - perfect for watching the sun set. Rest and relaxation is found in your luxurious master bath with whirlpool bath and 'his and her' walk-in closets provide ample storage space.

Width: 64' 8"
Depth: 62' 1"
Total Living: 2,107 sq. ft.

Price Tier: C

Main Ceiling: 8 ft.
Bedrooms: 4
Baths: 2 1/2
Foundation: Crawl, Slab, Basement, Daylight Basement

256 Olive Street

Fashion and function collaborate in this split-bedroom Nelson Design Group home tailor-made for your active lifestyle. Barrier-free transitions among the living areas create an ideal entertainment environment. Skylights bring natural lighting to the impressive great room and open, visitor-friendly kitchen that share a vaulted ceiling. The gorgeous master suite also features a vaulted ceiling, French doors leading to the bath, his and her walk-in closets and a large whirlpool tub. During harsh weather, the family can feel at ease in the built-in storm shelter.

Width: 63' 10"
Depth: 72' 2"
Total Living: 2,131 sq. ft.

Price Tier: C

Main Ceiling: 9 ft.
Bedrooms: 3
Baths: 2 1/2
Foundation: Crawl, Slab,
Optional Basement,
Optional Daylight Basement

562 Thomas Road

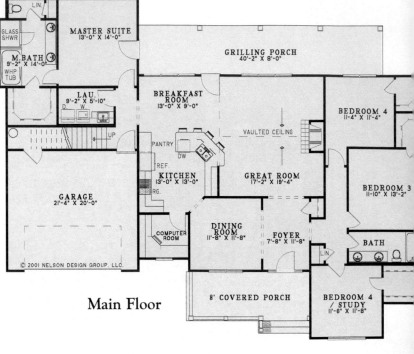

Main Floor

MASTER SUITE 13'-0" X 14'-0"
GLASS SHWR
M.BATH 9'-2" X 14'-0"
WHP TUB
LIN.
GRILLING PORCH 40'-2" X 8'-0"
BREAKFAST ROOM 13'-0" X 9'-0"
LAU. 9'-2" X 5'-10"
VAULTED CEILING
BEDROOM 4 11'-4" X 11'-4"
UP
PANTRY
DW
KITCHEN 13'-0" X 13'-0"
REF.
GREAT ROOM 17'-2" X 19'-4"
BEDROOM 3 11'-10" X 13'-2"
GARAGE 21'-4" X 20'-0"
COMPUTER ROOM
DINING ROOM 11'-8" X 11'-8"
FOYER 7'-8" X 11'-8"
BATH
LIN
© 2001 NELSON DESIGN GROUP, LLC.
8' COVERED PORCH
BEDROOM 4 / STUDY 11'-6" X 11'-8"

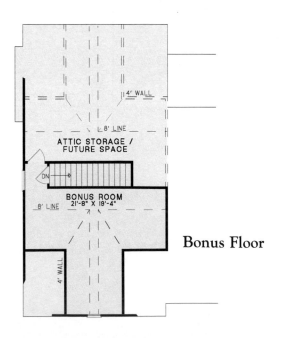

Bonus Floor

4' WALL
8' LINE
ATTIC STORAGE / FUTURE SPACE
DN
BONUS ROOM 21'-8" X 19'-4"
8' LINE
4' WALL

This traditional Nelson Design Group offering accentuates the neighborhood with a cozy covered porch. Inside, convenience expounds. The expansive great room offers vaulted ceilings and cozy fireplace. The kitchen, featuring a computer room and snack bar, opens to the breakfast room affording easy entry to the rear-grilling porch. One of the bedrooms can be converted into a study. All bedrooms offer spacious walk-in closets. The master bath showcases a whirlpool tub, double vanities, and glass shower.

Width: 69' 10"
Depth: 55' 6"
Total Living: 2,169 sq. ft. *
*Optional Bonus: 319 sq. ft.

Main Ceiling: 9 ft.
Bonus Ceiling: 8 ft.
Bedrooms: 4
Baths: 2
Foundation: Crawl, Slab

Price Tier: C

To order call 1.800.590.2423 or to view similar plans visit www.nelsondesigngroup.com

Main Floor

10x10 BOXED COLUMNS

CARPORT
22'-0" X 22'-0"

COVERED WALK

PORCH
12'-0" X 22'-0"

GLASS SHWR

LAU.
10'-2" X 7'-10"

BEDROOM 4
STUDY
10'-0" X 12'-2"

BEDROOM 3
13'-10" X 10'-0"

LIN.

BREAKFAST AREA
18'-10" X 9'-2"

BATH

BEDROOM 2
13'-4" X 11'-0"

DW.

ISLAND

DINING ROOM
14'-0" X 11'-0"

KITCHEN
13'-6" X 16'-6"

RG.

REF.

PANTRY

M.BATH
17'-10" X 14'-4"

WHP TUB

GLASS BLOCKS

SEAT

LIN.

FRENCH DOORS

GREAT ROOM
15'-0" X 19'-4"

BUILT-INS

MASTER SUITE
14'-8" X 14'-10"

UP

FOYER

PORCH
38'-8" X 8'-0"

© 1998 NELSON DESIGN GROUP, LLC.

10x10 BOXED COLUMNS

Bonus Floor

8' LINE

PROPOSED GAME ROOM
37'-0" X 33'-7"

8' LINE

5' WALL

340 Olive Street

R. Nelson

Mom will be so proud as she visits you in this delightful Nelson Design Group home. She'll marvel at the amount of space available throughout the design and find the unique island in the kitchen a clever idea. A convenient shower in the laundry room is ideal when the children stampede in covered with mud. After the kids are tucked away into bed for the evening, you can finally retreat to your master suite for your own relaxation. Solitude within the confines of the luxurious corner whirlpool bath is a wonderful way to unwind.

Width: 62' 10"
Depth: 91' 4"
Total Living: 2,186 sq. ft.*
*Optional Bonus: 1,283 sq. ft.

Main Ceiling: 9 ft.
Upper Ceiling: 8 ft.
Bedrooms: 4
Baths: 3
Foundation: Crawl, Slab, Basement, Daylight Basement

Price Tier: C

549 Madison Drive

Elevation A

Elevation B

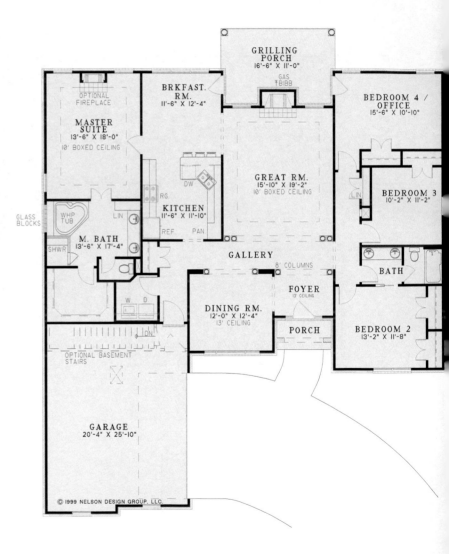

This exceptional Nelson Design Group home has a beautiful arched entry porch and exterior options for your perfect setting. High ceilings and eight-inch columns are used throughout the family areas including a formal dining room and expansive great room with boxed ceiling and cozy fireplace. A well-designed kitchen with bar seating and plenty of storage adjoins the breakfast room accessing a rear-grilling porch. The private master suite has an optional fireplace and luxurious bathroom including a large corner whirlpool tub. One of the three additional bedrooms makes for a perfect home office or library.

Width: 58' 0"
Depth: 69' 6"
Total Living: 2,189 sq. ft.

Price Tier: C

Main Ceiling: 9 ft.
Bedrooms: 4
Baths: 2
Foundation: Crawl, Slab,
Optional Basement,
Optional Daylight Basement

467 Kensington Cove

The exquisite exterior of this Nelson Design Group split-bedroom home hints at the stylish features waiting to be found inside. Meticulous living spaces evolve from the foyer and all share ten foot ceilings. Enjoy an appetizer by the fireplace or step outside and lounge on the festive patio until mealtime. The breakfast room merges with the kitchen allowing conversation during clean up. The master suite is accented by a boxed ceiling, 'his and her' walk-in closets and a marvelous step-up whirlpool tub.

Width: 65' 2"	Main Ceiling: 8 ft.
Depth: 63' 8"	Bedrooms: 4
Total Living: 2,210 sq. ft.	Baths: 2 1/2
	Foundation: Crawl, Slab

Price Tier: C

604 Cypress Drive

This craftsman style Nelson Design Group plan has everything that a family needs. A foyer leads into the formal dining room, which can be used as a study if desired. The great room with fireplace views the upper balcony and accesses the rear-grilling porch, perfect for entertaining. Nearby a breakfast room and kitchen combination with an angled bar counter provides extra seating, plenty of windows for natural light and is perfect for the ultimate Sunday brunch. The master suite has a private bath full of amenities. Upstairs houses the three additional bedrooms, full bath and optional game room.

Width: 41' 8"
Depth: 55' 6"
Main Floor: 1,449 sq. ft.
Upper Floor: 795 sq. ft.
Total Living: 2,244 sq. ft.*
*Optional Bonus: 181 sq. ft.

Main Ceiling: 9 ft.
Upper Ceiling: 8 ft.
Bedrooms: 4
Baths: 2 1/2
Foundation: Crawl, Slab,
              Optional Basement,
              Optional Daylight Basement

Price Tier: C

Main Floor

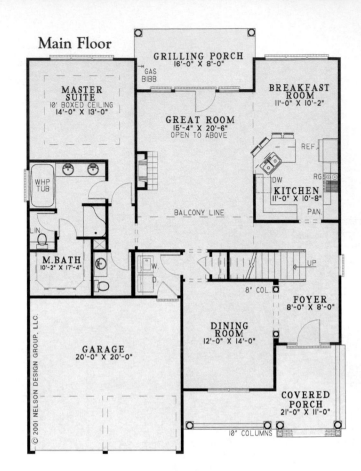

Upper Floor

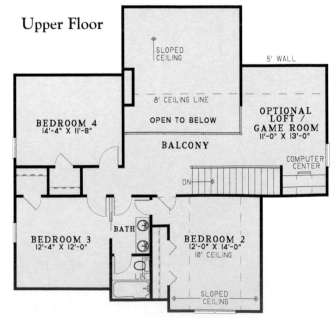

To order call 1.800.590.2423 or to view similar plans visit www.nelsondesigngroup.com

275 Olive Street

Main Floor

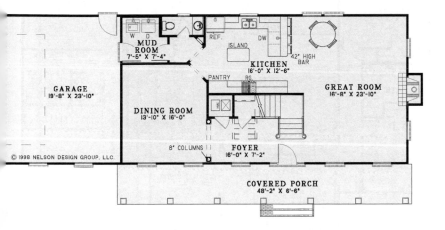

GARAGE
19'-8" X 23'-10"

MUD ROOM
7'-5" X 7'-4"

W D

REF. DW

ISLAND

KITCHEN
16'-0" X 12'-6"

42" HIGH BAR

PANTRY RG

DINING ROOM
13'-10" X 16'-0"

GREAT ROOM
16'-8" X 23'-10"

8" COLUMNS

FOYER
16'-0" X 7'-2"

© 1998 NELSON DESIGN GROUP, LLC.

COVERED PORCH
48'-2" X 6'-6"

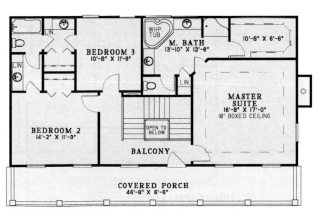

LIN

WHP. TUB

BEDROOM 3
10'-8" X 11'-9"

M. BATH
13'-10" X 12'-0"

10'-8" X 6'-6"

LIN

LIN

LIN

BEDROOM 2
14'-2" X 11'-9"

MASTER SUITE
16'-8" X 17'-0"
10' BOXED CEILING

OPEN TO BELOW

BALCONY

COVERED PORCH
46'-8" X 6'-6"

Upper Floor

This is definitely the life. A gorgeous Southern Traditional Nelson Design Group home offering almost everything. Family can gather around a cozy fireplace in the great room or enjoy the roomy kitchen/dining area. Magnificent columns welcome your guests into the grand dining room with fluid access to the kitchen for ease and meal preparation. A mud room with half bath is located at the garage entry. The children have the benefit of shared access to their bathroom upstairs with you close by in your master suite. A corner whirlpool tub will become a favorite haven for your relaxation, with a spacious walk-in closet conveniently located nearby.

Width: 69' 6"
Depth: 31' 0"
Main Floor: 1,154 sq. ft.
Upper Floor: 1,093 sq. ft.
Total Living: 2,247 sq. ft.

Price Tier: C

Main Ceiling: 9 ft.
Upper Ceiling: 9 ft.
Bedrooms: 3
Baths: 2 1/2
Foundation: Crawl, Slab, Basement, Daylight Basement

To order call 1.800.590.2423 or to view similar plans visit www.nelsondesigngroup.com

620 Emery Lane

Main Floor

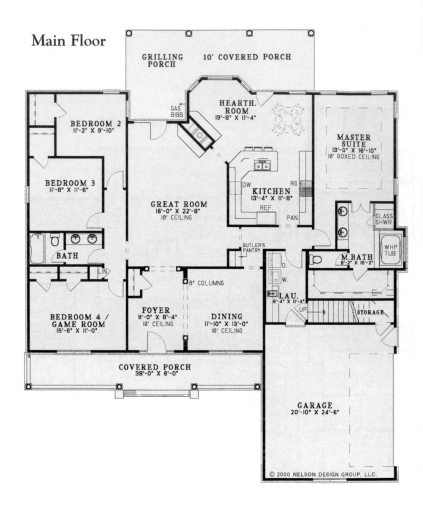

Round columns and ten-foot ceilings add elegance, while secluded bedrooms are pleasant retreats in this Nelson Design Group home. The formal dining room has access to the kitchen through a butler's pantry making hosting dinner parties much easier. After dinner enjoy coffee and conversation in front of the cozy double-sided hearth room fireplace or enjoy stargazing on the rear grilling porch. Once the evening has ended, retreat to your master suite enhanced by a ten foot boxed ceiling and spacious private bathroom packed with amenities. Conveniently located nearby is a laundry room with sink and countertop. Upstairs you'll find a full bathroom and a large bonus room.

Width: 61' 0"
Depth: 71' 8"
Total Living: 2,338 sq. ft.*
*Optional Bonus: 553 sq. ft.

Price Tier: C

Main Ceiling: 9 ft.
Bonus Ceiling: 8 ft.
Bedrooms: 4
Baths: 2
Foundation: Crawl, Slab,
Optional Basement,
Optional Daylight Basement

Bonus Floor

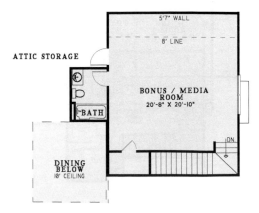

212

To order call 1.800.590.2423 or to view similar plans visit www.nelsondesigngroup.com

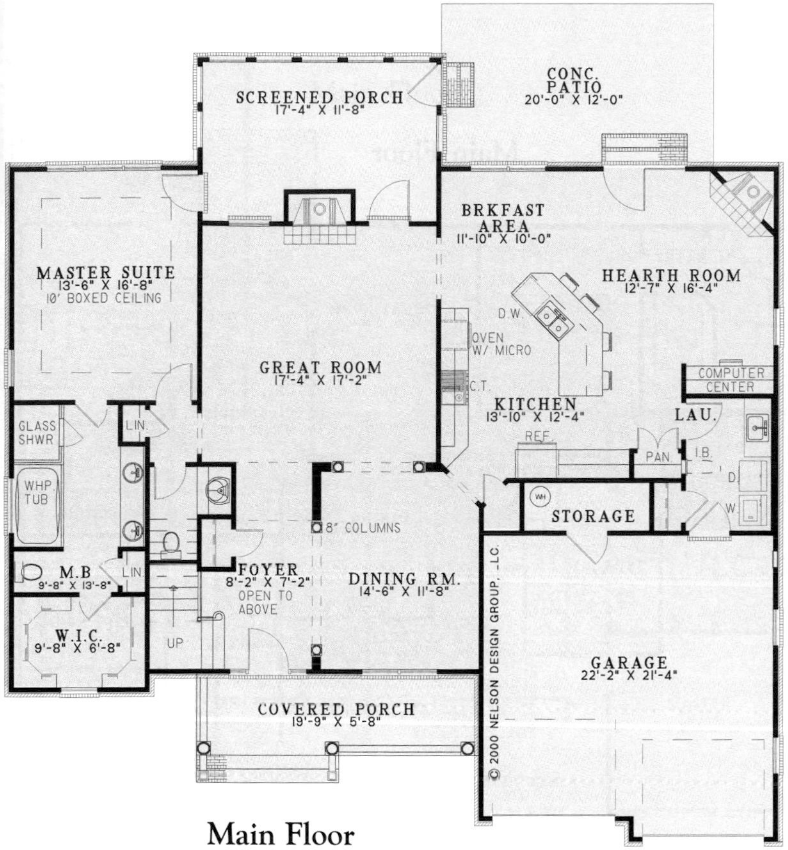

511 Magnolia Drive

Main Floor

Main Floor labels:
- SCREENED PORCH 17'-4" X 11'-8"
- CONC. PATIO 20'-0" X 12'-0"
- MASTER SUITE 13'-6" X 16'-8" 10' BOXED CEILING
- BRKFAST AREA 11'-10" X 10'-0"
- HEARTH ROOM 12'-7" X 16'-4"
- GREAT ROOM 17'-4" X 17'-2"
- D.W.
- OVEN W/ MICRO
- COMPUTER CENTER
- KITCHEN 13'-10" X 12'-4"
- LAU.
- GLASS SHWR
- LIN.
- REF.
- C.T.
- PAN.
- I.B.
- WHP TUB
- STORAGE
- W.H.
- D
- W
- M.B 9'-8" X 13'-8"
- LIN
- FOYER 8'-2" X 7'-2" OPEN TO ABOVE
- DINING RM. 14'-6" X 11'-8"
- 8" COLUMNS
- W.I.C. 9'-8" X 6'-8"
- UP
- GARAGE 22'-2" X 21'-4"
- COVERED PORCH 19'-9" X 5'-8"
- © 2000 NELSON DESIGN GROUP, LC

Upper Floor

Upper Floor labels:
- SLOPED CEILING
- WINDOW SEAT
- W.I.C. 6'-0" X 5'-11"
- OPEN TO BELOW
- BEDROOM 3 / LOFT 11'-3" X 18'-0"
- OPTIONAL WET BAR FOR LOFT ROOM
- BATH
- LIN
- DN.
- PLANT LEDGE
- FOYER BELOW 8'-2" X 12'-1"
- BEDROOM 2 12'-0" X 11'-0"
- BONUS ROOM 10'-0" X 21'-10"
- 8' LINE
- SLOPED CEILING

Neighbors will surely envy the elegant exterior of this charming Nelson Design Group home with its welcoming porch and gabled-roof line. Inside, the two-story foyer blends wonderfully with the column-accented formal dining room and opens into the vast great room anchored by a stately fireplace. Enjoy casual meals by the fireplace as the hearth room flows barrier-free into the breakfast area and kitchen. Upstairs the loft bedroom steals the show with its extra-wide window seat, walk-in closet and private entrance to the upstairs bath.

Width: 56' 8"	Main Ceiling: 9 ft.
Depth: 57' 4"	Upper Ceiling: 8 ft.
Main Floor: 1,776 sq. ft.	Bedrooms: 3
Upper Floor: 584 sq. ft.	Baths: 2 1/2
Total Living: 2,360 sq. ft.*	Foundation: Crawl, Slab,
*Optional Bonus: 262 sq. ft.	Optional Basement,
	Optional Daylight Basement

Price Tier: C

149 Kensington Cove

A sleek roofline and sheltered entry accent the stately elegance of this sprawling four-bedroom Nelson Design Group home. Once inside you will immediately notice the decorative columns leading to the formal dining room. The comforting great room fireplace serves as a central gathering point before heading through the atrium doors to the large covered porch. The family chef can entertain at the island bar while preparing the evening feast in the spacious kitchen. The deluxe master suite features his and her walk-in closets, private entrance to the porch, and a raised corner whirlpool bath.

Width: 67' 2"
Depth: 71' 8"
Total Living: 2,392 sq. ft.

Price Tier: C

Main Ceiling: 8 ft.
Bedrooms: 4
Baths: 2 1/2
Foundation: Crawl, Slab, Basement,
Daylight Basement

514 Kensington Cove

Elevation A

Main Floor

© 2001 NELSON DESIGN GROUP, LLC.

Bonus Floor

Elevation B

T he vast areas of this wide-open floor plan from Nelson Design Group provide the perfect atmosphere to host both formal and casual gatherings. Decorative columns adorn the transition from the extended foyer to the open areas of the formal dining and great rooms. Comfort abounds in the open kitchen area with its island bar, combined with the sunny breakfast room and built-in computer station. Optional gas fireplaces and built-ins provide just the right finishing touches to customize and personalize this astonishing home.

Width: 66' 4"
Depth: 54' 2"
Total Living: 2,394 sq. ft.*
*Optional Bonus: 202 sq. ft.

Price Tier: C

Main Ceiling: 9 ft.
Bonus Ceiling: 8 ft.
Bedrooms: 4
Baths: 2
Foundation: Crawl, Slab,
Optional Basement,
Optional Daylight Basement

204 Richmond Drive

C asual sensibility intertwined with exciting angles defines this dazzling four-bedroom Nelson Design Group home. The impressive gallery demands attention with its french door entry into the large study and boxed columns detailing the formal dining room and family room. The openness of the pass-through fireplace merging with the spacious kitchen and sunny breakfast room promotes a cozy and casual atmosphere ideal for family fun and entertainment. A large master suite includes wonderful amenities.

Width: 65' 8"
Depth: 61' 7"
Total Living: 2,439 sq. ft.

Price Tier: C

Main Ceiling: 9 ft.
Bedrooms: 4
Baths: 3
Foundation: Crawl, Slab, Basement,
Daylight Basement

152 Richmond Drive

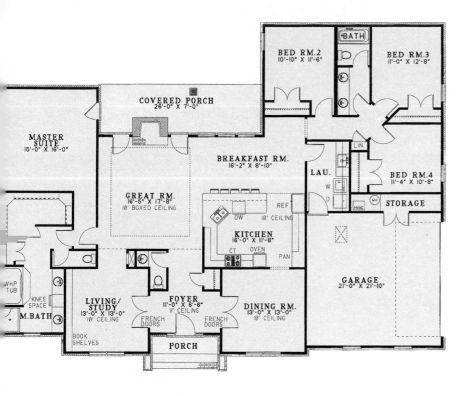

BED RM.2 10'-10" X 11'-6"

BED RM.3 11'-0" X 12'-8"

BATH

COVERED PORCH 26'-0" X 7'-0"

MASTER SUITE 15'-0" X 16'-0"

BREAKFAST RM. 16'-2" X 8'-10"

LAU.

LIN

BED RM.4 11'-4" X 10'-8"

GREAT RM. 16'-5" X 17'-8" 10' BOXED CEILING

REF 10' CEILING

STORAGE

HVAC

WHP TUB

KITCHEN 16'-0" X 11'-8"

DW

CT **OVEN** **PAN**

GARAGE 21'-0" X 21'-10"

KNEE SPACE

M.BATH

LIVING/ STUDY 13'-0" X 13'-0" 10' CEILING

FOYER 11'-0" X 6'-6" 11' CEILING

FRENCH DOORS

DINING RM. 13'-0" X 13'-0" 10' CEILING

FRENCH DOORS

BOOK SHELVES

PORCH

Nelson Design Group set the standard for homes to follow with the neo-traditional look of this all brick, four-bedroom design. Dramatic doors flank the foyer leading to the formal dining and living rooms. With a wall of built-in bookshelves, the living room could easily serve as a study or library. The magnificent great room harbors a stunning fireplace nestled between twin doors leading to a sprawling covered porch. A superb breakfast room is the perfect accent to the spacious kitchen with its functional eat-at bar.

Width: 70' 0"
Depth: 51' 10"
Total Living: 2,444 sq. ft.

Price Tier: C

Main Ceiling: 9 ft.
Bedrooms: 4
Baths: 2 1/2
Foundation: Crawl, Slab, Optional Basement, Optional Daylight Basement

128 Cherry Street

Capture the true essence of tradition in this Nelson Design Group home. Entering the home, you'll notice the attractive french doors opening to the study with an inviting private patio that is the perfect niche to finish that novel. While preparing dinner in your spacious kitchen, you can keep a close eye on the kids completing their homework in the convenient computer center. Dads will enjoy the rear covered porch accessible from several rooms. After the kids are tucked away, escape to your master suite with whirlpool bath.

Width: 67' 0"
Depth: 66' 0"
Total Living: 2,444 sq. ft.

Price Tier: C

Main Ceiling: 9 ft.
Bedrooms: 3
Baths: 2 1/2
Foundation: Crawl, Slab, Basement, Daylight Basement

To order call 1.800.590.2423 or to view similar plans visit www.nelsondesigngroup.com

Main Floor

DINING
15'-0" X 10'-8"

COVERED DECK
16'-0" X 6'-0"

MASTER BEDROOM
15'-8" X 13'-6"

12' TRAY CEILING

GREAT ROOM
16'-0" X 18'-4"
16' BEADED CEILING

8" COLUMNS

8" BOX BEAM

WALK-IN CLOSET

WALK-IN CLOSET

KITCHEN
15'-8" X 11'-7"

RG

DW   REF.

PAN.

PASS-THRU GAS FIREPLACE

8" BOX BEAM

WHP TUB

MASTER BATH
14'-8" X 11'-4"

LIN

D. W.

LAU.
8'-8" x 6'-2"

FOYER
16'-0" X 5'-0"

DN

TV CAB.

SHWR

P.R.

COVERED PORCH
20'-7" X 6'-0"

8" BOXED COLUMNS

GARAGE
21'-5" x 22'-0"

BRICK STEPS

© 1998 NELSON DESIGN GROUP, LLC.

Lower Floor

COVERED PATIO
16'-0" X 6'-0"

BEDROOM 2
15'-8" X 10'-0"

BONUS ROOM
16'-0" X 16'-4"

BATH

UP

BEDROOM 3
14'-8" X 12'-2"

MECH.   WH

HVAC

STORM / SAFE ROOM
10'-0" X 6'-0"

565 Thomas Road

A crisp autumn breeze touches your face as you enter this Nelson Design Group home. The great room with beaded ceiling and pass-through fireplace provides an excellent place for quality family time. This open floor plan creates an ambiance that is carried throughout this design. The children will love having a floor to themselves with a shared full bath and patio access. The master suite is adorned with twelve foot pan ceiling, large 'his and her' walk-in closets, and spacious master bath.

Width: 54' 0"	Main Ceiling: 8 ft.
Depth: 54' 8"	Lower Ceiling: 8 ft.
Main Floor: 1,484 sq. ft.	Bedrooms: 3
Lower Floor: 963 sq. ft.	Baths: 2 1/2
Total Living: 2,447 sq. ft.	Foundation: Daylight Basement

Price Tier: C

261 Poplar Avenue

Nelson Design Group has created this magnificent French Classic home that offers a split bedroom design. Greet your dinner guests on the charming front porch as you lead them into your spacious great room for conversation before the meal. The rear grilling porch can be accessed through the hearth room which makes it easy access for outdoor entertaining. The master suite and bath are full of amenities such as an optional fireplace, enormous walk-in closet, 'his and her' shower access, double vanities and a whirlpool bath.

Floor plan labels:

8' GRILLING PORCH / OPTIONAL SCREENED

HEARTH. ROOM 19'-8" X 12'-0" 9' CEILING

BRKFAST ROOM 9'-10" X 9'-10" 12' PAN CEILING

5' PORCH

BEDROOM 2 11'-2" X 9'-10"

MASTER SUITE 15'-0" X 16'-6" 9' BOXED CEILING

OPT. GAS FIREPLACE

KITCHEN 13'-4" X 12'-2"

GREAT ROOM 16'-0" X 23'-0" 10' CEILING

BEDROOM 3 11'-8" X 11'-6"

GLASS BLOCKS

DW RG.

PAN. REF.

WHP TUB DRAWERS

M.BATH 13'-8" X 18'-4"

LIN.

BATH

K.S. GLASS SHWR LIN.

COMPUTER CENTER

LAU. 6'-4" X 8'-6"

10' COLUMNS

FOYER 9'-8" X 9'-0" 10' CEILING

STRG.

DINING 12'-2" X 12'-0" 10' CEILING

BEDROOM 4 11'-6" X 11'-0"

OPTIONAL BASEMENT PLAN

3-CAR GARAGE 29'-10" X 20'-6"

6' COVERED PORCH 10' CEILING

© 2000 NELSON DESIGN GROUP, LLC.

Width: 68' 6"
Depth: 65' 0"
Total Living: 2,478 sq. ft.

Price Tier: C

Main Ceiling: 8 ft.
Bedrooms: 4
Baths: 2 1/2
Foundation: Crawl, Slab,
Optional Basement,
Optional Daylight Basement

479 Willow Lane

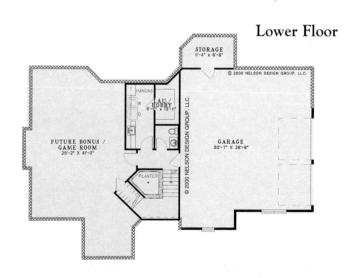

Main Floor

Floor plan labels:
- 10" COLUMNS
- GRILLING PORCH 24'-0" X 10'-0"
- BRKFAST ROOM 12'-0" X 11'-1"
- GAS BIBB
- WHP TUB
- BEDROOM 4 10'-0" X 11'-6"
- GREAT ROOM 17'-0" X 19'-0"
- DW
- KITCHEN 12'-0" X 13'-6"
- SHWR
- M.BATH 16'-8" X 12'-0"
- SEAT
- LIN
- BUILT-INS
- BEDROOM 3 11'-5" X 11'-7"
- REF.
- PAN.
- R.G.
- WINDOW SEAT
- WHP TUB
- R.A.
- PLANTER
- DN
- DN
- 8' COLUMNS
- MASTER SUITE 16'-8" X 16'-5" 10' BOX CEILING
- BATH 11'-5" X 9'-4"
- LIN
- FOYER
- DINING ROOM 11'-6" X 13'-8"
- BEDROOM 2 / STUDY 10'-11" X 12'-8"
- COVERED PORCH 8'-8" X 7'-0"
- DN
- DN

Lower Floor

Floor plan labels:
- STORAGE 11'-4" X 6'-8"
- © 2000 NELSON DESIGN GROUP, LLC.
- HANGING
- AU / HOBBY 6'-4" X 13'-11"
- FUTURE BONUS / GAME ROOM 25'-2" X 41'-0"
- GARAGE 30'-7" X 28'-8"
- PLANTER
- UP

T his trendy Nelson Design Group home with its mutiple-material exterior is equally suited for formal business entertaining or the casual excitement of a family get together. Greeted by the lovely planter, one can't help but notice the warm, comfortable feeling generated by the corner fireplace and how the great room flows effortlessly into the breakfast room and kitchen. Any overnight guests will enjoy bedroom details such as an extended window seat, walk-in closets and a bath rivaling many master baths. A glorious master suite includes an entire wall of built-ins surrounding elegant French door entry into the deluxe bath.

Width: 64' 0"	Main Ceiling: 9 ft.
Depth: 49' 4"	Lower Ceiling: 8 ft.
Main Floor: 2,249 sq. ft.	Bedrooms: 4
Lower Floor: 246 sq. ft.	Baths: 2 1/2
Total Living: 2,495 sq. ft. *	Foundation: Daylight Basement
*Optional Bonus: 776 sq. ft.	

Price Tier: C

541 Timber Drive

Main Floor

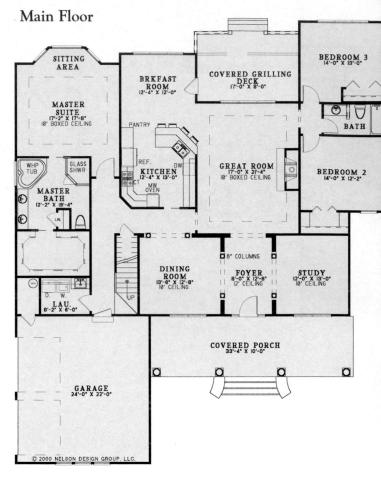

SITTING AREA

MASTER SUITE
17'-2" X 17'-8"
10' BOXED CEILING

BRKFAST ROOM
12'-4" X 12'-0"

COVERED GRILLING DECK
17'-0" X 8'-0"

BEDROOM 3
14'-0" X 13'-0"

PANTRY

WHP TUB

GLASS SHWR

REF.

KITCHEN
12'-4" X 13'-0"

MW OVEN

DW

GREAT ROOM
17'-0" X 21'-4"
10' BOXED CEILING

BATH

BEDROOM 2
14'-0" X 12'-2"

MASTER BATH
12'-2" X 19'-4"

LIN.

8" COLUMNS

DINING ROOM
13'-6" X 12'-8"
10' CEILING

FOYER
8'-0" X 12'-8"
12' CEILING

STUDY
12'-0" X 13'-0"
10' CEILING

D.W.

LAU.
8'-2" X 6'-0"

UP

COVERED PORCH
33'-4" X 10'-0"

GARAGE
24'-0" X 22'-0"

© 2000 NELSON DESIGN GROUP, LLC.

A large front porch adorns this cedar shake and siding Nelson Design Group design. High ceilings are carried throughout this plan and columns separate the foyer from formal dining room and study. This split bedroom plan has a luxurious master suite with all the amenities and enjoys privacy from the other two bedrooms. The large great room with cozy fireplace views a large covered grilling porch for ultimate family gatherings. Extra seating is available at the angled bar counter separating the kitchen and large breakfast room. An upstairs gives two options for a bonus room or fourth bedroom with full bath.

Width: 62' 2"
Depth: 73' 0"
Total Living: 2,499 sq. ft.*
*Optional Bonus A: 421 sq. ft.
*Optional Bonus B: 438 sq. ft.

Price Tier: C

Main Ceiling: 9 ft.
Upper Ceiling: 8 ft.
Bedrooms: 4
Baths: 3
Foundation: Crawl, Slab,
Optional Basement,
Optional Daylight Basement

Bonus Floor A

5' WALL

8' LINE

OPTIONAL BEDROOM 4
14'-0" X 20'-10"

BATH

8' LINE

5' WALL

Bonus Floor B

5' WALL

8' LINE

BONUS ROOM
20'-2" X 20'-10"

DN.

8' LINE

5' WALL

To order call 1.800.590.2423 or to view similar plans visit www.nelsondesigngroup.com

118 Country Club Drive

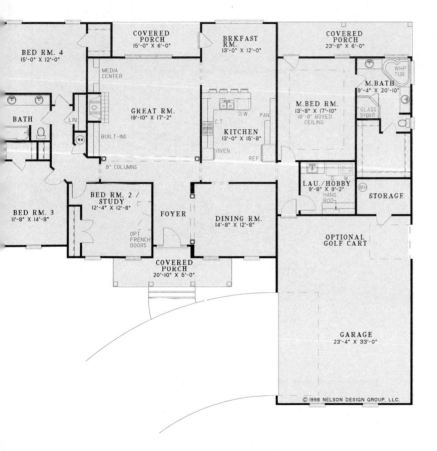

T he dignified exterior of this Nelson Design Group home conceals an exciting floor plan and surprising detail that waits inside. The extended foyer opens into a sprawling great room with a fireplace anchoring a wall filled with built-in bookshelves and media center. The cozy breakfast room allows casual dining as well as swift access to the rear porch and adjoining kitchen. Setting for the night is a breeze with your own private covered porch and extraordinary corner whirlpool tub.

Width: 72' 10"
Depth: 67' 0"
Total Living: 2,502 sq. ft.

Price Tier: D

Main Ceiling: 9 ft.
Bedrooms: 4
Baths: 2
Foundation: Crawl, Slab, Basement, Daylight Basement

585 Laurel Street

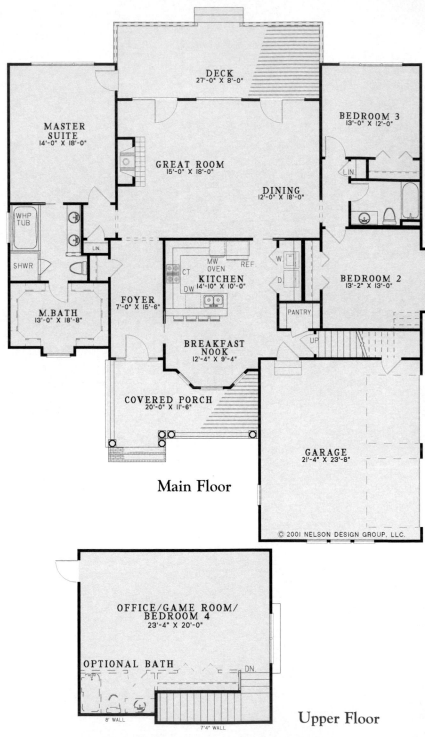

Main Floor

DECK
27'-0" X 8'-0"

MASTER SUITE
14'-0" X 18'-0"

GREAT ROOM
15'-0" X 18'-0"

DINING
12'-0" X 18'-0"

BEDROOM 3
13'-0" X 12'-0"

LIN.

WHP TUB

LIN.

SHWR

M.BATH
13'-0" X 18'-8"

FOYER
7'-0" X 15'-6"

MW OVEN
CT
KITCHEN
14'-10" X 10'-0"
DW

REF.

W D

BEDROOM 2
13'-2" X 13'-0"

PANTRY

UP

BREAKFAST NOOK
12'-4" X 9'-4"

COVERED PORCH
20'-0" X 11'-6"

GARAGE
21'-4" X 23'-8"

© 2001 NELSON DESIGN GROUP, LLC.

OFFICE/GAME ROOM/ BEDROOM 4
23'-4" X 20'-0"

OPTIONAL BATH

DN.

8' WALL   7'4" WALL

Upper Floor

This Nelson Design Group home is enhanced with craftsman style railing and a wooden porch extending a warm welcome to family and friends. Wasted space isn't an issue with this historical plan packed full of amenities. The kitchen and breakfast bay area enjoy a front view with plenty of natural lighting and large walk-in pantry near the upstairs access. A great room and dining area share a large fireplace and enjoy double access to the rear deck. The master suite is separate from the other bedrooms for added privacy. In addition, enjoy a home office or an extra bedroom with full bath for a growing family.

Width: 56' 4"
Depth: 68' 6"
Main Floor: 2,071 sq. ft.
Upper Floor: 443 sq. ft.
Total Living: 2,514 sq. ft.

Main Ceiling: 9 ft.
Upper Ceiling: 8 ft.
Bedrooms: 4
Baths: 3
Foundation: Crawl, Slab

Price Tier: D

228

371 Dogwood Avenue

Welcome your guests in the warm foyer of this Nelson Design Group home before leading them into the impressive dining room with magnificent columns framing the entry. After dinner, your guest will enjoy conversation in the spacious great room complete with fireplace and built-ins. Beautiful french doors open to the quiet study where you'll be able to concentrate on that work away from the office. The rear porch is attainable through the breakfast room and your secluded master suite. The children and guests can enjoy their own privacy with this split bedroom design.

Width: 70' 4"	Main Ceiling: 9 ft.
Depth: 57' 2"	Bedrooms: 3
Total Living: 2,534 sq. ft.	Baths: 2
	Foundation: Crawl, Slab

Price Tier: D

249 Kensington Cove

© 1998 NELSON DESIGN GROUP, LLC.

This enchanting Nelson Design Group home is well-suited for entertaining as well as relaxing. Guests are free to mingle in the voluminous great room warmed by the radiant fireplace. Afterwards they can continue out into the sun room via the french door as they comment on the exquisite detailing of the gourmet kitchen. Enjoy coffee while sitting by the bay-windowed breakfast room watching the sunrise. The master wing includes stylish detailing such as a private porch entrance, dual walk-in closets and a large bath with a large whirlpool tub and separate glass shower.

Width: 67' 2"
Depth: 71' 8"
Total Living: 2,537 sq. ft.

Price Tier: D

Main Ceiling: 9 ft.
Bedrooms: 4
Baths: 2 1/2
Foundation: Crawl, Slab, Basement, Daylight Basement

GARAGE
25'-4" X 32'-2"

ATTIC STORAGE

UP.

BRKFST. ROOM
10' CEILING
14'-5" X 10'-2"

GRILLING PORCH
10' CEILING
18'-2" X 6'-8"

MASTER SUITE
10' BOXED CEILING
15'-0" X 13'-0"

WHP. TUB

M.BATH
10'-8" X 10'-4"

SEAT

STORAGE BINS

BENCH

STOR.

WH   HVAC

KID'S NOOK

42" HIGH BAR

DW

KITCHEN
10' CEILING
14'-5" X 16'-0"

CT

BUILT-INS

GREAT ROOM
10' BOXED CEILING
18'-2" X 19'-6"

LIN

W.I.C
12'-6" X 6'-0"

2860

BEDROOM 2
13'-2" X 12'-0"

PANTRY

OVEN
MW

REF.

BATH

D.

LIN

LAU.
6'-5" X 9'-6"

W.

DINING ROOM
12'-2" X 12'-2"

FRENCH DOORS

FOYER
11' CEILING
7'-8" X 11'-10"

OFFICE / GUEST ROOM
10' CEILING
11'-10" X 12'-2"

HANGING

BEDROOM 3
10' CEILING
14'-0" X 12'-8"

14" COLUMNS

COVERED PORCH
14' CEILING
33'-6" X 8'-0"

539 Madison Drive

From the moment you step upon the covered front porch of this traditional Nelson Design Group home you will revel in the comfort eluding from the heart of your hosts. The great room boasts a cozy fireplace to warm yourself on cold winter nights. The kitchen welcomes you with a raised snack bar open to the breakfast room and accessing the rear-grilling porch. As evening draws to an end you find that your hosts have converted the office into a suite prepared for you with a walk-in closet and private bath. As you drift off to dreams, your hosts find themselves beside the fireplace of the master suite or relaxing in the whirlpool tub of the master bath.

Width: 74' 7"
Depth: 70' 6"
Total Living: 2,556 sq. ft.

Main Ceiling: 9 ft.
Bedrooms: 4
Baths: 3
Foundation: Crawl, Slab

Price Tier: D

597 Hampton Circle

Main Floor

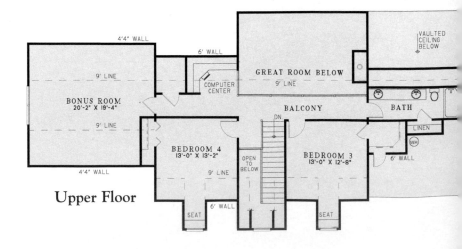

COVERED GRILLING PORCH
34'-8" X 10'-0"

STORAGE
10'-4" X 7'-8"

LAU.
9'-6" X 7'-8"

BREAKFST. RM.
10'-10" X 13'-0"

GREAT RM.
20'-8" X 17'-0"

MEDIA CENTER

GLASS SHWR

WHP TUB

M. BATH
14'-8" X 8'-8"

VAULTED TO SECOND STORY 9' CEILING

C.T. M.W.

KITCHEN
13'-0" X 16'-0"

BALCONY LINE

GARAGE
20'-2" X 21'-4"

OVEN

PANTRY   REF

DW

SHELVES

GLASS SHWR

MASTER SUITE
14'-8" X 14'-8"

DINING RM.
13'-0" X 12'-2"

OPEN TO ABOVE

STUDY/BEDROOM 2
13'-0" X 11'-6"

UP

© 2001 NELSON DESIGN GROUP, LLC

12' COLUMNS

COVERED PORCH
34'-8" X 8'-0"

12' COLUMNS

Covered porches and columns are used on both the front and rear of this traditional Nelson Design Group home. The master suite and an additional bedroom or study are on the main level for privacy and convenience. A vaulted ceiling, balcony and built-in media center enhance the great room while open to the breakfast room. The upstairs has a balcony overlooking the great room and has two bedrooms, full bath, built-in computer nook and a large bonus room.

Width: 70' 2"
Depth: 51' 4"
Main Floor: 1,813 sq. ft.
Upper Floor: 790 sq. ft.
Total Living: 2,603 sq. ft.*
*Optional Bonus: 410 sq. ft.

Main Ceiling: 9 ft.
Upper Ceiling: 9 ft.
Bedrooms: 4
Baths: 2 1/2
Foundation: Crawl, Slab,
Optional Basement,
Optional Daylight Basement

Price Tier: D

Upper Floor

4'4" WALL

6' WALL

VAULTED CEILING BELOW

9' LINE

GREAT ROOM BELOW
9' LINE

COMPUTER CENTER

BONUS ROOM
20'-2" X 19'-4"

BALCONY

BATH

9' LINE

DN

LINEN

WH

BEDROOM 4
13'-0" X 13'-2"

OPEN TO BELOW

BEDROOM 3
13'-0" X 12'-8"

6' WALL

4'4" WALL

9' LINE

SEAT

6' WALL

SEAT

To order call 1.800.590.2423 or to view similar plans visit www.nelsondesigngroup.com

Main Floor

Bonus Floor

380 Cherry Street

This stately Nelson Design Group plan will be the talk of the neighborhood. The column lined foyer and dining room view an open great room with french door access to the rear grilling porch. This split bedroom floor plan allows two bedrooms both accessing a full bath off the hearth room - perfect for weekend guests. The kitchen and breakfast room can seat many guests. The kids can enjoy the upstairs bonus area. A master suite full to the brim with amenities awaits the head of the house after working in the study on that special project.

Width: 67' 6"
Depth: 73' 10"
Total Living: 2,606 sq. ft.*
*Optional Bonus: 751 sq. ft.

Main Ceiling: 9 ft.
Bonus Ceiling: 8 ft.
Bedrooms: 4
Baths: 2 1/2
Foundation: Crawl, Slab, Basement, Daylight Basement

Price Tier: D

502 Willow Lane

Main Floor

MASTER SUITE
20'-0" X 13'-4"
10' BOXED CEILING

GRILLING PORCH
32'-8" X 9'-0"

BEDROOM 2
12'-0" X 13'-4"

WHP TUB

M.BATH
16'-6" X 15'-2"

BONUS AREA ABOVE

H.B.

8" COLUMNS

LIN.

BATH

GLASS SHOWER

LIN.

BRKFAST / HEARTH
13'-4" X 20'-0"

LIVING RM.
16'-4" X 24'-0"

D.W.

LAU.

KID'S NOOK

PASS-THRU

BEDROOM 3
12'-0" X 11'-0"

PAN.

KITCHEN
12'-0" X 16'-6"

CT

REF.

FRENCH DOORS

GARAGE
22'-2" X 21'-0"

OVEN

FOYER
11'-6" X 9'-4"

STUDY / BEDROOM 4
11'-0" X 12'-0"

BATH

© 2000 NELSON DESIGN GROUP, LLC.

DINING
12'-0" X 15'-4"
11' CEILING

COVERED PORCH
19'-2" X 10'-4"

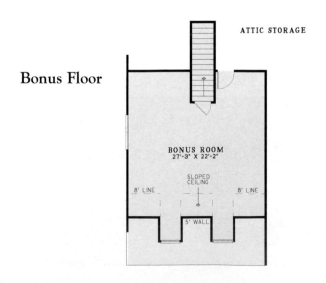

Bonus Floor

ATTIC STORAGE

BONUS ROOM
27'-3" X 22'-2"

SLOPED CEILING

8' LINE

8' LINE

5' WALL

Don't be fooled by the traditional country appearance of this Nelson Design Group home. Inside you'll find exciting angles, a unique use of available space and enough open area to host the little league team dinner. Coming in from the garage, the kids have their very own nook to keep track of their stuff. The uniquely-designed kitchen is capable of serving any living area in the house, including the nearby grilling porch. The fireplace in the hearth room is centrally located so it also warms the living room. Walk-in closets accompany most bedrooms while two of the three secondary bedrooms boast private bathroom entrances as well.

Width: 66' 4"
Depth: 64' 0"
Total Living: 2,624 sq. ft.*
*Optional Bonus: 561 sq. ft.

Price Tier: D

Main Ceiling: 9 ft.
Bonus Ceiling: 8 ft.
Bedrooms: 4
Baths: 3
Foundation: Crawl, Slab,
Optional Basement,
Optional Daylight Basement

Main Floor

12" COLUMN

GRILLING PORCH
15'-8" X 10'-0"

GAS BIBB

VAULTED CEILING

VAULTED CEILING

UP

MASTER SUITE
13'-0" X 18'-6"

GREAT ROOM
22'-0" X 22'-0"
OPEN TO ABOVE

HEARTH ROOM
15'-8" X 12'-4"

BALCONY LINE

FRENCH DOORS

GLASS SHWR

42" HIGH BAR

M. BATH
13'-0" X 16'-8"

WHP TUB

BREAKFAST ROOM
9'-0" X 10'-0"

DW

RG

8" COLUMNS

BALCONY LINE

FOYER
7'-6" X 14'-4"

LIN

KITCHEN
11'-0" X 12'-8"

REF

PANTRY

DINING ROOM
13'-0" X 12'-8"

OPEN TO ABOVE

LAUNDRY
10'-2" X 5'-10"

D W

PANTRY

COVERED PORCH
35'-2" X 8'-0"
10' CEILING

STORAGE
13'-8" X 3'-8"

WH

KID'S NOOK

12" COLUMN

BENCH W/ STORAGE BINS & HANGING

GARAGE
20'-0" X 23'-0"

© 2001 NELSON DESIGN GROUP, LLC.

Upper Floor

5' WALL

8' LINE

VAULTED CEILING

OPEN TO BELOW

BATH

BONUS ROOM
OPT. BEDROOM 4
15'-4" X 18'-6"

COMPUTER CENTER

BALCONY

DN

LIN

ATTIC STORAGE

BEDROOM 2
13'-4" X 11'-0"

OPEN TO FOYER

BEDROOM 3
13'-0" X 13'-4"

8' LINE

5'7" WALL

VAULTED CEILING

547 Autumn Drive

Nelson Design Group has created a beautiful country split bedroom design. Traditions will begin in the expansive great room with vaulted ceilings. Holiday dinners will be easy in the kitchen with easy access to the formal dining room as well as breakfast and hearth rooms with fireplace. The kid's nook provides ample space for storing backpacks and gear. Parents can rest easy in the privacy of the master suite with ten foot boxed ceiling and french door access to the master bath. Upstairs the children have space of their own including a place to finish their homework at the computer center.

Width: 55' 6"		Main Ceiling: 9 ft.
Depth: 69' 6"		Upper Ceiling: 8 ft.
Main Floor: 1,990 sq. ft.		Bedrooms: 4
Upper Floor: 695 sq. ft.		Baths: 2 1/2
Total Living: 2,685 sq. ft.*		Foundation: Crawl, Slab,
*Optional Bonus: 301 sq. ft.		Optional Basement,
		Optional Daylight Basement

Price Tier: D

327 Willow Lane

Main Floor

SEAT
LIN
GLASS SHWR
WHP TUB
M.BATH
9' CEILINGS
16'-0" X 16'-8"
HIS'
HER'S
M.U.
MASTER SUITE
10' BOXED CEILING
16'-8" X 16'-8"
ATRIUM DOORS
SCREENED PORCH
13'-6" X 15'-0"
FRENCH DOOR
FRENCH DOOR
SUN ROOM
21'-0" X 8'-8"
SKYLIGHT
SKYLIGHT
BEDROOM 4
15'-4" X 12'-0"
BRKFAST ROOM
10' CEILING
13'-6" X 9'-6"
FRENCH DOORS
MEDIA CENTER
COVERED PORCH
16'-4" X 8'-0"
8" COLUMNS
TO BONUS AREA ABOVE
DESK
GREAT ROOM
10' CEILING
21'-0" X 17'-0"
BATH
DW
KITCHEN
10' CEILING
13'-6" X 10'-4"
PAN
REF
LAUNDRY
12'-10" X 5'-11"
© 1998 NELSON DESIGN GROUP, LLC.
8" RND COL
FOYER
12' CEILING
7'-4" X 10'-11"
BEDROOM 3
11'-6" X 12'-0"
LIN
GARAGE
20'-4" X 25'-6"
DINING ROOM
10' CEILING
12'-6" X 16'-2"
BEDROOM 2/ STUDY
10' CEILING
11'-0" X 13'-0"
VAULTED CEILING
PORCH
10' CEILING
31'-6" X 8'-0"
8" BOX COL

Upper Floor

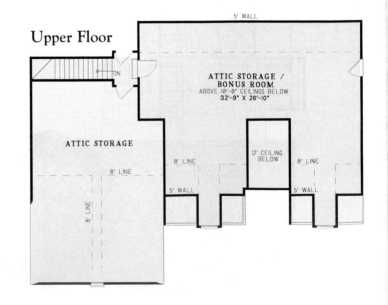

5' WALL
DN.
ATTIC STORAGE / BONUS ROOM
ABOVE 10'-0" CEILINGS BELOW
32'-9" X 26'-10"
ATTIC STORAGE
8' LINE
8' LINE
12' CEILING BELOW
8' LINE
8' LINE
5' WALL
5' WALL
5' WALL

A splendid arched entry accented with elegant dual columns and flanked by charming dormers meshes cleanly with the smooth stucco and rock exterior of this Nelson Design Group offering. The sun room demands attention with its elegant french door entries, twin sky lights and quick access to three distinct areas of the home and the back yard. The screened porch is sure to be a hit with the beautiful atrium doors leading to the master suite and adjacent placement next to the kitchen.

Width: 84' 6"
Depth: 58' 6"
Total Living: 2,742 sq. ft.*
*Optional Bonus: 916 sq. ft.

Price Tier: D

Main Ceiling: 9 ft.
Bedrooms: 4
Baths: 2 1/2
Foundation: Crawl, Slab, Basement, Daylight Basement

Main Floor

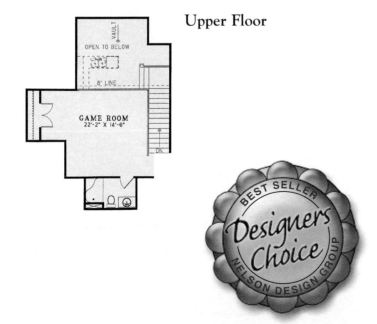

GLASS BLOCKS

WHP TUB

M. BATH
19'-4" X 11'-4"

PLANTER

10' BOX COL.

PLANTER

10' PORCH

LIN.

ATRIUM DOOR

MASTER SUITE
19'-4" X 13'-8"

DESK

ATRIUM DOOR

MEDIA CENTER

BREAKFAST ROOM
12'-2" X 8'-4"

BEDROOM 3
15'-9" X 12'-2"

OPEN ABOVE

GREAT ROOM
20'-2" X 20'-6"

DW

UP

LAU.
9'-10" X 10'-6"

D

W

ISLAND

OVEN

STOR.

KNEE SPACE

LIN.

KITCHEN
12'-2" X 16'-2"

TC CT

REF

BATH

NICHE

PAN.

BATH

WINDOW SEAT

BEDROOM 2
13'-2" X 14'-8"

FOYER
10' CEILING

DESK

8' COLUMN

DINING
9' CEILING
12'-4" X 12'-8"

GARAGE
21'-4" X 32'-8"

PORCH
31'-0" X 8'-0"

10' COLUMNS

© 1998 NELSON DESIGN GROUP, LLC.

Upper Floor

VAULT

OPEN TO BELOW

8' LINE

GAME ROOM
22'-2" X 14'-6"

DN

BEST SELLER
Designers Choice
NELSON DESIGN GROUP

209 Olive Street

Memories will be cherished forever in this southern traditional Nelson Design Group home. Receive your dinner guests in the open foyer before seating them in the beautiful dining room. The children will enjoy the amenities in their rooms such as walk-in closets, built-in desks, and private baths that will alleviate morning chaos over equal bath time. You will enjoy amenities such as an atrium door to the rear porch for moonlight talks, 'his and her' walk-in closets, and a gorgeous whirlpool bath with glass blocks for enhanced lighting and privacy.

Width: 69' 0"	Main Ceiling: 9 ft.
Depth: 69' 10"	Upper Ceiling: 8 ft.
Main Floor: 2,352 sq. ft.	Bedrooms: 3
Upper Floor: 349 sq. ft.	Baths: 4 1/2
Total Living: 2,701 sq. ft.	Foundation: Crawl, Slab, Basement, Daylight Basement

Price Tier: D

327 Willow Lane

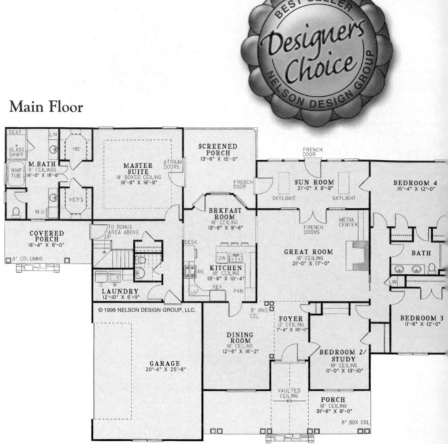

Main Floor

SEAT
GLASS SHWR
WHP TUB
M.BATH
9' CEILINGS
16'-0" X 16'-8"
HIS'
HER'S
LIN
M.U.
MASTER SUITE
10' BOXED CEILING
16'-8" X 16'-8"
ATRIUM DOORS
SCREENED PORCH
13'-6" X 15'-0"
FRENCH DOOR
FRENCH DOOR
SUN ROOM
21'-0" X 8'-8"
SKYLIGHT   SKYLIGHT
BEDROOM 4
15'-4" X 12'-0"
COVERED PORCH
16'-4" X 8'-0"
8' COLUMNS
TO BONUS AREA ABOVE UP
BRKFAST ROOM
10' CEILING
13'-6" X 9'-6"
FRENCH DOORS
MEDIA CENTER
GREAT ROOM
10' CEILING
21'-0" X 17'-0"
BATH
DESK
DW
KITCHEN
10' CEILING
13'-6" X 10'-4"
RG.
PAN.
REF
LAUNDRY
12'-10" X 5'-11"
8' RND COL
LIN
BEDROOM 3
11'-6" X 12'-0"
© 1998 NELSON DESIGN GROUP, LLC.
FOYER
12' CEILING
7'-4" X 10'-11"
GARAGE
20'-4" X 25'-6"
DINING ROOM
10' CEILING
12'-6" X 16'-2"
BEDROOM 2/ STUDY
10' CEILING
11'-0" X 13'-10"
VAULTED CEILING
PORCH
10' CEILING
31'-6" X 8'-0"
8' BOX COL

Upper Floor

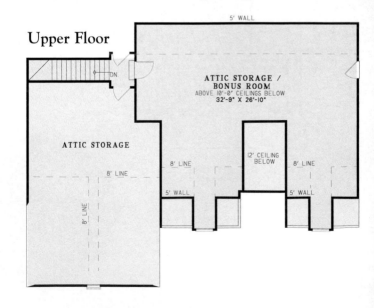

5' WALL
DN.
ATTIC STORAGE / BONUS ROOM
ABOVE 10'-0" CEILINGS BELOW
32'-9" X 26'-10"
ATTIC STORAGE
8' LINE
8' LINE
12' CEILING BELOW
8' LINE
8' LINE
5' WALL
5' WALL

A splendid arched entry accented with elegant dual columns and flanked by charming dormers meshes cleanly with the smooth stucco and rock exterior of this Nelson Design Group offering. The sun room demands attention with its elegant french door entries, twin sky lights and quick access to three distinct areas of the home and the back yard. The screened porch is sure to be a hit with the beautiful atrium doors leading to the master suite and adjacent placement next to the kitchen.

Width: 84' 6"
Depth: 58' 6"
Total Living: 2,742 sq. ft.*
*Optional Bonus: 916 sq. ft.

Price Tier: D

Main Ceiling: 9 ft.
Bedrooms: 4
Baths: 2 1/2
Foundation: Crawl, Slab, Basement, Daylight Basement

To order call 1.800.590.2423 or to view similar plans visit www.nelsondesigngroup.com

Main Floor

GLASS BLOCKS

WHP TUB

SEAT GLASS SHWR.

M.BATH
11'-8" X 16'-6"

MASTER SUITE
16'-0" X 18'-10"

12" COLUMNS

GRILLING PORCH
26'-0" X 7'-6"

BREAKFAST AREA
10' CEILING
12'-0" X 10'-0"

UP

LAUNDRY
11'-2" X 8'-2"

W   D

ATRIUM DOORS

MEDIA CENTER

GREAT ROOM
10' CEILING
20'-10" X 18'-10"

PAN.

REF.

DW.

STRG.
7'-2" X 9'-2"

HVAC

WH

KITCHEN
10' CEILING
12'-0" X 13'-10"

RG

BUILT-INS.

8" COLUMNS

FOYER
10' CEILING
8'-6" X 7'-4"

DINING ROOM
10' CEILING
11'-4" X 12'-0"

FORMAL LIVING
10' CEILING
12'-0" X 14'-0"

PORCH
8'-6" X 5'-8"

ARCH OPENING

GARAGE
20'-0" X 35'-8"

© 1993 NELSON DESIGN GROUP, LLC.

Main Floor

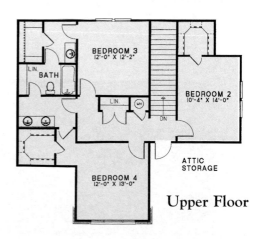

BEDROOM 3
12'-0" X 12'-2"

LIN.

BATH

LIN.

BEDROOM 2
10'-4" X 14'-0"

WH

DN

ATTIC STORAGE

BEDROOM 4
12'-0" X 13'-0"

Upper Floor

348 Willow Lane

The stately exterior of this Nelson Design Group home opens to a spacious and well-organized interior. The foyer, highlighted by graceful columns, separates the formal living and dining areas. Built-in bookshelves and media center surround the great room's elegant fireplace. Stylish atrium doors provide access to the grilling porch where the family chef prepares the night's cuisine. All three secondary bedrooms offer walk-in closets.

Width: 54' 2"
Depth: 73' 6"
Main Floor: 1,895 sq. ft.
Upper Floor: 889 sq. ft.
Total Living: 2,784 sq. ft.

Main Ceiling: 9 ft.
Upper Ceiling: 8 ft.
Bedrooms: 4
Baths: 2 1/2
Foundation: Crawl, Slab, Basement, Daylight Basement

Price Tier: D

129-2 Olive Street

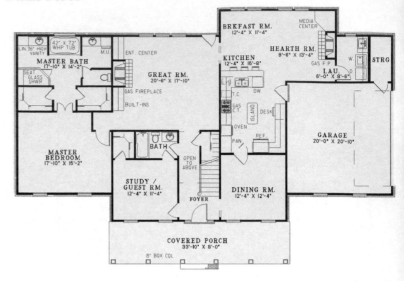

BRKFAST RM. 12'-4" X 11'-4"
MEDIA CENTER
HEARTH RM. 9'-6" X 13'-4"
MASTER BATH 17'-10" X 14'-2"
LIN. 36" HIGH VANITY
42" X 72" WHP TUB
M.U.
ENT. CENTER
GREAT RM. 20'-6" X 17'-10"
KITCHEN 12'-4" X 15'-8"
GAS F.P.
LAU. 6'-0" X 8'-6"
STRG
W. D.
SEAT GLASS SHWR
GAS FIREPLACE
BUILT-INS
T.C.
GAS C.T.
DW
ISLAND
DESK
OVEN
PAN.
REF
MASTER BEDROOM 17'-10" X 15'-2"
BATH
OPEN TO ABOVE
GARAGE 20'-0" X 20'-10"
STUDY / GUEST RM. 12'-4" X 11'-4"
FOYER
DINING RM. 12'-4" X 12'-4"
COVERED PORCH 33'-10" X 8'-0"
8" BOX COL.

Upper Floor

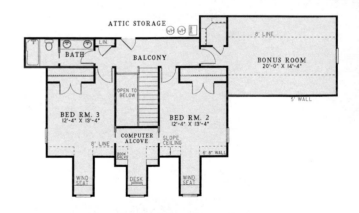

ATTIC STORAGE
BATH
LIN.
8' LINE
BALCONY
BONUS ROOM 20'-0" X 14'-4"
OPEN TO BELOW
5' WALL
BED RM. 3 12'-4" X 13'-4"
BED RM. 2 12'-4" X 13'-4"
8' LINE
COMPUTER ALCOVE
SLOPE CEILING
BOOK SHELF
6' 8" WALL
WIND SEAT
DESK
WIND SEAT

Picture yourself welcoming friends and family to Sunday dinner in this Nelson Design Group home. There will be plenty of room for buffet in your spacious kitchen with a hearth room and breakfast room. Afterwards, you can watch the ballgame in your great room with fireplace. Overnight guests will appreciate the convenient private bath available to them. Your secluded master bath includes marvelous 'his and her' walk-in closets and relaxing whirlpool bath. Upstairs, the unique computer alcove allows the children to finish their school projects with ease.

Width: 72' 4"
Depth: 48' 4"
Main Floor: 1,977 sq. ft.
Upper Floor: 812 sq. ft.
Total Living: 2,789 sq. ft.*
*Optional Bonus: 286 sq. ft.

Main Ceiling: 9 ft.
Upper Ceiling: 8 ft.
Bedrooms: 4
Baths: 3
Foundation: Crawl, Slab, Basement, Daylight Basement

Price Tier: D

Main Floor

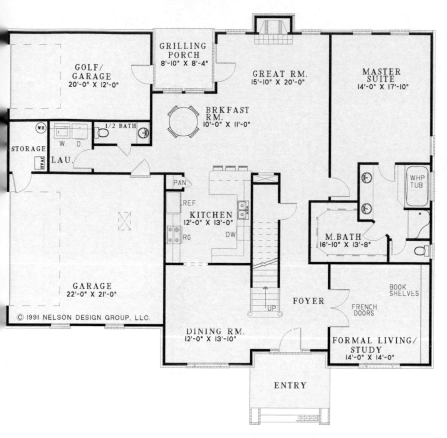

GOLF/ GARAGE
20'-0" X 12'-0"

GRILLING PORCH
8'-10" X 8'-4"

GREAT RM.
15'-10" X 20'-0"

MASTER SUITE
14'-0" X 17'-10"

BRKFAST RM.
10'-0" X 11'-0"

STORAGE

W. D.

1/2 BATH

LAU.

WH

PAN.

REF.

KITCHEN
12'-0" X 13'-0"

DW

RG

WHP TUB

M.BATH
16'-10" X 13'-8"

GARAGE
22'-0" X 21'-0"

© 1991 NELSON DESIGN GROUP, LLC.

UP

FOYER

BOOK SHELVES

FRENCH DOORS

DINING RM.
12'-0" X 13'-10"

FORMAL LIVING/ STUDY
14'-0" X 14'-0"

ENTRY

Upper Floor

ATTIC STORAGE

BATH

LIN.

BATH

LOFT
10'-8" X 16'-0"

LIN.

BEDROOM 4
11'-2" X 12'-2"

DN

COMPUTER CENTER

HVAC

BEDROOM 2
12'-0" X 13'-0"

FOYER
OPEN TO BELOW

BEDROOM 3
14'-0" X 11'-2"

125 Hickory Place

Upon entering this French Classic Nelson Design Group home notice the ambiance that is radiated throughout this design. French doors access the formal living area or study with built-in bookshelves. The spacious great room opens to the kitchen, and the breakfast room has a great rear view along with easy access to the grilling porch for the grill masters. The master suite provides all the seclusion needed at the end of the day, complete with master bath and a huge walk-in closet. The kids will have a floor of their own featuring a computer center and two full baths.

Width: 60' 4"	Main Ceiling: 9 ft.
Depth: 55' 2"	Upper Ceiling: 9 ft.
Main Floor: 1,834 sq. ft.	Bedrooms: 4
Upper Floor: 968 sq. ft.	Baths: 3 1/2
Total Living: 2,802 sq. ft.	Foundation: Crawl, Slab, Optional Basement, Optional Daylight Basement

Price Tier: D

592 Olive Street

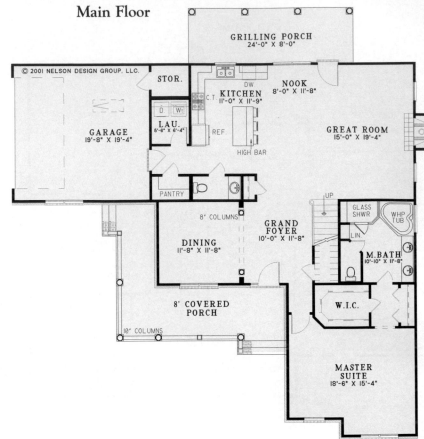

GRILLING PORCH
24'-0" X 8'-0"

© 2001 NELSON DESIGN GROUP, LLC.

STOR.

NOOK
8'-0" X 11'-8"

KITCHEN
11'-0" X 11'-9"

GARAGE
19'-8" X 19'-4"

LAU.
5'-6" X 6'-4"

REF.

GREAT ROOM
15'-0" X 19'-4"

HIGH BAR

PANTRY

8" COLUMNS

GRAND
FOYER
10'-0" X 11'-8"

UP

GLASS
SHWR

WHP
TUB

LIN.

DINING
11'-8" X 11'-8"

M.BATH
10'-10" X 11'-8"

8' COVERED
PORCH

W.I.C.

10" COLUMNS

MASTER
SUITE
18'-6" X 15'-4"

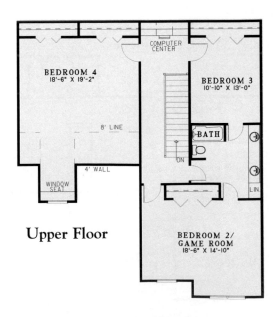

COMPUTER
CENTER

BEDROOM 4
18'-6" X 19'-2"

BEDROOM 3
10'-10" X 13'-0"

8' LINE

BATH

4' WALL

DN

LIN.

WINDOW
SEAT

Upper Floor

BEDROOM 2/
GAME ROOM
18'-6" X 14'-10"

A combination of brick and siding are just right for this traditional, yet up to date home. The grand foyer introduces a main floor allowing privacy for the exquisite master suite while lending to spacious living areas. The step saver kitchen has an island bar with seating, a view of the grilling porch and adjoins the great room for cozy entertaining options. The upstairs includes a centrally located computer center, three additional bedrooms and a shared bathroom.

Width: 61' 4"
Depth: 62' 0"
Main Floor: 1,610 sq. ft.
Upper Floor: 1,200 sq. ft.
Total Living: 2,810 sq. ft.

Price Tier: D

Main Ceiling: 9 ft.
Upper Ceiling: 8 ft.
Bedrooms: 4
Baths: 2 1/2
Foundation: Crawl, Slab,
Optional Basement,
Optional Daylight Basement

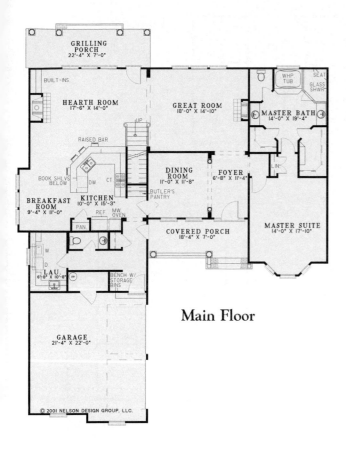

Main Floor

GRILLING PORCH
22'-4" X 7'-0"

BUILT-INS

HEARTH ROOM
17'-6" X 14'-0"

GREAT ROOM
18'-0" X 14'-10"

WHP TUB

SEAT

GLASS SHWR

MASTER BATH
14'-0" X 19'-4"

RAISED BAR

UP

BOOK SHLVS BELOW

DW

CT

DINING ROOM
11'-0" X 11'-8"

FOYER
6'-8" X 11'-4"

BUTLER'S PANTRY

BREAKFAST ROOM
9'-4" X 11'-0"

KITCHEN
10'-0" X 15'-3"

REF

MW OVEN

PAN

W

D

LAU.
6'-8" X 10'-8"

BENCH W/ STORAGE BINS

COVERED PORCH
18'-4" X 7'-0"

MASTER SUITE
14'-0" X 17'-10"

GARAGE
21'-4" X 22'-0"

© 2001 NELSON DESIGN GROUP, LLC.

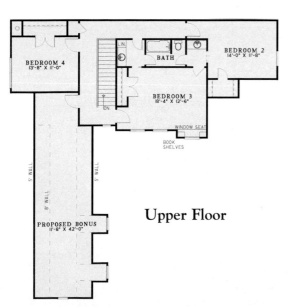

Upper Floor

BEDROOM 4
13'-8" X 11'-0"

LIN

BATH

BEDROOM 2
14'-0" X 11'-8"

DN

BEDROOM 3
18'-4" X 12'-6"

WINDOW SEAT

BOOK SHELVES

5' WALL

5' WALL

8' WALL

PROPOSED BONUS
11'-8" X 42'-0"

572 Brittany Lane

The beautiful covered front porch alludes to the comfort contained within this Nelson Design Group home. The great room offers a cozy fireplace to gather your friends and family. The kitchen offers a snack bar with bookshelves below and a butler's pantry for storage. The hearth room features a warm fireplace and access to the rear-grilling porch. The master suite is illuminated with bay windows as the bath offers 'his and her' walk-in closets, glass shower with seat, and whirlpool tub. Traveling upstairs the children will enjoy the privacy of their own floor, a proposed bonus room and full bath access.

Width: 57' 0"
Depth: 71' 8"
Main Floor: 1,921 sq. ft.
Upper Floor: 965 sq. ft.
Total Living: 2,886 sq. ft.*
*Optional Bonus: 528 sq. ft.

Main Ceiling: 9 ft.
Upper Ceiling: 8 ft.
Bedrooms: 4
Baths: 2 1/2
Foundation: Crawl, Slab

Price Tier: D

603 Autumn Drive

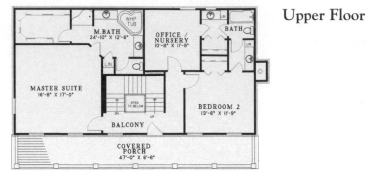

Upper Floor

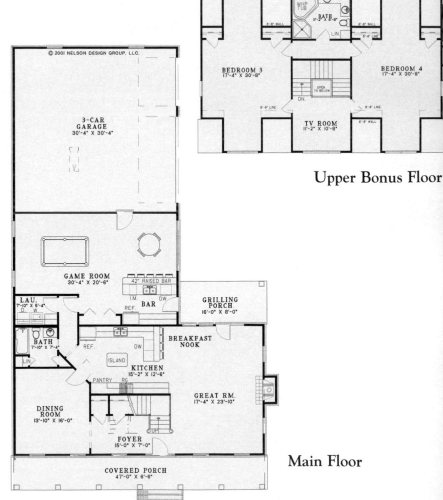

Upper Bonus Floor

Main Floor

This Nelson Design Group plan has beautifully crafted columns and a large porch with covered balcony making this the home the talk of the neighborhood. The main level contains a large game room with kitchenette accessible to the rear-grilling porch for the ultimate in entertaining. The second level has a lovely master suite with private bath, an additional bedroom as well as a nursery or home office with private vanities and full bath. The third level or bonus area, has two large bedrooms with access to a convenient TV room.

Width: 49' 6"
Depth: 82' 6"
Main Floor: 1,801 sq. ft.
Upper Floor: 1,089 sq. ft.
Total Living: 2,890 sq. ft.*
*Upper Bonus: 1,148 sq. ft.

Main Ceiling: 9 ft.
Upper Ceiling: 9 ft.
Upper Bonus Ceiling: 8 ft.
Bedrooms: 3
Baths: 3
Foundation: Crawl, Slab, Optional Basement, Optional Daylight Basement

Price Tier: D

Main Floor

© 1994 NELSON DESIGN GROUP, LLC.

GARAGE
31'-4" X 21'-4"

METAL RAIL

GRILLING PORCH
22'-4" X 8'-0"

GAS
BIBB

PANTRY

REF

K.S.
WHP TUB
GLASS
SHWR

M. BATH
23'-8" X 9'-8"

LIN.

WH

MW
OVEN

CT

GREAT RM.
21'-10" X 19'-8"

KITCHEN
12'-4" X 18'-0"

DW

MASTER
SUITE
15'-8" X 12'-4"

LAU.
D W

FRENCH
DOORS

BREAKFAST
ROOM
12'-4" X 10'-0"

STUDY
11'-0" X 12'-8"

FOYER
OPEN TO
ABOVE

DINING RM.
11'-0" X 13'-8"

UP

PORCH
9'-10" X 4'-0"
8" COLUMNS

Upper Floor

BEDROOM 4
13'-10" X 11'-10"

LIN

LIN

BATH

BATH

BEDROOM 3
11'-0" X 15'-8"

DN.

OPEN TO
BELOW

BEDROOM 2
11'-0" X 15'-8"

PLANT
LEDGE

482 Dogwood Avenue

Elegant quoin corners add definition to this Nelson Design Group brick home. Upon entering, a grand foyer opens above allowing natural light to shine throughout. Just off the foyer is a spacious formal dining room adjoining the breakfast room and open to the kitchen. This expansive kitchen has an island cooktop, plenty of storage and additional bar seating. The master suite has a private study for the ultimate quiet space, and french doors leading into a magnificent private bath. The second level has three additional bedrooms each with a walk-in closet and private access to a bathroom.

Width: 69' 2"
Depth: 72' 4"
Main Floor: 1,999 sq. ft.
Upper Floor: 923 sq. ft.
Total Living: 2,922 sq. ft.

Main Ceiling: 9 ft.
Upper Ceiling: 8 ft.
Bedrooms: 4
Baths: 3 1/2
Foundation: Crawl, Slab,
Optional Basement,
Optional Daylight Basement

Price Tier: D

164 Brittany Lane

Main Floor

GRILLING PORCH
31'-6" X 10'-0"

FIXED FRENCH DOORS

FRENCH DOORS

GREAT RM.
18'-2" X 14'-0"

BREAKFAST ROOM
11'-6" X 14'-0"

D.W.

DINING RM.
11'-6" X 13'-0"

COMPUTER DESK

KITCHEN
12'-6" X 14'-0"

C.T.

REF.

PANTRY

8" COLUMNS

UP

BATH

FORMAL LIVING
11'-6" X 16'-10"

GARAGE
22'-4" X 25'-0"

GUEST RM.
11'-0" X 11'-2"

FOYER
8'-10" X 18'-8"
OPEN ABOVE

UP

PORCH

© 1994 NELSON DESIGN GROUP, LLC.

As your guests enter this traditional Nelson Design Group home they are touched by the grandeur of the formal living room with columns framing the dining room. The kitchen boasts an island cook top, snack bar and walk-in pantry. The great room features a beautiful fireplace and french door access to the rear grilling proch. As you ascend the grand stairway in the foyer, you are encompassed by convenience as you find all four bedrooms tucked privately away. Mom affords herself the luxury of a long soak in the whirlpool tub, as the children lay nestled within their own rooms or busy utilizing the bonus room.

Width: 55' 4"
Depth: 53' 10"
Main Floor: 1,547 sq. ft.
Upper Floor: 1,395 sq. ft.
Total Living: 2,942 sq. ft.*
*Optional Bonus: 366 sq. ft.

Price Tier: D

Main Ceiling: 9 ft.
Upper Ceiling: 8 ft.
Bedrooms: 5
Baths: 4
Foundation: Crawl, Slab,
Optional Basement,
Optional Daylight Basement

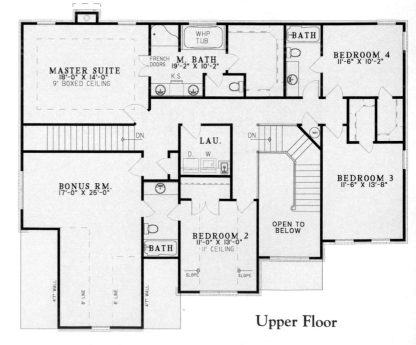

WHP TUB

BATH

MASTER SUITE
18'-0" X 14'-0"
9' BOXED CEILING

FRENCH DOORS

M. BATH
19'-2" X 10'-2"

K.S.

BEDROOM 4
11'-6" X 10'-2"

DN

LAU.
D. W.

DN

BONUS RM.
17'-0" X 25'-0"

BEDROOM 3
11'-6" X 13'-8"

OPEN TO BELOW

47" WALL

8' LINE

8' LINE

47" WALL

BATH

BEDROOM 2
11'-0" X 13'-0"
11' CEILING

SLOPE

SLOPE

Upper Floor

345 Sunset Drive

Floor plan labels:

- BATH
- BEDROOM 4 11'-2" X 15'-4"
- LIN
- ATRIUM DOORS
- BREAKFAST AREA 12' CEILING 10'-0" X 10'-8"
- LANAI 18'-4" X 11'-8"
- SITTING ROOM 11'-4" X 8'-6"
- BEDROOM 3 13'-2" X 13'-2"
- BUILT-INS
- GREAT ROOM 12' CEILING 18'-6" X 19'-6"
- 42" HIGH BAR
- DW
- KITCHEN 12'-8" X 16'-6"
- ATRIUM DOORS
- REF
- CT
- ISLAND
- 12' CEILING
- MASTER SUITE 14'-2" X 18'-8"
- WET BAR
- BUTLER'S PANTRY
- OVEN
- LIVING ROOM 12' CEILING 13'-0" X 19'-10"
- BEDROOM 2 13'-2" X 14'-10"
- BATH
- PAN
- LAU. 10'-4" X 8'-8"
- W D
- 8" COLUMNS
- FOYER 12' CEILING 8'-6" X 6'-2"
- LIN
- M.BATH 16'-4" X 21'-4"
- DINING 10' BOXED CLNG 16'-10" X 12'-2"
- PORCH 11'-2" X 11'-6"
- LIN
- KNEE SPACE
- LIN
- GLASS SHWR SEAT
- 3 CAR GARAGE 22'-4" X 31'-8"
- WHP TUB
- 2X4 BOXED COLUMNS

© 1996 NELSON DESIGN GROUP, LLC.

This sprawling four-bedroom plan from Nelson Design Group centers on an ultra functional kitchen accessing all living areas with ease. A handy eat-at bar and island help make this kitchen any gourmet's dream. Separate living and great rooms each flaunt gas fireplaces and lots of open space. All three secondary bedrooms feature private bath entrances. The exquisite master suite presents a radiant fireplace, large sitting area, private entrance to the lanai and a massive bath that includes his and her walk-in closets and an oversized whirlpool bath.

Width: 73' 6"
Depth: 80' 6"
Total Living: 2,951 sq. ft.

Price Tier: D

Main Ceiling: 9 ft.
Bedrooms: 4
Baths: 3
Foundation: Crawl, Slab, Basement, Daylight Basement

598 Brittany Lane

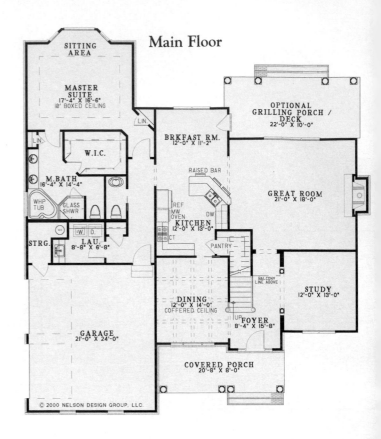

Main Floor

SITTING AREA

MASTER SUITE
17'-4" X 16'-6"
10' BOXED CEILING

LIN.

LIN.

W.I.C.

BRKFAST RM.
12'-0" X 11'-2"

OPTIONAL GRILLING PORCH / DECK
22'-0" X 10'-0"

M. BATH
16'-4" X 14'-4"

RAISED BAR

WHP TUB

GLASS SHWR

REF
MW OVEN
DW

KITCHEN
12'-0" X 13'-0"

GREAT ROOM
21'-0" X 18'-0"

STRG.

LAU.
8'-8" X 6'-8"

W. D.

CT

PANTRY

BALCONY LINE ABOVE

STUDY
12'-0" X 13'-0"

GARAGE
21'-0" X 24'-0"

DINING
12'-0" X 14'-0"
COFFERED CEILING

UP

FOYER
8'-4" X 15'-8"

COVERED PORCH
20'-8" X 8'-0"

© 2000 NELSON DESIGN GROUP, LLC.

Upper Floor

ATTIC STORAGE

5' WALL

BATH

W.I.C.

8' LINE

COMPUTER CENTER

LIN.
LIN.

BEDROOM 3
16'-2" X 12'-0"

FUTURE OFFICE / GAME ROOM
21'-0" X 21'-5"

8' LINE

W.I.C.

BATH

DN

5' WALL

BEDROOM 4
12'-0" X 11'-8"

BEDROOM 2
12'-4" X 11'-8"

ATTIC STORAGE
8'-4" X 19'-4"

OPT. 5' WALL

8' LINE

OPT. 5' WALL

OPEN TO BELOW

A s you step from the covered front porch into the foyer of this beautiful Nelson Design Group home, you feel comfortable. Breakfast begins at the raised snack bar in the kitchen. As evening draws near and your guests begin to arrive, gather round the fireplace adorning the great room for fellowship and drinks. An optional grilling porch is offered for additional gathering space. As your guests leave, retreat to the comfort of your whirlpool tub as your spouse completes a novel in the bay window sitting area of the master suite. Upstairs the children have their own privacy with two full baths, a computer center and future game room.

Width: 57' 2"
Depth: 63' 4"
Main Floor: 1,930 sq. ft.
Upper Floor: 1,022 sq. ft.
Total Living: 2,952 sq. ft.*
*Optional Bonus: 471 sq. ft.

Price Tier: D

Main Ceiling: 9 ft.
Upper Ceiling: 8 ft.
Bedrooms: 4
Baths: 3 1/2
Foundation: Crawl, Slab,
Optional Basement,
Optional Daylight Basement

388 Madison Drive

Main Floor

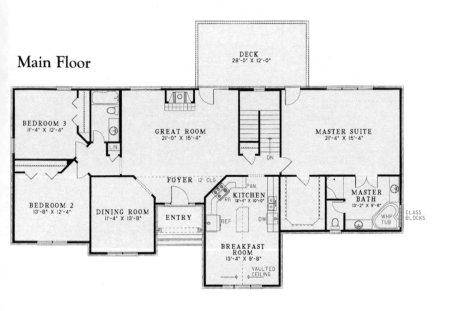

Lower Floor

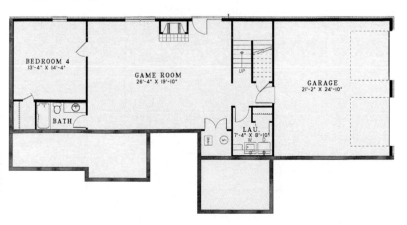

Elevation A

Elevation B

The brick arched entry of this French Traditional Nelson Design Group home presents an air of grandeur. The great room offers a grand fireplace for gathering around glowing embers and atrium doors that guests may pass through to the rear deck. Vaulted ceilings in the kitchen and breakfast rooms exemplify a stately gesture. The master suite offers an expansive walk-in closet and access to rear deck. Enter the master bath via french doors, step into the whirlpool tub accented with glass blocks as the steam envelopes you. As you travel to the lower floor you will find a game room with a cozy fireplace for entertaining options and an additional bedroom with full bath for your overnight guests.

Width:	70' 6"	Main Ceiling:	9 ft.
Depth:	48' 0"	Lower Ceiling:	8 ft.
Main Floor:	2,005 sq. ft.	Bedrooms:	4
Lower Floor:	1,047 sq. ft.	Baths:	3
Total Living:	3,052 sq. ft.	Foundation:	Daylight Basement

Price Tier: E

362 Cherry Street

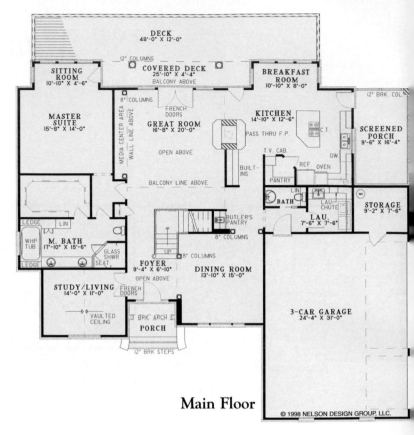

Main Floor

© 1998 NELSON DESIGN GROUP, LLC.

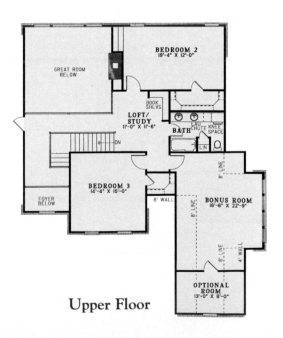

Upper Floor

Invite the family to your house for the holidays in this impressive Nelson Design Group split bedroom home. Enticing french doors open to your private study. A comfortable great room displays a distinctive fireplace that is shared with the kitchen. You can utilize the side screened porch as a convenient grilling porch. Slip off for the evening to your master suite with a sitting room that opens to the rear covered deck. On the upper floor, the children's rooms have spacious closets, and you have the opportunity for a home office and game room with the ample bonus and optional rooms available.

Width: 66' 8"
Depth: 60' 4"
Main Floor: 2,107 sq. ft.
Upper Floor: 1,001 sq. ft.
Total Living: 3,108 sq. ft.*
*Optional Bonus: 485 sq. ft.

Main Ceiling: 9 ft.
Upper Ceiling: 8 ft.
Bedrooms: 3
Baths: 2 1/2
Foundation: Crawl, Slab,
Optional Basement,
Optional Daylight Basement

Price Tier: E

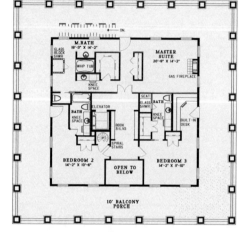

Main Floor

Upper Floor

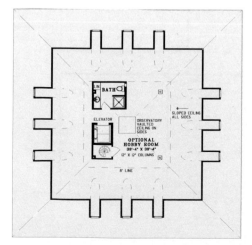

Upper Bonus Floor

606 Dogwood Avenue

We have created a Southern plantation style home that emulates tradition, at its finest. Wrap around porches with boxed columns will welcome family and friends with the opportunity for sipping lemonade while engaging in outdoor conversation. Bedrooms on the upper floor enable close monitoring of the younger children. Access all floors of this home by the elevator or beautiful spiral staircase to the optional hobby room and observatory.

Width: 60' 2"
Depth: 60' 2"
Main Floor: 1,600 sq. ft.
Upper Floor: 1,530 sq. ft.
Total Living: 3,130 sq. ft.*
*Upper Bonus Floor: 1,744 sq. ft.

Main Ceiling: 9 ft.
Upper Ceiling: 9 ft.
Upper Bonus Ceiling: 8 ft.
Bedrooms: 3
Baths: 3 1/2
Foundation: Crawl, Slab

Price Tier: E

600 Brittany Lane

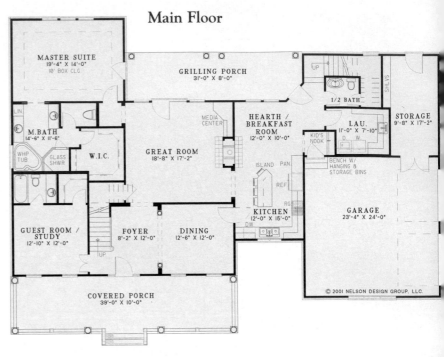

Main Floor

MASTER SUITE
19'-4" X 14'-0"
10' BOX CLG

GRILLING PORCH
31'-0" X 8'-0"

1/2 BATH

STORAGE
9'-8" X 17'-2"

LIN

M.BATH
14'-6" X 11'-6"

MEDIA
CENTER

HEARTH /
BREAKFAST
ROOM
12'-0" X 10'-0"

LAU.
11'-0" X 7'-10"

KID'S
NOOK

W.I.C.

GREAT ROOM
18'-8" X 17'-2"

WHP
TUB

GLASS
SHWR

ISLAND   PAN.

BENCH W/
HANGING 8
STORAGE BINS

REF

GUEST ROOM /
STUDY
12'-10" X 12'-0"

FOYER
8'-2" X 12'-0"

DINING
12'-6" X 12'-0"

KITCHEN
12'-0" X 15'-0"

GARAGE
23'-4" X 24'-0"

UP

COVERED PORCH
39'-0" X 10'-0"

© 2001 NELSON DESIGN GROUP, LLC.

This wonderful Nelson Design Group home has five bedrooms and serves a large family well. The coziest room in the house, aside from the master suite, is a hearth room perfect for quality family time. The kitchen has a view of the front yard, island bar seating and a swinging door to the formal dining room. In addition, the great room fireplace and media center will make entertaining a pleasure while grilling on the rear porch. For added convenience, both the master suite and an additional bedroom are on the main level. Upstairs is complete with three bedrooms, two full bathrooms and large bonus room.

Upper Floor

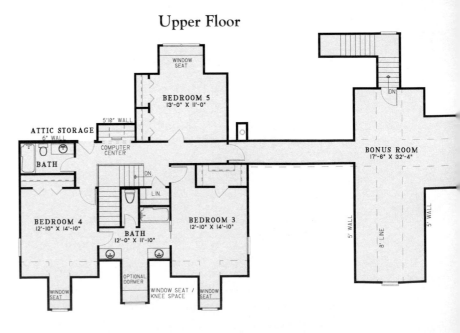

WINDOW
SEAT

BEDROOM 5
13'-0" X 11'-0"

ATTIC STORAGE
6' WALL

5'10" WALL

COMPUTER
CENTER

BONUS ROOM
17'-6" X 32'-4"

BATH

DN

BEDROOM 4
12'-10" X 14'-10"

DN

L.IN.

BEDROOM 3
12'-10" X 14'-10"

BATH
12'-0" X 11'-10"

WINDOW
SEAT

OPTIONAL
DORMER

WINDOW SEAT /
KNEE SPACE

WINDOW
SEAT

5' WALL

8' LINE

5' WALL

Width: 75' 0"
Depth: 54' 6"
Main Floor: 2,025 sq. ft.
Upper Floor: 1,130 sq. ft.
Total Living: 3,155 sq. ft.*
*Optional Bonus: 572 sq. ft.

Main Ceiling: 9 ft.
Upper Ceiling: 8 ft.
Bedrooms: 5
Baths: 4 1/2
Foundation: Crawl, Slab,
       Optional Basement,
       Optional Daylight Basement

Price Tier: E

Main Floor

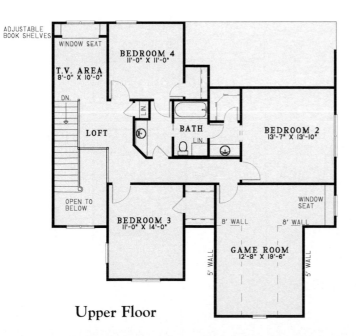

GRILLING PORCH 16'-4" X 7'-0"

GAS BIBB

MASTER SUITE 14'-2" X 16'-4" 10' BOXED CLG

M. BATH 13'-3" X 16'-4"

60'X60' WHP TUB

LIN K S

GLASS SHWR SEAT

W.I.C.

BUILT-INS

FRENCH DOORS

HEARTH ROOM 17'-8" X 10'-8"

ARCHED OPENING

BATH

GUEST ROOM / TEENAGE ROOM 11'-10" X 14'-0"

8" COLUMNS

DW

KITCHEN 11'-0" X 12'-8"

CT

PANTRY

MW OVEN

REF

L.A.U. 10'-2" X 6'-6"

W D

STOR.

HANGING

GREAT ROOM 16'-0" X 22'-8" 10' BOXED CLG

UP

FOYER

COVERED PORCH 24'-6" X 8'-0"

12" COLUMNS

DINING ROOM 11'-0" X 14'-0"

GARAGE 22'-0" X 21'-0"

© 2001 NELSON DESIGN GROUP, LLC.

Upper Floor

ADJUSTABLE BOOK SHELVES

WINDOW SEAT

T.V. AREA 8'-0" X 10'-0"

BEDROOM 4 11'-0" X 11'-0"

DN.

LOFT

LIN

BATH

LIN

BEDROOM 2 13'-7" X 13'-10"

OPEN TO BELOW

BEDROOM 3 11'-0" X 14'-0"

8' WALL

8' WALL

WINDOW SEAT

5' WALL

GAME ROOM 12'-8" X 19'-6"

5' WALL

534 Autumn Drive

Y ou'll find yourself lost in thought as you relax on the covered front porch of this Nelson Design Group home. As you enter the foyer carefully concealing a large walk-in pantry, you will be transfixed by the abundant convenience of the floor plan. The great room has a cozy fireplace and access to the rear-grilling porch for those summer barbeques. The kitchen snack bar makes breakfast easy. Your guests will find a suite complete with full bath amenities awaiting them. Romantic evenings may be enjoyed around the fireplace in the hearth room. As you adjourn to your master bath with corner whirlpool tub, the kids enjoy the privacy of the upper floor with bonus room and TV area boasting a window seat.

Width: 58' 6"	Main Ceiling: 9 ft.
Depth: 60' 6"	Upper Ceiling: 9 ft.
Main Floor: 2,021 sq. ft.	Bedrooms: 5
Upper Floor: 1,227 sq. ft.	Baths: 3
Total Living: 3,248 sq. ft.	Foundation: Crawl, Slab

Price Tier: E

564 Brittany Lane

Main Floor

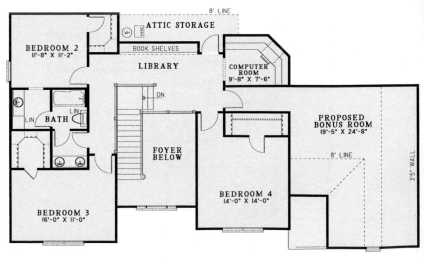

Upper Floor

Pure luxury and elegance describe this exceptional Nelson Design Group home. The formal dining room and kitchen are separated by a butler's pantry adding a buffer for a busy kitchen during meal preparation. This wonderful kitchen has bar counter seating and a large walk-in pantry. On the opposite side of this home is the master suite complete with an adjoining study or nursery. The private master bath is full of amenities including 'his and her' walk-in closets. The upstairs has three additional bedrooms, a shared bath and a library wall near the computer room.

Width: 69' 0"
Depth: 52' 10"
Main Floor: 2,184 sq. ft.
Upper Floor: 1,099 sq. ft.
Total Living: 3,283 sq. ft.*
*Optional Bonus: 494 sq. ft.

Price Tier: E

Main Ceiling: 9 ft.
Upper Ceiling: 8 ft.
Bedrooms: 5
Baths: 2 1/2
Foundation: Crawl, Slab,
    Optional Basement,
    Optional Daylight Basement

Main Floor

MASTER SUITE
22'-0" X 14'-0"
10' BOXED CEILING

GRILLING PORCH
46'-0" X 10'-0"

FRENCH DOORS

SEAT
SHWR

HEARTH ROOM
14'-0" X 17'-4"

BREAKFAST ROOM
12'-4" X 9'-8"

HIGH BAR

LIN.

36" HIGH VANITY

LAUNDRY
9'-0" X 6'-10"

WHP TUB GLASS BLOCKS

COMPUTER CENTER

KITCHEN
12'-0" X 15'-0"

GREAT ROOM
19'-3" X 18'-8"
10' CEILING

M. BATH
12'-8" X 18'-8"

DW

CT

BATH
10'-0" X 7'-10"

DBL OVEN

REF

BUILT-INS

STORAGE
9'-0" X 4'-0"

PAN.

STOR.

UP

GARAGE
22'-0" X 20'-0"

BEDROOM 2 / STUDY
12'-0" X 11'-4"

FOYER
10' CEILING

DINING ROOM
11'-8" X 13'-4"

OPTIONAL FRENCH DOORS

BEDROOM 3
14'-0" X 12'-0"

© 1996 NELSON DESIGN GROUP, LLC.

COVERED PORCH
33'-0" X 8'-0"

Upper Floor

BEDROOM 4
10'-8" X 20'-0"

5' WALL

8' CEILING LINE

6'4" WALL

GAME ROOM
19'-3" X 24'-0"

ATTIC STORAGE

UP

BATH

DN

8' CEILING LINE

8' WALL

240 Linden Avenue

This Nelson Design Group home is extremely practical to build because of its simple box design and spacious interior. The great room features a fireplace nestled between built-ins and an abundance of windows providing a lovely rear view. Nearby is a breakfast bay area open to the kitchen and cozy hearth room including a convenient computer center with nearby storage closet. The opposite side of this home includes a private master suite with boxed ceiling and french door entry to a bathroom full of amenities. An impressive staircase in the great room leads up to a full bath, extra large bedroom and spacious game room with options galore.

Width: 71' 4"
Depth: 66' 0"
Main Floor: 2,746 sq. ft.
Upper Floor: 820 sq. ft.
Total Living: 3,566 sq. ft.

Price Tier: F

Main Ceiling: 9 ft.
Upper Ceiling: 8 ft.
Bedrooms: 5
Baths: 3
Foundation: Crawl, Slab, Optional Basement, Optional Daylight Basement

255

To order call 1.800.590.2423 or to view similar plans visit www.nelsondesigngroup.com

573 Linden Avenue

Main Floor

GLASS SHWR
KS
M.BATH
11'-0" X 24'-6"
SEAT
WHP TUB
LEDGE
MASTER SUITE
14'-6" X 24'-6"
SITTING AREA
ATRIUM DOOR
MEDIA CENTER
FRENCH DOOR
BEDROOM 2
12'-0" X 12'-0"
FRENCH DOORS
BUILT-INS
GALLERY
BUILT-INS
BATH
LIN
BEDROOM 3
12' CEILING
11'-8" X 15'-0"
9' CEILING LINE
FOYER
14' CEILING
10'-0" X 13'-0"
14" COLUMNS
ARCHED OPENING
GRILLING PORCH
22'-8" X 11'-0"
GREAT ROOM
10' CEILING
20'-10" X 18'-0"
UP
OPTIONAL BASEMENT
PAN
DINING ROOM
14' CEILING
12'-10" X 12'-6"
BEDROOM 4 / IN-LAWS SUITE
11' BOXED CEILING
14'-0" X 17'-0"
WHP TUB
KITCHENETTE
RG
REF
BREAKFAST ROOM
12'-0" X 9'-0"
DESK
KITCHEN
14'-0" X 16'-0"
DW
BOOK SHLVS
REF
OVEN MW
T.C.
LAU.
9'-6" X 6'-1"
W D
STORAGE
7'-2" X 4'-4"
GARAGE
20'-0" X 28'-2"

© 2001 NELSON DESIGN GROUP, LLC.

Upper Floor

6' WALL
6' WALL
8' LINE
GAME ROOM / OFFICE
24'-6" X 14'-2"
BATH
LIN
8' LINE
8' LINE

An arched opening with columns welcomes guests into this remarkable Nelson Design Group home. High ceilings are used throughout and massive fourteen-foot ceilings are used in the foyer and dining room. The kitchen is fit for a gourmet cook with a work island and adjoins a large breakfast room with a wall of windows for plenty of natural lighting. A glorious master suite and "mother-in-law" quarters are opposite each other giving the family many options. This home has a great room with built-in media center and french doors to a rear-grilling porch. The upstairs has a full bathroom and large game room or home office with abundant storage.

Width: 70' 0"
Depth: 81' 0"
Main Floor: 3,051 sq. ft.
Upper Floor: 517 sq. ft.
Total Living: 3,568 sq. ft.

Price Tier: F

Main Ceiling: 10 ft.
Upper Ceiling: 8 ft.
Bedrooms: 4
Baths: 4 1/2
Foundation: Crawl, Slab,
Optional Basement,
Optional Daylight Basement

To order call 1.800.590.2423 or to view similar plans visit www.nelsondesigngroup.com

Main Floor

Upper Floor

143 Olive Street

Holidays will be remembered when celebrating in this Nelson Design Group home. Upon entering the open foyer, your guests will enjoy the private sitting room to reminisce the days gone by. Your guests will enjoy the hearth room with coffee and conversation over a roaring fire. Entertain in the formal living area with handy wet bar. After your guests leave, retire to your spacious master suite with a fabulous corner whirlpool bath and corner glass shower. Upstairs, you'll find the children playing in their bedrooms with their own private window seats. A proposed bonus room offers numerous possibilities.

Width: 92' 5"
Depth: 64' 0"
Main Floor: 2,651 sq. ft.
Upper Floor: 1,089 sq. ft.
Total Living: 3,740 sq. ft.*
*Optional Bonus: 497 sq. ft.

Main Ceiling: 10 ft.
Upper Ceiling: 9 ft.
Bedrooms: 4
Baths: 4 1/2
Foundation: Crawl, Slab, Optional Basement, Optional Daylight Basement

Price Tier: F

591 Hampton Circle

Elevation A

Elevation B

Main Floor

GRILLING PORCH
36'-0" X 12'-0"

HEARTH ROOM
13'-0" X 12'-0"

MEDIA CENTER

MASTER SUITE
17'-0" X 19'-0"

GREAT ROOM
19'-10" X 22'-2"
OPEN TO UPPER FLOOR

KITCHEN
13'-0" X 13'-8"

BATH

M.BATH
11'-10" X 23'-8"

GUEST ROOM/STUDY
13'-0" X 16'-10"

GRAND FOYER
11'-6" X 13'-8"

DINING ROOM
15'-2" X 12'-2"

LAU.

KID'S NOOK

PORTICO
9'-0" X 6'-0"

Upper Floor

OPEN TO GREAT ROOM

BATH

BEDROOM 5
19'-4" X 14'-0"

3 CAR GARAGE
23'-4" X 34'-4"

© 2001 NELSON DESIGN GROUP, LLC.

COMPUTER CENTER

BEDROOM 3
11'-6" X 14'-0"

BEDROOM 4
13'-0" X 12'-6"

GAME / TV ROOM
12'-0" X 16'-4"

ATTIC STORAGE / FUTURE SPACE
15'-8" X 24'-7"

This beautiful Nelson Design Group home beckons you into the grand foyer accented by corner niches. The great room pleads for entertaining opportunities with media center. The kitchen features a large pantry and the snack bar opens to the fireplace accented hearth room. The master suite affords entry to the rear-grilling porch while the bath stands ready for relaxation in the whirlpool tub, glass shower and large walk-in closet. Ascending the stairway the remaining bedrooms share full bath access and central computer center. A game/TV room stands ready for entertaining with window seat accents.

Width: 69' 4"
Depth: 89' 10"
Main Floor: 2,636 sq. ft.
Upper Floor: 1,310 sq. ft.
Total Living: 3,946 sq. ft.*
*Optional Bonus: 539 sq. ft.

Price Tier: F

Main Ceiling: 9 ft.
Upper Ceiling: 8 ft.
Bedrooms: 5
Baths: 3 1/2
Foundation: Crawl, Slab,
Optional Basement,
Optional Daylight Basement

Main Floor

SCREENED PORCH
22'-8" X 10'-3"

BUILT-INS | BUILT-INS

OPT. GAS FIREPLACE

HEARTH ROOM
14'-0" X 16'-0"

42" HIGH BAR

1M WET BAR

KITCHEN
19'-8" X 15'-8"

HANGING ROD

DW

REF

DESK

LAU.
10'-0" X 12'-8"

PANTRY

COVERED DECK
26'-8" X 14'-0"

GREAT ROOM
18'-6" X 16'-6"

DESK

PANTRY

OPT GAS FIREPLACE

WALL NICHE | WALL NICHE

DN

GARAGE
22'-0" X 34'-0"

8" COLUMNS

DINING
11'-8" X 14'-0"

8' CLG

UP
FOYER
14'-0" X 18'-4"

PORCH
14'-0" X 5'-0"
VAULTED ◆ ◆ VAULTED

MASTER SUITE
18'-0" X 17'-6"

WHP TUB

GLASS BLOCKS

MASTER BATH
14'-2" X 13'-2"

GLASS SHWR

LIN

LIN

L.B.

BATH

GUEST ROOM/ STUDY
15'-0" X 12'-0"

Upper Floor

4' WALL

9' LINE

GAME ROOM
23'-7" X 13'-9"

9' LINE

9' LINE

SLOPED CEILING

9' LINE

OPEN TO BELOW

8' LINE

BEDROOM 2
16'-10" X 11'-0"

9' LINE

BUILT-INS | WALL NICHE | BUILT-INS

ATTIC STORAGE

BATH

DN

VAULTED CEILING

BEDROOM 3
12'-0" X 14'-0"

OPEN TO BELOW

VAULTED CEILING

VAULTED CEILING

Lower Floor

BEDROOM 4
12'-8" X 13'-6"

POOL ROOM
17'-8" X 24'-0"

ATRIUM DOORS

BATH

REF | 1M | MEDIA CENTER

GOLF CART STORAGE
13'-4" X 16'-0"

STRG.

TV AREA
11'-6" X 16'-4"

STRG.

STORAGE
14'-4" X 12'-0"

403 Huntington Avenue

Deceiving in its façade, this home from Nelson Design Group is both spacious and comfortable. A stunning stairway is centered in the two-story foyer, and beyond is the great room, also with a double-height ceiling, which overlooks a huge covered deck and separates living areas from sleeping quarters. The kitchen, laundry, pantry and hearth room are situated on the garage side of the house, while the master suite is located opposite. The upper floor hosts two bedrooms, a bath and a game room, and the lower level contains a fourth bedroom, bath and billiards room with kitchenette.

Width: 70' 0"
Depth: 75' 10"
Main Floor: 2,777 sq. ft.
Upper Floor: 1,170 sq. ft.
Total Living: 3,947 sq. ft.*
*Optional Lower Floor: 1,616 sq. ft.

Main Ceiling: 10 ft.
Upper Ceiling: 9 ft.
Lower Bonus Ceiling: 9 ft.
Bedrooms: 4
Baths: 4, 2-1/2
Foundation: Crawl, Slab, Daylight Basement

Price Tier: G

501 Brittany Lane

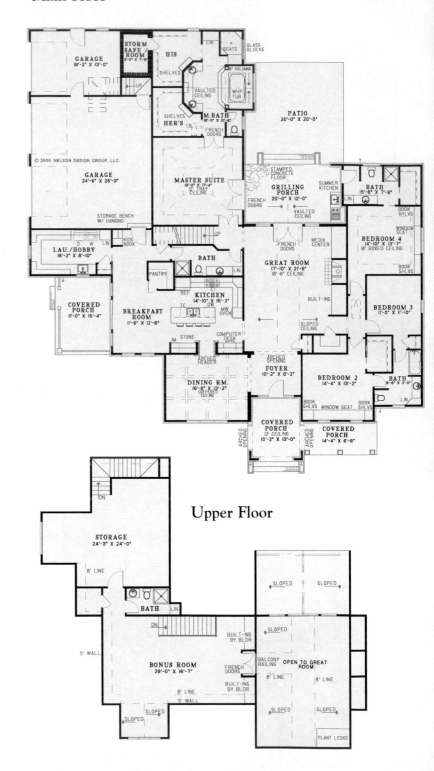

A lovely stone entry, arched windows and covered porches welcome you into this enchanting Nelson Design Group home. Special ceiling designs and arches are carried throughout the home adding elegance to this extraordinary home. A family oriented kitchen and breakfast room access the side porch perfect for large family gatherings. The master suite is a spectacular world of its own and has features including french doors, columns, vaulted ceiling as well as a safe room and is placed away from the three additional bedrooms. You must study this plan to fully appreciate the ultimate amenities within.

Width: 79' 10"
Depth: 86' 8"
Main Floor: 3,354 sq. ft.
Upper Floor: 615 sq. ft.
Total Living: 3,969 sq. ft.

Price Tier: F

Main Ceiling: 9 ft.
Upper Ceiling: 9 ft.
Bedrooms: 4
Baths: 4
Foundation: Crawl, Slab,
Optional Basement,
Optional Daylight Basement

Upper Floor

Main Floor

© 1993 Nelson Design Group, LLC

Upper Floor

584 Hickory Place

French classic design and ambiance culminate in this Nelson Design Group home. The great room features vaulted ceilings, built-in media center, fireplace and french door entry to the rear-grilling porch. The kitchen offers an island bar for culinary preparation. The wine cellar stands ready for the quiet nights at home as you relax in the master suite sitting room warmed by the corner fireplace. The master bath contains separate walk-in closets and whirlpool tub illuminated by skylights. Two bedrooms with desks and shared access to a full bath are found on the upper floor. An additional bedroom features bay window and another private bath. A bonus room and storage area complete the design.

Width: 79' 10"
Depth: 60' 6"
Main Floor: 2,861 sq. ft.
Upper Floor: 1,600 sq. ft.
Total Living: 4,461 sq. ft.*
*Optional Bonus: 250 sq. ft.

Main Ceiling: 10 ft.
Upper Ceiling: 9 ft.
Bedrooms: 5
Baths: 4 1/2
Foundation: Crawl, Slab,
Optional Basement,
Optional Daylight Basement

Price Tier: G

505 Dogwood Avenue

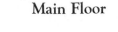

Main Floor

Front View

Rear View

Lower Floor

Entering this stately Nelson Design Group home you become overwhelmed by the expansive floor plan. The great room features vaulted ceilings, a grand fireplace, and amazing rear view. The open kitchen offers the chef ample counter space utilizing the island bar to showcase their culinary exquisiteness. The master suite has a cozy fireplace while the bath presents a column accented whirlpool tub and glass shower. Each of the remaining bedrooms offer a walk-in closet. As you descend the spiral staircases to the lower level you'll enter an array of activity rooms to include an exercise, hobby, and game room with access to a full bath and walk-in closet.

Width: 84' 2"
Depth: 62' 0"
Main Floor: 3,062 sq. ft.
Lower Floor: 1,766 sq. ft.
Total Living: 4,828 sq. ft.

Main Ceiling: 9 ft.
Lower Ceiling: 9 ft.
Bedrooms: 4
Baths: 4
Foundation: Basement, Daylight Basement

Price Tier: G

621 Birchwood Lane

Main Floor

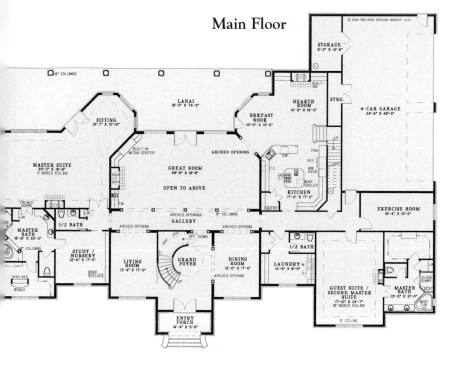

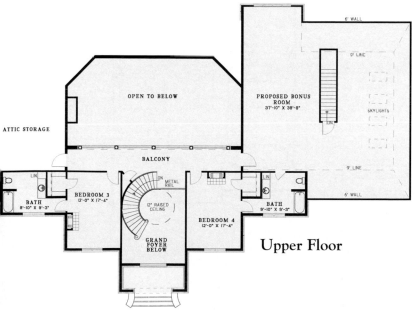

Upper Floor

This absolutely exquisite design by Nelson Design Group is a dream home come true. A grand foyer separates a formal living room and dining room and has stairs leading to a balcony overlooking the enormous great room. The main master suite has a large sitting bay, private access to the study and french door entry to a luxurious master bath. Upstairs, placed above the four-car garage, is a large bonus room with skylights and an additional stairwell to the main floor hearth room. The expansive kitchen adjoins both breakfast nook and hearth room and is located near the second master suite for an abundance of options. Fireplaces are placed throughout for warmth while a rear column-lined Lanai is perfect for entertaining as well as relaxing.

Width: 117' 8"	Main Ceiling: 10 ft.
Depth: 84' 8"	Upper Ceiling: 9 ft.
Main Floor: 5,338 sq. ft.	Bedrooms: 4
Upper Floor: 1,050 sq. ft.	Baths: 4, 2-1/2
Total Living: 6,388 sq. ft.*	Foundation: Crawl, Slab,
*Optional Bonus: 1,460 sq. ft.	Optional Basement,
	Optional Daylight Basement

Price Tier: G

215 Birchwood Lane

This magnificent Nelson Design Group home is designed with inviting appeal. You'll marvel at the openness as one room welcomes you to the next. Relax in your comfortable hearth room as the cook prepares dinner in the gourmet kitchen. The children will be entertained by the convenient computer center tucked away just off the kitchen. After dinner, retreat to your fully appointed and private master suite and bath with soothing whirlpool bath. On the upper level, the children will discover plenty of open space with their own private bath, spacious bedrooms and game room for the entire family.

Width: 121' 10"
Depth: 95' 5"
Main Floor: 4,774 sq. ft.
Upper Floor: 2,564 sq. ft.
Total Living: 7,338 sq. ft.*
*Optional Bonus: 2,015 sq. ft.

Main Ceiling: 12 ft.
Upper Ceiling: 10 ft.
Bedrooms: 4
Baths: 4 1/2
Foundation: Crawl, Slab, Opt. Basement,
Opt. Daylight Basement

Price Tier: G

Main Floor

Upper Floor

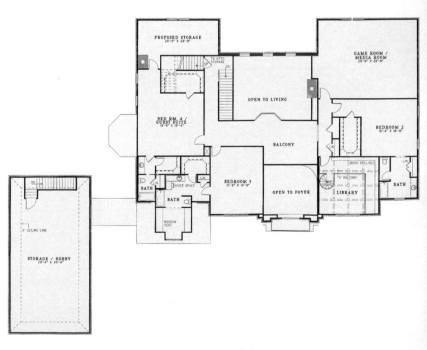

... more plans

Address http://www.nelsondesigngroup.com/

Marketing

Nelson Design Group offers a wide variety of marketing tools that will assist you in selling your homes. Because we cater daily to a diverse marketplace with a broad mix of consumers, real estate professionals and home builders, we know what buyers want, how builders build, and how to design and market homes that sell quickly.

NDG offers a complete product line of marketing materials including full color feature sheets, framed and matted color renderings, streetscapes and outdoor promotional signage allowing the builder or developer to have cost effective marketing materials on their homes and for their business.

Our in-house marketing and design staff provides you with everything you need to develop a turn-key marketing program and we can answer any questions you or your staff may have. We provide valued expertise throughout all phases of development from site selection and layout to final marketing strategies.

"When building in the Dallas/Fort Worth Metro, you must come to the realization that you are competing in one of the largest, fastest growing New Home markets in the World. Knowledge, hard work and dedication only get you started here. It was essential for us to find the competent resources that could handle all of our development planning, home design, marketing and plan costing needs. I can't tell you how pleased I was to find a company that had all of this to offer. Our business has increased over ten times since we began our relationship with **Nelson Design Group** *and it has been a pleasure having them as an intricate part of our team. Thank you for your vision of what builders and developers really need."*

KENMARK HOMES

That Works

Selling Your Home Faster

Feature Sheets

These 8 1/2" x 11" feature sheets include specifications, highlights and sales features describing each home plan as well as your company information. Customized logo work is available for an additional price.

Price: $50.00

per 100 quantity

Outdoor Posters

These 24" x 36" full color laminated posters are perfect for displaying at the Open House, Grand Opening, Sales Office or the Model Home. Metal Sign Holders & Brochure Box are available...

Price: Laminated Poster......$199.00

Metal Sign Holder:......$75.00   Brochure Box:......$45.00

Individuals shopping for a new home tend to drive by after work hours when no one is on the job site. These outdoor posters and feature sheets give the potential buyer much needed plan specs and your contact information to help you sell your home faster.

Framed Prints

Greet clients with an attractive display perfect for hanging in your office lobby or in a show home. Each finished 20" x 24" framed and matted print includes design highlights and your company's information.

Price: Gold Frame......$150.00   Black Frame......$89.00

Big Image On A Small Budget

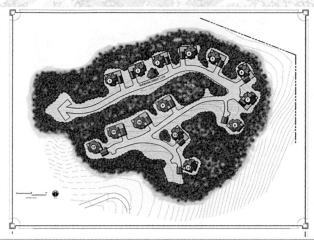

Land Use Planning & Design

Nelson Design Group works with builders and developers during the conceptualization phase of land use planning. We provide valuable expertise from site selection to proper land use. We can recommend the appropriate lot sizes to maximize the best use for the land and assist in creating effective neighborhoods. Our services during these early development stages help builders avoid costly revisions in design and engineering.

Identity Packages

Nelson Design Group's in-house design department can develop a professional image for your firm including company logos and brochures.

Professional Services

Utilizing Nelson Design Group's advertising services, you will save money and time in developing your marketing strategies. Nelson Design Group has a staff of experienced specialists to assist you in every phase of your project. We provide the following services: News Releases, Ad Design, Grand Opening Coordination and Home Development Consultation.

Development and Collection Portfolios

Builders will find individual designs and also several different groups of plans such as our new Wellington and Renaissance Collections. Our designs have complimentary themes that work together to build a single home, a neighborhood or a full-scale development.

Multi-Media Support

Nelson Design Group's website provides a builder with the opportunity to promote their firm's website and also link to our home plan search page. Nelson Design Group can also assist in the marketing of your firm and developments.

269

Tru-Cost
ESTIMATING

Tru-Cost Estimating is a valuable tool for planning and constructing your new home. Tru-Cost is available for each of NDG's plans.

We provide a complete estimate, similar to a bid, that will act as a checklist for all items you will need to select or coordinate during your building process. Tru-Cost will provide you a direct comparison to track your cost and help you stay within budget.

Tru-Cost has options that allow you to customize your estimate, to include labor rates and material prices for your area and can be imported into Tru-Cost software. The key to a successful project is to have a realistic budget, Tru-Cost is the solution.

Estimating Your Home Cost...

Tru-Cost ESTIMATING

Tru-Cost is adaptable to a variety of estimating techniques and methods. By utilizing a ledger entry format, creating a bid is as simple as selecting items from the Master Database.

Tru-Cost Estimating provides a simplified method for calculating costs for equipment, labor, material and subcontractors, thus creating more accurate bids and easier cost tracking. Tru-Cost has multiple reports that assist a variety of tasks, from ordering materials to negotiating price with clients. Tru-Cost can automatically update pricing on previous bids to meet current prices within the Master Database.

Ledger Entry Form

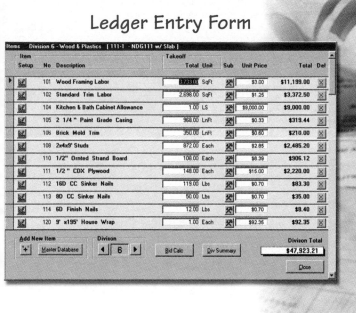

Itemized Listing

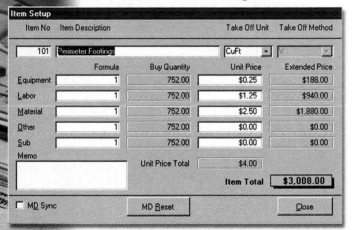

Advantages

– Quick startup

– Save time with material databases

– Import estimates from NDG

– Create a variety of reports

– Export reports to Excel or Palm Pilot

– Technical Support

– 16 Standard Construction Divisions

Bid Overview

Bid Calculations				
	Base Cost	Adjust %	Adjustment	Adjusted Cost
Equipment	$13,188.00	10.00%	$1,318.80	$14,506.80
Labor	$28,342.00	10.00%	$2,834.20	$31,176.20
Materials	$62,292.22	10.00%	$6,229.22	$68,521.44
Other	$4,309.65	10.00%	$430.97	$4,740.62
Sub Bid	$71,537.17	10.00%	$7,153.72	$78,690.88
Total	$179,669.04		$17,966.90	$197,635.94
Overhead & Profit		10.00%		$19,763.59
Bid Price				$217,399.53

Recalc   Report   Close

Features

– Organize subcontractor bids

– Itemize materials per category

– Easy to adjust material takeoff quantities

– Adjust overhead and profit margins

– Mark up individual categories, equipment, labor, materials, etc.

– Step-by-step instructional and interactive tutorial

273

Nelson Design Group LLC

RESIDENTIAL PLANNERS - DESIGNERS

Home Plan Books

Nelson Design Group wants to ensure that our customers, whether consumers or builders, have the most helpful designs available. At NDG, we are constantly developing new plan publications in addition to our permanent collection. These books are valuable tools in selecting the home of your dreams, providing easy-to-read floor plans and specs, and detailed artistic renderings in full color. Each book showcases new plan collections, with minimal duplication, for optimum variety.

Builder Edition - Volume I.........(Black/White – 80 pages).........$10

Builder Edition - Volume II........(Black/White – 80 pages).........$10

"NewBeginnings"...................(Full Color – 156 pages).........$15

Builder's Special Edition I..........(Full Color – 288 pages).........$20

Builder's Special Edition II.........(Fulll Color – 288 pages).........$20

All 5 Plan Books...$50

(shipping and handling not included)

274

Big Image On A Small Budget?

Feature Sheets
8.5" x 11" customized color rendering with floor plan, your color logo and customized bullet points. . . . . . . 100 sheets/pack - 20% discount with 2 packs or more. . . **$50**

Framed Prints
Professionally framed and matted 20" x 24" color renderings customized with your logo, floor plan and bullet points.

Black Metal. **$89**

Gold Wood. **$150**

Outdoor Signage
24" x 36", similar to above but in vertical format laminated and weatherproofed, customized and ready for display in front of your construction site.

Color Laminated. **$195**

Free blueprint of yard sign holder with sign purchase

Interior Signage
24" x 36", customized and ready for mounting on foamcore backing. Perfect for displaying on easels at Open Houses, Grand Openings, Sales Offices, Model Homes, etc.

Full Color. **$150**

Brochures
Have your own customized brochure introducing and promoting your company or development as well as your benefits with photos and logo display. . . . . **Call**

Logo and Artwork
Nelson Design Group's graphics and marketing team will develop a professional logo or other art design for your company, development, etc. . . . . From **$250**

Dura-trans
Special backlit 'Dura-tran' color images ready for display. Available in a variety of custom sizes. . . . . **$125** to **$195**

Specialty Printing
Nelson Design Group can handle most every requirement: business cards, letterhead, envelopes, presentation folders, thank-you cards - and more. . . . . **Call**

Video Presentations
We can produce a video presentation for you to play on VHS videotape and/or CD. Ask for the Nelson Design video as an example!. . . . . **Call**

3-D Virtual Reality Tours
Nelson Design Group provides this cutting edge service allowing you to view the home interior through 3-D visualization. . . . . **Call**

Promotion, Ad Placement, Public Relations And More!
Nelson Design Group has experienced professionals to assist you in every phase of your marketing program. . . . . **Call**

CUSTOMER INFORMATION

Name: _____

Company Name: _____

Address: _____

City: _____ State: _____ Zip: _____

Phone: _____ Fax: _____

E-mail Address: _____

Credit Card #: _____ Exp. Date: _____

☐ VISA ☐ MasterCard ☐ AmEx ☐ Discover

☐ Check/Money Order Enclosed (U.S. Funds)

BLUEPRINT PRICING

Price Tier	Square Feet	One Set	Four Sets	Eight Sets	Twelve Sets	Repro Sets	CAD Disk
A	0-1499	$400	$435	$475	$520	$585	$1,060
B	1500-1999	$440	$475	$515	$560	$630	$1,105
C	2000-2499	$480	$515	$555	$605	$670	$1,145
D	2500-2999	$550	$585	$635	$675	$755	$1,430
E	3000-3499	$610	$645	$685	$730	$805	$1,480
F	3500-3999	$650	$685	$730	$780	$855	$1,530
G	4000 and up	$700	$735	$775	$820	$900	$1,575

NUMBER OF SETS

☐ **ONE SET** (stamped "not for construction")
Recommended for preview study

☐ **FOUR SETS**
Recommended for bidding

☐ **EIGHT SETS**
Recommended for construction

☐ **TWELVE SETS**
Recommended for multiple bids

☐ **REPRODUCIBLE SETS**
Recommended for construction/modifications

☐ **CAD Disks**
DXF/DWG Files

Prices are subject to change. Special or grouped plans may vary in price.

SHIPPING AND HANDLING

	1-3 Sets	4-7 Sets	8 or more Sets	Repro Sets	CAD Disk
U.S. Regular (5-6 business days)	$17.50	$20.00	$25.00	$17.50	$15.00
U.S. Express (2-3 business days)	$35.00	$40.00	$45.00	$35.00	$30.00
Canada Regular (5-7 business days)	$40.00	$45.00	$50.00	$40.00	$35.00
Canada Express (2-4 business days)	$55.00	$60.00	$65.00	$55.00	$50.00
Overseas/Airmail (7-10 business days)	$70.00	$80.00	$90.00	$70.00	$60.00

	Plan # ____	Plan # ____	Plan # ____
Source Code:			
Price Tier			
Number of Sets			
Blueprint Cost			
Additional Sets @ $40 each			
Right Readable-Reversed Sets @ $50			
Tru-Cost Estimating @ $125			
CAD Disk			
Reproducible Sets			
☐ Crawl			
☐ Slab			
☐ Basement			
☐ Basement (Opt.) @ $250			
☐ Daylight Basement			
☐ Daylight Basement (Opt.) @ $250			
Tru-Cost Software @ $595			
☐ Other			
Sub-Total			
Shipping & Handling			
TOTAL			

Additional Sets - Additional individual sets of plan ordered at point of sale are **$40** each.

Right Readable-Reversed Plans - A **$50** surcharge. From the total number of sets you order above, all plans will be reversed. You pay only **$50**. Note: All plans are produced using computers, and all text is reversed as well.

All Nelson Design Group, LLC sales are non-credit purchases. The total amount is due when your order is placed. Orders may not be returned or exchanged. All orders are final.

MAIL TO: **Nelson Design Group, LLC**
100 E. Huntington, Suite C, Jonesboro, AR 72401
Phone: 870-931-5777 • Fax: 870-931-5792
www.nelsondesigngroup.com

For Ordering and Technical Assistance call:
800-590-2423

275

WHAT'S INCLUDED IN YOUR PLANS?

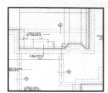

FOUNDATION PLANS

(1/4" or 1/2" = 1')

Most plans are available with a slab or crawl space foundation. Optional walkout style basement (three walls masonry with a wood framed rear wall with windows and doors) or full basement are available if plan allows, at an additional cost. Please call for details.

FLOOR PLANS

(1/4" = 1')

Each home plan includes the floor plan showing the dimensioned locations of walls, doors and windows as well as a schematic electrical layout.

ELEVATION SETS

(1/4" = 1')

All plans include the exterior elevations (front, rear, right and left) that show and describe the finished material of the house.

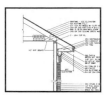

DETAIL SECTION(S)

(1/4" or 1/2" = 1')

The building sections are vertical cuts through the house showing floor, ceiling and roof height information.

KITCHEN AND BATH ELEVATIONS

(1/2" = 1')

The kitchen and bath elevations show the arrangement and size of each cabinet and other fixtures in the room. These drawings give basic information that can be used to create customized layouts with a cabinet manufacturer.

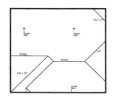

ROOF OVERVIEW PLAN

(1/4" = 1')

This is a "bird's eye" view showing the roof slopes, ridges, valleys and any saddles.

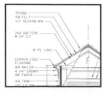

MISCELLANEOUS DETAILS

(3/4" = 1')

These are included for many interior and exterior conditions that require more specific information for their construction.

ADDITIONAL PLAN SERVICES

FLOOR FRAMING PLANS

(1/4" = 1'-0")

Each floor framing plan shows each floor joist indicating the size, spacing and length. All beams are labeled and sized.

$100.00 (includes one floor. Additional floors $50.00 each)

CEILING JOIST FRAMING PLAN

(1/4" = 1'-0")

The ceiling joist framing plan shows each ceiling joist indicating the size, spacing and length. All beams are labeled and sized.

$100.00

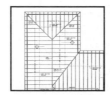

ROOF FRAMING PLAN

(1/4" = 1'-0")

The roof framing plan shows each rafter, valley, hip and ridge indicating the size, spacing and length. All beams are labeled and sized.

$100.00

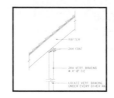

MISCELLANEOUS FRAMING DETAILS

Each framing plan sheet includes any framing details that are needed (boxed ceiling details, connection details, etc.) All of the framing is designed using conventional framing materials. Open web trusses are used in most one-and-a-half story and two-story plans.

CAD DISKS

CAD Disks are available on all plans. Standard formats are DWG and DXF. See order form for pricing.

RIGHT-READABLE REVERSED PLANS

Right-readable reversed plans are available should you wish to build your home reverse of the one shown in our book. The lettering and dimensions appear right reading. From the total number of sets ordered, all plans will be reversed. Check the appropriate area on the area form or let us know when ordering.

REPRODUCIBLES

With the purchase of a reproducible set (vellums), a license and copyright release are also provided. Similarly, the purchase of reproducible home plans carries the same copyright protection as mentioned in this book. It is generally allowed to make up to a maximum of 10 copies for the construction of a single dwelling only. To use any plans more than once, and to avoid any copyright licenses infringement, it is necessary to contact Nelson Design Group, LLC to receive a release and a license for any extended usage. Nelson Design Group, LLC will make special provisions for plan usage within developments when previous arrangements have been made directly with Nelson Design Group, LLC.

ADDITIONAL PLAN SERVICES PROVIDED BY NELSON DESIGN GROUP

TRU-COST ESTIMATING

Nelson Design Group developed the Tru-Cost Estimating system to be a valuable tool for builders to use in the planning and construction of new homes. We have combined a thorough database of items required for construction. We offer three different options for our customers by providing estimates for all of our Stock Plans, as well as Modified and Custom Plans. Our Custom Estimate is not only available for our plans, it's also offered for our customer's plans. The Custom Estimate service allows the customer to modify or change any of the pricing or materials they may wish to use.

Base NDG Plan Estimate	**$125.00**
Revised Estimate for NDG Stock Plan	**$250.00**
Custom Estimate starting at	**$500.00**
Estimating Software	**$595.00**

Nelson Design Group, LLC Home Plans do not carry an architect/engineer stamp. Code Compliance: Our plans are drawn to meet the 1995 CABO One & Two Family Dwelling Code and the 1994 Standard Building Code with the 1996 Georgia amendments. Many states and counties amend the codes in their area. Consult your local building officials to determine the plan, code and site requirements.
Heated and Cooled Square Footage calculations are made from outside the exterior frame wall and do not include decks, porches, garages, basements, attics, fireplaces, etc. We include two story and vaulted areas only once in the calculations of the first floor. Stairs are counted once. Balconies and open walkways in two-story and vaulted areas are included in square footage of the second floor.

MODIFY YOUR STOCK PLAN

Not only do we have numerous designs prepared for various sized homes, we encourage the modification of our stock plans to meet personal specifications. Nelson Design Group will help you fulfill your dreams with a customized computer area, media center, hearth room, privacy nooks or whatever your needs entail.

Modification work has a per plan set up charge and hourly fee or, is priced per total square footage under roof depending on the changes required and the complexity. To receive an estimated fee and completion time for modifications please call **1-800-590-2423** or fax a copy of the floor plan and the changes you wish to make, along with your daytime phone number to 870-931-5792.

The reproducible cost and the set up fee are required before revisions can be made, and the remaining fees are to be paid prior to shipping.

Any modifications made to the vellums by parties other than Nelson Design Group, LLC voids any warranties expressed or implied including the warranties of fitness for a particular purpose and merchantability. We recommend that an engineer in your area review your plans before actual construction begins due to local codes.

Foundation Alterations
Optional Basement Foundation - $250.00
Optional Daylight Basement Foundation - $250.00
Monolithic Slab - $250.00

Interior/Exterior Alterations
Siding to Brick - $250.00
Brick to Siding - $250.00
Hip Roof to Gable - $250.00 and up
Gable to Hip Roof - $250.00 and up
Flat Ceilings to Vaulted Ceilings - $250.00

Garage Alterations
Side Load to Front Entry - $250.00
Front Entry to Side Load - $250.00
Two Car to Three Car - $375.00

Call our modification department for questions regarding these or other modifications.

COPYRIGHT LAWS

Reproduction of the illustration and working drawings of these home plans, either in whole or in part, including any form and/or preparation of derivative works thereof, for any reason without prior written permission is strictly prohibited. The purchase of a set of home plans in no way transfers any copyright or other ownership interest in it to the buyer except for a limited license to use that set of home plans for the construction of one, and only one, dwelling unit. The purchase of an additional set(s) of that home plan at a reduced price from the original set or as part of a multiple set package does not convey to the buyer a license to construct more than one dwelling. This is also the case with reproducible vellum, CAD disks or any multimedia.

Similarly, the purchase of reproducible vellum carries the same copyright protection as mentioned above. It is generally allowed to make up to a maximum of 10 copies for the construction of a single dwelling only. To use any plans more than once, and to avoid any copyright licenses infringement, it is necessary to contact the plan designer to receive a release and a license for any extended usage. Nelson Design Group, LLC will make special provisions for plan usage within developments when previous arrangements have been made directly with Nelson Design Group, LLC.

Whereas a purchaser of reproducible is granted license to make copies, it should be noted that as copyright material, making photocopies from blueprints is illegal.

Copyright and licensing of home plans for construction exist to protect all parties. It respects and supports the intellectual property of the original architect or designer. Copyright law has been reinforced over the past few years. Willful infringement could cause settlements for statutory damages up to $100,000.00 plus attorney fees, damages and loss of profits.

84 LUMBER
Build on what we know.™

84lumber.com

WHO WE ARE

84 Lumber Company is the largest privately held supplier of building materials in the United States. Founded in 1956 by Joe Hardy in the town of Eighty Four, Pennsylvania, 20 miles south of Pittsburgh, 84 Lumber is still growing. In 2002, we opened 20 new stores, raising the company's store count to 437 locations in 34 states coast-to-coast. In two of the past three years, 84 Lumber sold more building materials to professional contractors and remodelers than any other supplier, with 2002 sales exceeding $2 billion.

OUR MISSION

84 Lumber Company is dedicated to being the low cost provider of lumber and building materials to professional builders, remodelers and dedicated do-it-yourselfers, while adding value to our quality products through a trained, knowledgeable and motivated team of professional sales associates.

WHAT WE OFFER

- Competitive Prices
- Top Quality Products
- Knowledgeable Associates
- Special Order Program
- Convenient Hours
- Professional Delivery

INVENTORY & VOLUME BUYING POWER

With over 400 stores and a centralized buying system, customers can take advantage of our national purchasing power to save money and add more to their bottom line. Through our established relationships with national suppliers and bulk buying power, you can rely on 84 to have the products and quantities you need.

- Lumber
- Plywood
- Insulation
- Trim
- Mouldings
- Flooring
- Siding
- Drywall
- Decks
- Trusses
- Roofing
- Skylights
- Engineered Lumber
- Hardware
- Doors and Windows
- Kitchens and Baths
- Storage Buildings
- 84 Home Packages

MEETING THE NEEDS OF PROFESSIONAL BUILDERS

To meet the special needs of the professional builder, 84 Lumber has assembled a well-trained contractor sales force of more than 1,200 associates nationwide, with each of the company's stores having two to four contractor sales representatives (CSR's) on staff. Each new CSR goes through an extensive training and development program, and attends on-going courses throughout their career to stay current on the latest building trends and new services available. Our CSR's truly understand that every contractor has their own unique set of needs relating to service, product selection, delivery, and financing, just to name a few. Our CSR's strive to learn the operation of each contractor's business so that 84 Lumber may serve you as efficiently as possible.

FINANCING OPTIONS

84 Lumber provides many fast, builder-friendly financing options with our same down-to-earth value and convenience.

SPECIAL ORDER PROGRAM & BUILDING COMPONENTS

While our stores are well stocked with many basic building materials, we also have an outstanding special order program which allows virtually any custom product to be ordered through any 84 Lumber store associate or CSR. We will cater to a wide range of tastes by ordering those hard-to-find products, to be delivered when you need them, in most cases, directly to a job site if requested. 84 Lumber also operates building component manufacturing facilities in major markets, producing roof and floor trusses, as well as wall panels to help builders become more efficient and profitable.

COMPUTERIZED BIDS AND PRICING

Give us your materials list, blueprints, sketches or ideas and we will process your estimate within 24 hours and your blueprint take-off within 48 hours. If you're not ready to start your next project now, 84 offers a 30-day price guarantee. Pay for the materials now to lock in current prices, and you'll have up to 30 days to pick up your materials without any change in cost to you!

FAST AND RELIABLE DELIVERY

We know your time is important, and we won't waste it. Careful scheduling assures that materials are delivered to the job site when you need them. If you prefer, our convenient "drive up and load" sheds with express loading allow you to spend more time on your project and less time pulling carts through those crowded "superstores".

For the 84 Lumber location nearest you call:
1-800-359-8484

WHEN YOU FOLLOW A RECIPE, CAN YOUR KITCHEN KEEP UP?

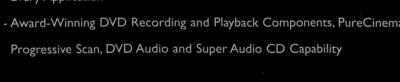

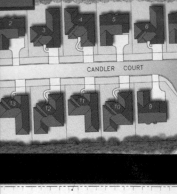

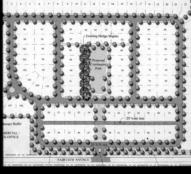

We Take Your Ideas to the Next Level...

Featured project development by Sapphire Lakes,

land planning by Luther E. Smith & Associates, PA

www.bhmdesign.com
866.684.3820
Asheville, North Carolina

BHMdesign

LiveSouth.com

The best source for choosing your place in the South

PRO SOUND COMES HOME TO RESIDENTIAL NEW CONSTRUCTION AND RETROFITS

SPECIFYING AND INSTALLING JBL FOR RESIDENTIAL SOUND SYSTEMS NOT ONLY GIVES YOU THE BENEFITS OF OUR SOUND QUALITY AND REPUTATION FOR RELIABILITY. IT OFFERS THE PEACE OF MIND ASSOCIATED WITH CHOOSING THE BRAND PROFESSIONALS IN THE MUSIC AND MOVIE INDUSTRIES RELY ON.

IN 1928, WHEN JAMES B. LANSING HELPED MAKE MOVIES TALK, QUALITY SOUND REPRODUCTION WAS LITERALLY UNHEARD OF. THE COMPANY LANSING FOUNDED WENT ON TO HELP DEFINE THE CONCEPT OF HIGH FIDELITY. WE HAVEN'T LOOKED BACK SINCE.

TODAY, JBL IS THE SYSTEM OF CHOICE FOR MORE THAN 80% OF ALL DOLBY® DIGITAL CINEMA INSTALLATIONS. WE'RE IN THE FINEST CONCERT HALLS AND AT MAJOR ROCK CONCERTS, AND WE CONTINUE TO PRODUCE THE MONITOR SPEAKER OF CHOICE FOR TOP RECORDING STUDIOS. JBL'S RESIDENTIAL PRODUCTS ARE FURTHER EXAMPLES OF OUR CONTINUED COMMITMENT TO ADVANCED SOUND REPRODUCTION TECHNOLOGY.

NOTHING QUITE COMPARES TO LISTENING TO YOUR FAVORITE MUSIC OR WATCHING THE LATEST MOVIES WHILE EXPERIENCING ALL THE INTENSITY AND NUANCES OF A LIVE PERFORMANCE...RIGHT AT HOME!

WE'RE NOT JUST BRINGING PRO SOUND HOME – WE'RE HELPING YOU PUT IT RIGHT INTO WALLS, CEILINGS AND PATIOS.

   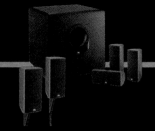 

| IN-WALL AND CEILING LOUDSPEAKERS | BOOKSHELF LOUDSPEAKERS | FLOORSTANDING LOUDSPEAKERS | POWERED SUBWOOFERS | SURROUND CINEMA LOUDSPEAKER SYSTEMS | STUDIO MONITORS | ALL-WEATHER LOUDSPEAKERS |

PRO SOUND COMES HOME™

JBL

JBL Consumer Products
250 Crossways Park Drive, Woodbury, NY 11797
8500 Balboa Boulevard, Northridge, CA 91329
818.895.8187 www.jbl.com
©2002 JBL, Incorporated
H A Harman International Company

Why an L.J. Smith Stair System is the best choice...

It's important to us that your stairway is not only functional and beautiful, but that it safely carries you and your loved ones from one floor to another for decades to come. L.J. Smith's stairway components are uniquely designed so they provide the strongest, most durable and attractive stairway, when installed properly. You will have piece of mind knowing you made the right choice with the stair components manufacturer who is recognized as the leader and innovator in the industry for over one hundred years...L.J. Smith.

Custom pre-built straight, circular and spiral stairways are also available from Woodsmiths Design and Manufacturing, a division of L.J. Smith. Woodsmiths uses only genuine L.J. Smith stair parts in their wood stairs, however, their abilities also include carved wood turnings, glass, metals and even molded plastics.

For more information on L.J. Smith products, visit www.ljsmith.net, contact your local lumber dealer or call us at (740) 269-2221.
For more information on Woodsmiths Design & Manufacturing capabilities, visit www.woodsmiths.net or call us at (800) 874-2876.

Windsor Knows Me and My Business.

"Windsor knows what it takes to make me happy. It means delivering the garage doors I need *exactly when I need them.* It takes *competitive pricing* to keep me in the game and *product quality* that lasts long after the walk-through and the homeowners move in. Windsor knows I need a *broad line* of decorative panel designs, colors and glass inserts to increase my profit margins while giving each home it's own unique look. They also know that *service* is more than just a word, it's action backed by a proven North American network of local Windsor subcontractors. But most of all, Windsor knows that *when it's all said and done,* if my homeowners are happy...*I'm happy*... For All the Right Reasons."

BUILDER
W
FRIENDLY

WINDSOR DOOR
For All the Right Reasons.

www.windsordoor.com

GARAGE DOORS, INSTALLATION & SERVICE

Little Rock, AR: 501/562-1872   Marysville, CA: 530/743-1851   TECHNICAL SUPPORT: 1-800-WINDSOR

Today's homebuyer is looking at closets in a different way...

Are you?

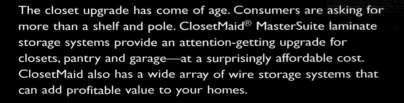

The closet upgrade has come of age. Consumers are asking for more than a shelf and pole. ClosetMaid® MasterSuite laminate storage systems provide an attention-getting upgrade for closets, pantry and garage—at a surprisingly affordable cost. ClosetMaid also has a wide array of wire storage systems that can add profitable value to your homes.

Get ahead of your prospects—and the competition. Contact your ClosetMaid dealer or call 1-800-221-0641.

© ClosetMaid Corporation 2002

Nature provides the drama.
Pozzi provides the stage.

Tina Ferguson,
Frame Builder

Pozzi® wood windows and patio doors are the ideal setting for nature's enchanting story. Artisans, like Tina Ferguson, ensure their energy efficient creations are as stunning as any landscape. Each carefully crafted frame, sash and panel, whether straight or arched, can be enhanced with aluminum cladding. This cladding comes in 12 standard, 19 Designer Choice™ or unlimited custom colors. With all these choices, and experts like Tina, obtaining windows is enjoyable, as well as effortless.

POZZI
WOOD WINDOWS®
Part of the JELD-WEN® family

"Handcrafted in Bend, Oregon"
Free catalog:
1-800-257-9663 ext. P12.
www.pozzi.com